THOSE INCREDIBLE CHRISTIANS

by the same author

THE JEW OF TARSUS, a life of Paul

SAINTS AGAINST CAESAR
the Story of the First Christian Community

THE AUTHENTIC NEW TESTAMENT,
a modern translation of the New Testament

SECRETS OF THE DEAD SEA SCROLLS

THE BIBLE WAS RIGHT

THE SONG OF SONGS

A POPULAR DICTIONARY OF JUDAISM

THE PASSOVER PLOT

HUGH J. SCHONFIELD

THOSE INCREDIBLE CHRISTIANS

PUBLISHED BY
BERNARD GEIS ASSOCIATES

Distributed by Grove Press, Inc.

Library of Congress Catalog Card Number: 68–16148

First Printing

To

RICHARD E. MEIER

in deep appreciation of his liberal mind,
staunch friendship and constant
encouragement, I gratefully and
affectionately dedicate this work.

Contents

Introduction

CHRISTIANITY for most of those who profess it, and for most others as well, is a religion, and they are not aware that it was ever anything else. It is supposed that this religion was instituted by Jesus and his Apostles and commonly accepted that a sufficient description of its beginnings is contained in the New Testament and that its basic tenets are summarised in the Creeds. Jesus is often referred to as the Founder of Christianity, as if he belonged to that select company of great teachers of religion who have appeared at various times. Christians think of him specially as God incarnate. It is in any case considered that he claimed to be in a position to communicate important spiritual truths, and by so doing to gather about him a body of those committed to their acceptance.

The Christian Scriptures appear to sanction such a view, yet the evidence when strictly examined tells heavily against the proposition that Jesus had any intention to furnish a revelation of God or to found a religion. He was a Jew addressing himself to fellow Jews, for whom there was no requirement that he should make God known, since this had already been achieved by Moses and by the ancient prophets and sages whose inspiration both he and his audience acknowledged. What Jesus proclaimed was repentance and the requirements of the Kingdom of God, the advent of which was the Jewish Hope, and he felt charged with this responsibility as the Messiah identified with the inauguration of that Kingdom.

There could be no question for him of a new religion arising from his teaching and activities, quite apart from it being needless, firstly because he believed the coming of the Kingdom of God to be imminent, and secondly because the Scriptures declared that redeemed Israel would be the instrument for bringing the knowledge of God to the nations.

In the event, Christianity did become a new religion and progressively divested itself of association with the Jewish people and the Jewish Faith. How and why this transformation took place it is the purpose of this book to reconsider. The task is timely because current thinking is challenging almost all the doctrines by which Christianity was constituted as a religion in its own right. Even among those who continue to affirm them there is a widespread feeling that the Church has let Christ down, not only because of its differences and disunity, but because of its abject failure to convert mankind to the ways of peace and righteousness. Conceivably what is now called for may be something much more revolutionary than either new theologising or ecumenism, something which would take Christians back beyond the New Testament, there to rediscover a lost Hebrew Gospel with a less complicated and more electrifying message vital for humanity today.

Of course the sense of compulsion would have to be very great to produce any far-reaching surrender of long established convictions. It would be a bitter pill to swallow that an institution professing to be of Divine origin and continually guided by the Holy Spirit should have to confess itself to have been in grievous error for some nineteen centuries. What would become of the indoctrinated flock, amounting to many millions, theologically unable to distinguish between their right handand their left? Resentment is already rife against defecting divines.

So far no need has been seen by the entrenched forces of Christianity for any radical changes of belief. The kind of questioning and modernisation which is going on can be deceptive. Far more attention is being paid to the potentialities of consolidation and a united front.

I have been able to assess the situation much more acutely since the publication of my previous book *The Passover Plot*. In that work, which has been read and discussed far more widely than I could possibly have contemplated, I rejected after protracted and thorough research the traditional portrayal of Jesus and revealed him as a Jew, who at a psychological moment in Jewish history courageously, steadfastly and with deep insight acted on the conviction that he was the Messiah his afflicted people were awaiting. I showed him to have been a man of faith, but not more than man, who employed his natural intelligence to bring to fruition the predictions which in the manner of his time he believed must be accomplished. The theme of the book, in certain of its features, administered a jolt to those who held confidently that whether one agreed with it or not the story of Christ was fixed for all time in the form in which the Church had presented it. The reactions, both favourable and unfavourable, were impressive and highly illuminating. Letters, some anonymous and some even threatening, flooded in, multitudes of articles were written and sermons preached. I was interviewed by many sections of the Press, invited to speak to all kinds of audiences in Britain and America, interrogated and criticised in radio and television programmes. The upshot was that the writing of the present volume became essential.

From the adverse comments it was evident that to a surprising extent Christian belief in God depended not so much on a spiritual sense of his Being as upon a demonstration of his existence in having manifested himself uniquely in a human personality, that of Jesus Christ. Through the atoning death of Christ the guilt of sin had been taken away, and through his resurrection the believer was assured of his own blissful immortality. In other words, it was upon an image of God partaking strongly of the characteristics of ancient heathenism that Christian faith was still largely founded. Times and conditions had changed, but in religion venerable attitudes persisted. The revelations of Frazer in *The Golden Bough* had not got through to the masses, nor George Bernard Shaw's preface to *Androcles and the Lion*. Homer W. Smith's *Man and His Gods* might never have been written. Christians remained related under the skin to the devotees of Adonis and Osiris, Dionysus and Mithras. When, therefore, in *The Passover Plot* I showed that Jesus had never claimed deity, and that this had been ascribed to him later, that he had sought to avoid death on the Cross on grounds made clear to him from his interpretation of the Messianic prophecies, and that his bodily resurrection had failed to materialise, I found myself assailed by an outburst of deep-seated emotions. For simple believers I was destroying their faith, I was taking away their God. It was as if I had deliberately smashed the idol of some primitive tribe.

The animus of some people left me gasping. The vaunted love which was declared to be the hallmark of the Christian appeared to be conspicuously absent from their composition. In extreme cases antisemitism reared its ugly head. My being a Jew was sufficient warrant for deciding that I was writing polemically in a conspiratorial attempt to discredit Christianity. Of course no one in his senses has imagined this, and no one reading my book carefully and honestly could entertain such a foolish notion. My work in fact sustained faith, faith in the God whom Jesus the Jew worshipped, and upheld the greatness of the man who believed himself to have been charged by God with a unique mission, that of Messiah the king of Israel of the line of David. What my investigation had removed was not basic Christianity, but the Gentilism which had invested it with the trappings of a different religious environment of thought. There had to be an acute perception of the pressures of that environment to explain the palimpsest of a Jesus of theology imposed upon the Jesus of history.

Naturally, most Christian clerics will not be prepared to admit, at least not very emphatically, that the Jesus of history was other than the Jesus of theology. The more scholarly may venture on a halfway admission, which amounts to contending that the Church under inspiration became better informed about Jesus than he was about himself. Liberal theologians are doing a deal of pouring new wine into old wineskins these days. What is not readily perceived is the root cause why Christian thinking, instinctively as it would seem, shapes itself to a pattern involving the apprehension of God through the personality of a man. There is still a primordial fear of an Otherness beyond the grasp of human definition and explanation. The mind, therefore, inclines either to doubt or deny the existence of what we call God, or seeks comfort in the proposition that the Otherness can be brought into association with ourselves in a manner which sublimates our fear of the alien. The view has great attractions which posits a specific relationship between God and man, as of creator to creature, father to child, and envisages a love-initiative on God's part to assure man of the reality of this relationship, most convincingly by his having entered into and embraced the conditions of humanity. The idea that Otherness does not have to be hostile and can have a participation in all Being distinct from kinship in kind and character has not yet widely commended itself. After all, we have not so far succeeded in accepting Otherness as congenial even within the limited framework of our own species.

There is no need for me to enlarge on the particular reactions of the different Christian communions: they were as typical as once had been those of the Pharisees and Sadducees. Leaving aside the disagreements with certain of my conjectures, which did not offend me in the least, what was encouraging was that for many *The Passover Plot* had rendered an evident service in that there had flooded in upon them a surprised awareness of the play of forces which had affected Jesus and his followers. The mists were dispersed with their roseate glow of myth and marvel. Here starkly revealed were the actualities of the period, and no one confronted with them who was neither fanatic nor intellecutally dishonest could ever again dismiss them from consideration. To quibble was idle when the whole brooding scene clamoured for a new evaluation of what had transpired.

The open-minded Christian was brought sharply back to the Jewishness of which he had been little conscious. The Messianism to which Christianity owed its original inspiration now began to appear not as a virtual irrelevancy, except for Jews, but as a primary factor which offered potentialities for the future of Christianity, not as a religion and not religionless, but as a commitment to the politics of the Kingdom of God.

The effect of my book was imperfect, however, because its theme did not permit of sufficient explanation of how Christianity became what it has been. It was still left to very sincere people to question whether the Church could have been so radically wrong in its beliefs as I had indicated. It seemed to them that if I was right the Church had all along been propagating falsehood, and I was asked repeatedly how I accounted for the success and endurance of Christianity and the beneficial results it had had on the lives of many millions. For the questioners these considerations established the veracity of the Christian testimony. They chose to ignore that these criteria applied to all religions, some of them much older than Christianity, and to disregard what they did know of the less favourable aspects of Christianity. For the most part they had no inkling that there was more to be learnt which threw a different light on the story of its development.

The Church has all along contended for obedient faith on the basis that what it taught had been Divinely revealed. By this dogmatism it has achieved a mastery over human reason, and has been able to bring within the area of its own rulings matters which in fact were the fruits of its own very human speculations and contrivances. The asserted operation of the Holy Spirit could be and has been employed to sanction the most perverse and unspiritual judgments of men. If it is too late in the day for a mythical and mystical view of Jesus, it is equally too late for a similar view of the Church.

Ecclesiolatry and Bibliolatry have to be discarded in favour of an emancipated approach which is free from any imposed restrictions and reservations. We have to see ourselves as fully at liberty to take account of the psychology, characteristics and circumstances of individuals in determining the worth of what they may have said or written. No longer are we to believe anything as guaranteed to be true because of the status or special illumination of whoever may have affirmed it.

In this healthy atmosphere of unimpeded inquiry the subject ponderously termed Ecclesiastical History has to be flung open to study and discussion in a spirit of frank re-examination. This particularly applies to the critical formative period. While there is a vast literature on the subject, and courses in it are provided for Divinity students, it is rare to find it treated objectively and without a conscious Christian bias. The result has been a considerable failure to discern the motivations which operated in various connections. One of the great difficulties which confronts the impartial investigator is that the available documentation is very largely one-sided. So many records have been lost or were wilfully destroyed which reflected the position and arguments of those who opposed the direction the Church was taking under the impact of powerful influences. This lack has to be compensated for to the fullest extent that is practicable by a keen exploration of the indications which have survived.

In general about the rise of Christianity the average Christian is abysmally ignorant. There has been no serious inducement for him to regard this as a matter on which he should be well-informed. What impression the simple believer has received of the Early Church outside the Bible is largely one of a persecuted Faith, which produced saints and martyrs who joyfully went to a tortured death rather than betray their convictions. Thus both the commendation and defence of Christianity which is normal rests on the assumption that its main lines were fixed from the beginning and are represented in the New Testament. Discussion, therefore, is centred upon the interpretation of the New Testament instead of being related to a series of circumstances over a protracted period which are outside the province of the New Testament as much as and even more than within it.

The Passover Plot came as a shock in no small measure because it introduced a variety of historical factors and additional relevant information of which many Christians were only partially aware and of which little account had consequently been taken in reaching convictions about Jesus. The reader was brought into contact with knowledge which both seriously impugned certain things in the Gospel story and also put a different complexion on much of its content. The intentionally dramatic title of the book permitted this knowledge to reach those who most needed to be better instructed.

It is possible that *Those Incredible Christians* will administer a greater shock since it utilises the same kind of resources in dealing with the formation of the Christian Faith and discloses by what circumstances and devious means it was accomplished. On the showing of the evidence Christianity as we know it is far removed from the original terms of its expression, and this would have been much clearer and more convincing were it not for the loss and suppression of material testimony and the ineffectiveness due to ascertainable causes of those in a position to correct the falsifications of gifted and eloquent teachers whose ideas were more appealing to Gentiles.

There were scholars in the nineteenth century who were able to discern a great deal of what occurred, all credit to them, and no doubt this will be mentioned by those who will wish to urge that I am saying nothing new. But neither novelty nor sensationalism is my object, though I have in fact been able to make some additional contribution to what could be comprehended previously. If I permitted myself to be deterred by what my critics are bound to contend I would forfeit all claim to have my honesty of purpose respected. I both know in advance, and have taken carefully into account, the kind of comments which will be made adverse to myself and to what I have set down, and those whose business it must be to try to counter the effect of this book have my understanding sympathy. I believe that even those disposed to be hostile will receive some benefit and illumination, especially from the way in which to an unusual extent I have placed Christian affairs in juxtaposition with Jewish affairs, and have brought out what is pertinent to a correct apprehension of the phenomenon of Christianity by revealing the interplay between internal and external circumstances. For the general reader, I imagine, no small part of the attraction of the work will lie in his being introduced to these matters and to a great number of ancient records for the first time.

Let me, then, briefly outline as I see it the nature and significance of this book for all who are much exercised by the question of the relevance of Christianity today. My view is that such a question cannot be answered effectually without a penetrating exposition of Christian Origins which for obvious reasons the ecclesiastical authorities are not in a position to offer.

The ground covered is roughly the first hundred and fifty years of the Christian movement, though of necessity there is an overlap at either end. If we are able to dismiss from our minds even minimally the impressions we have received from previous reading and instruction the story may grip our imagination and carry us along by its own intrinsic fascination and excitement. We may find ourselves appreciating responsively possibilities we had never before entertained. The whole ideology of Messianism is still strange to most people because it is without parallel in secular and religious thought and history. When they have supposed that they had got the hang of it they have largely got it wrong, as often appears in modern usage of the term. It was even stranger to the Graeco-Roman world into which it erupted, with Christianity initially as its most dramatic expression, and could not be sustained in an environment which feared it and could not assimilate it.

In the event Christianity survived and flourished at the cost of change and accommodation. Our story is concerned starkly with this process. It is not a pretty story, for all the nobility, sincerity and idealism of many associated with it. Here with the lid off we can see this religion in the making, not without vision and a sense of revelation, but substantially as a result of competing influences and pressures, conflicts, intrigues, sufferings and disillusionments. Our picture is drawn from life as distinguished from pious fancy; but sometimes we do glimpse the shining through of something splendid, something which is at odds with what Christianity has chiefly emphasised, which indicates that the original Messianic enterprise was not wholly abandoned and could again burst forth and potently take over whenever the Church is ready for it.

In the preparation of the book I have consulted a great many modern treatises which are not named, and absence of direct reference does not imply either neglect or lack of appreciation. The authorities to which I am indebted and which are listed in the Notes and Bibliography are chiefly those which relate to particular themes, which often I have not dealt with at length, and to translations of early documents. I have laid under some contribution researches contained in two earlier works of mine, *The Jew of Tarsus* and *Saints Against Caesar*, published between 1945 and 1950, because these were indispensable and the books themselves have long been out of print. All the quotations from the New Testament, unless otherwise stated, are from my own translation entitled *The Authentic New Testament*, and acknowledgment is made to the British publishers, Dennis Dobson. A hardcover edition for publication in the United States is being undertaken by Bernard Geis Associates.

THOSE INCREDIBLE CHRISTIANS

I

The Kingdom of Arrogance

FOR almost two thousand years the story of Christianity has been linked with that of Rome, at first as enemy, later as ally, and finally as spiritual heir. When we think of the Church institutionally it is natural to do so in a Roman context. There is a mystery here which gravely affects the character and validity, and indeed the future of the Christian Faith, and the investigation of it cannot be other than timely even though it means treading again certain well-trodden paths as well as breaking fresh ground.

The mystery, for those who can consider history as not entirely fortuitous and devoid of meaning, was present from the start, since the rise of Christianity coincided with the first century of the Roman Empire. Jesus of Nazareth, in whose name the Christian message was proclaimed, was himself born in the reign of Caesar Augustus, first emperor of the new Roman regime in a land of which lately Rome had taken control. From the beginning Christianity had the Roman Empire as the main sphere of its activities and of its conflicts, and its remarkable achievement after some three centuries as a persecuted superstition was to be adopted as the state religion of that Empire.

Put in this way the story is one of persistence culminating in triumph. It has been and can be so represented, and with considerable justification. The gods and their temples were vanquished, and in due course the grandiose pagan title of Pontifex Maximus formerly held by the emperors was transferred to the head of the Roman Church. But what could have made such a long detested and proscribed faith acceptable to the Romans? Was there more than the sign of the Cross vouchsafed to the Emperor Constantine? Did Christianity become acceptable because circumstances had changed and because Christianity had substantially departed from its original positions? Was the triumph in reality that of Caesar and not of Christ?

These are searching questions, and the quest for answers calls for an observant and critical understanding of Christianity in its formative period.

We have to approach the evidence with a keen eye for what is significant at every stage, conscious that we are dealing with human personalities and motivations. The fact that we are dealing with the genesis of a religion, which like all religions is attributed to a Divine revelation or illumination, must not inhibit us from conducting our inquiry at the level of mundane causes and effects. The believer will naturally hold that we are thereby wilfully neglecting what is of paramount importance; but he in turn may be rendering himself blind to what is capable of explanation in other terms than supernatural intervention. It is much more consequential to be aware of the contributions of people and events to the moulding of developments in their rational interpretation, since in this way it will be determined more effectively whether there is anything over and above of which we are required to take account.

We are to think of our task, then, as primarily one of historical investigation and of honest reporting of what we discover, treating Christianity as a phenomenon arising from certain conditions and attitudes of mind as other faiths and ideologies have done. When we come to conclusions these must be reached with the whole panorama of the period environment spread out before us.

The world with which our story is concerned is that over

which Rome held sway, and chiefly its central area, the lands bordering the Mediterranean, the 'middle of the earth' sea. It was a region which had been the home of ancient civilisations, and was now dominated by a power unlike any of its imperial predecessors.

Rome had been imperial in its conquests and policies long before Octavian, as Caesar Augustus, obtained an authority which marked the beginning of what is known as the Empire. Technically Rome continued to be a Republic, governed in the name of 'Senate and People', but effectively for a considerable time the emperor was supreme ruler of all countries under Roman control.

For the Jews in their homeland and to an extent for the early Christians the institution of the Empire was an emphatic evil. They saw in it, as we shall illustrate later, a sign of the Last Days, a diabolical contrivance to withstand the coming of the Kingdom of God. To stress why at this juncture Christ should have come into the world Christian protagonists have inclined to paint a grim picture of the moral sickness and degradation of that age, the loosening of religious ties and the abandonment of hope in the future.

But the creation of the Empire did not present that appearance to many others, and the world did not seem to be in any special plight. This was not a time of great uncertainty, of grave danger and unusual turpitude. To the contrary, there were many indications of a marked betterment. Under the leadership of Augustus there was a peace that had not been known for many years. Piracy in the Mediterranean had virtually been extinguished, giving opportunity for increased seaborne commerce. Transport and communications were improved. The machinery of government had been drastically overhauled. New instructions had been given to Rome's agents and representatives abroad, which cut down extortion and self-enrichment by officials in the Provinces. The internal self-government of countries was subjected to a minimum of interference where loyalty to Rome was assured. The due performance of religious rites was encouraged. More foreigners could become Roman citizens, and more slaves could acquire their freedom. Rome exacted tributary fees for its services, but these were not unduly burdensome taking into account the benefits received. No doubt the Romans could be said by us nowadays to have most successfully run a large-scale Protection Racket, but they had no criminal intent. Rome was not loved by the subject peoples, and did not expect to be; but the orderly rule and security it offered was widely appreciated. In the fashion of the East the city of Rome was worshipped as a goddess and Caesar as a god, the Saviour of the World.

In this reverence there was much sincerity and genuine thankfulness; it was not merely sycophantic flattery. 'The most comprehensive compliment that Augustus ever received', writes Dr. Grant, 'was paid him during the last days of his life, off the Campanian coast. When the ship on which he was making for Capreae sailed by Puteoli, it passed a merchantman that had just arrived from Alexandria. Dressed in white, decked with garlands, and burning incense, the crew and passengers of the Alexandrian ship saluted Augustus, calling out that it was to him that they owed their lives, their liberty and their prosperity.'[1]

The Romans themselves were very conscious of the improvements brought about by Augustus. Virgil the poet, inspired by the Cumean Sibyl and other sources, had seen a fresh beginning of the cycle of time, the coming of a new Golden Age.[2] There was widespread revulsion against strife and political disorder, a spiritual discontent. The reign of Augustus brought a return of energy and invigoration. There was a leadership now to inspire and give promise of greater things in store. Those hopes were largely frustrated during the ensuing reign of Tiberius; but the spirit that had been quickened was not extinguished. Rome sought to harness it to herself, so that people should not look elsewhere for salvation.

The Romans accepted as a matter of course that praise and

devotion were their due. They were a serious-minded people, who took themselves and their civilising mission very seriously. They were strong on law and institutions, but lacking in artistry and imagination. Virgil had expressed this too:

> Others, no doubt, will better mould the bronze
> To the semblance of soft breathing, draw from marble
> The living countenance; and others plead
> With greater eloquence, or learn to measure,
> Better than we the pathways of the heaven,
> The risings of the stars; remember, Roman,
> To rule the people under law, to establish
> The way of peace, to battle down the haughty,
> To spare the meek. Our fine arts, these, forever.[3]

The fine arts were by no means despised, though it was considered that their products should be collected rather than executed by Romans. Their real business, entrusted to them by the gods, was to govern the peoples, not unkindly but firmly. The historian Tacitus puts into the mouth of Cerialis, commander in Gaul and the Rhineland in the Year of the Four Emperors (A.D. 68–69), an eloquent statement of Rome's function in an address to the defeated rebel tribe of the Treveri.

'There were always kings and wars throughout Gaul until you submitted to our laws. Although often provoked by you, the only use we have made of our rights as victors has been to impose on you the necessary costs of maintaining peace. For you cannot secure tranquillity among nations without armies, nor maintain armies without pay, nor provide pay without taxes. . . . If the Romans are driven out—which Heaven forbid—what will follow except universal war among all peoples? The good fortune and order of eight hundred years have built up this mighty fabric which cannot be destroyed without overwhelming its destroyers.'[4]

The Romans, from their point of view, were a superior

race with a superior way of life, Divinely entrusted with rulership, and to a remarkable extent—not only by military prowess—they succeeded in impressing on many peoples that they were the ordained custodians of peace and good order. They were strong in managerial qualities, which enabled them to be effective farmers, industrialists and administrators, jurists, planners and generals. These qualities were particularly in evidence among those of the old patrician families and the better educated, who tended to regard manual labour and petty tradesmanship as beneath their dignity. Land cultivation, however, was widely held to be an honest Roman toil and associated with physical exercise, otherwise encouraged by sports and games.

There was a vast gulf between the extremes, the patricians and the plebs. The Roman commons, whose poverty and misery was acute, especially under urban conditions, had to be kept under control. When the support of the plebs was needed in the name of democracy this was found to be obtainable by timely gifts of food and money and lavish free entertainments.

On the whole, the Romans were highly conservative and traditional. The family was of great importance. Religion also centred on the family, the nation being but a larger family. The home in all its contexts was under the protection of guardian-divinities, Penates, while the continuity of family life was sustained by other spiritual influences, the Lares. Moral instruction was strict, and equally regard for religious rites and ceremonies. Many of these had been inherited from the Etruscans, and the Romans were obsessed by the belief that the fortunes of their race depended on the maintenance and exactness of their observances and their devotion to the gods. Piety and conformity were the watchwords. But inevitably the Romans were also highly superstitious. 'If there be gods,' even the more rational thinkers urged, 'they must care for man; and if they care for him, then too they necessarily must supply him with tokens of their will and of the future.'[5]

Astrology was an alien art, but numerous forms of augury and divination were practised.

The rigidities of habit and custom, which were the hallmarks of the good citizen, had their effects in a seething discontent beneath the surface, which erupted violently from time to time both in individuals and factions. Politics provided one emotional outlet, and gambling another. Otherwise steam could be let off by witnessing cruel sports, shows and dangerous games, the more bloody and bizarre the better.

By various means, conquest, inheritance and diplomacy, Rome had acquired a vast empire. But the movement outward from Italy also brought about a movement inward, especially from the eastern Mediterranean lands. The remains of the older civilisations had for centuries been overlaid by Greek culture, a process speeded up after the victories of Alexander the Great. When the Romans moved into Asia Minor, Syria and Egypt they encountered a different and disturbing way of life, flamboyant, exotic and temperamentally alien. The Romans were both attracted and repelled. The art, the craftsmanship the ideas and philosophies were a great enrichment. Greek culture became essential to the equipment of the educated Roman. But the moral standards of the East, its flagrant vices, its chicanery and individualism, offended the Roman sense of virtue. Once imperialism got going, however, very little that was effective could be done to keep out all that was characteristic of the Hellenised Orient. No walls or fortresses could obstruct it. It invaded Rome along the Roman roads. It entered with every cargo of slaves and merchandise. As the Roman poet Juvenal expressed it:

> Long since into Tiber
> Syrian Orontes has come flooding in,
> Carrying language and manners on its flood,
> The flutist, and the harp with slanting strings,
> Outlandish drums too, and the girls whose trade
> Is to accost one at the Circus doors.[6]

Tacitus, the historian, speaks similarly of Rome as 'the common sewer into which everything infamous and abominable flows like a torrent from all quarters of the world'.[7]

This influx had begun to have its effects before the Empire as such existed, considerably modifying the older puritanism and piety. In the second century B.C. it had still been possible for a Greek like Polybius to write in the following terms:

'The quality in which the Roman commonwealth is most distinctly superior is in my opinion the nature of their religious convictions. . . . These matters are clothed in such pomp and introduced to such an extent into the public and private life of the Romans that nothing could exceed it, a fact which will surprise many. My own opinion at least is that they have adopted this course for the sake of the common people. It is a course which perhaps would not have been necessary had it been possible to form a state composed of wise men, but since every multitude is fickle, full of lawless desires, unreasoned passion, and violent anger, the multitude must be held in by invisible terrors and suchlike pageantry.'[8]

But now there was a change of times as the cults of the nations made an increasing impact on Roman society. That of Cybele had been imported before the close of the third century B.C., that of Dionysus and of Isis followed. Under the name of Chaldeans the eastern astrologers invaded Rome. The enticement of orgiastic practices, initiations, and the promise of well-being in the after life, brought decay to the old Roman religious institutions. There were moments of resistance, and actions taken to curb certain unwelcome developments and the more debasing rites. The Chaldeans were temporarily expelled. But Rome could not be at the heart of an empire without all the blood streams of that empire flowing into its veins and permeating the body politic. Augustus won applause for his efforts to revive Roman faith and purity of living. But the tide could not be stemmed, and something new was demanded to restore and consolidate Romanism.

This involved more than reforms and legislation; for now Rome was more than a state, it was a whole diverse world. Up to a point the alien elements could be absorbed and integrated, by identifying the gods of the nations with Roman deities, by the adoption of foreigners by Roman families, by giving Roman education and training to the sons of ruling houses and chiefs from the Provinces, by extending the privileges of Roman citizenship, by admitting men of other races to the lower and even higher ranks of the army and the civil service. Yet all such provisions, while they assisted the process of Romanisation, also contributed to transforming the character of the state and thus made possible changes which had been rejected when advanced by Julius Caesar. The Senate became less effective, the army more politically powerful, the emperor as the embodiment of the Empire became less Roman and far more autocratic, so long as he could count on the support of the legions and immediately of the Praetorian Guard. The time would come for the acceptance as emperor of men of provincial origin. It was seen needful to cultivate a Roman mystique, belief in Rome's paternal benevolence, world mission and invincible might. Under the Empire Rome was converted into a living legend.

The methods adopted were various, and partly derived from the East. There was the lavish building of imposing commemorative monuments and temples adorned with inscriptions bearing witness to Roman glory and achievements. Circuses, theatres and triumphal arches were everywhere in evidence. Another powerful instrument of propaganda was the coinage. Not only did this make the image and dignities of the emperors familiar to their subjects, the reverse of the coins was employed to illustrate and spell out the benefits of Roman rule, subtly indoctrinating every user. Artists, authors, poets played their part in fostering the Roman legend. It acquired the character of a dogma that the world owed to Rome peace and order, and that if the Empire should ever fall that world would return to darkness and primeval chaos.

But what chiefly served to invest the Empire with a mystical quality was the sanction of religion. Anciently the East had seen in its rulers the earthly embodiment of the protecting tribal or state deity, and the Hellenes had been even more generous in apotheosising great men and heroes and ascribing to them Divine origin. The practice was not unknown to Rome, where Romulus was identified with the god Quirinus, and in the first century B.C. Julius Caesar, even hailed as Jupiter-Julius, was declared to have become a god shortly after his death. Under Augustus it became a matter of state policy to encourage, mainly in the Provinces, the organisation of a cult having as its object the worship of Rome as a goddess and of the emperor as a god. The beginnings of this cult had appeared in the East long before the Empire. Smyrna had erected a temple to Rome as early as 195 B.C. But it was the hegemony of Augustus which quite naturally directed to him the worship accorded to deity as the son and representative of Zeus the father of the gods, as well as adopted son of the deified Julius. This circumstance was now employed as a valuable instrument for fostering loyalty to Rome and the cohesion of the Empire. This was achieved by the conjoining of the worship of Roma and Augustus. Provincial Councils were created to attend to the ceremonies of the cult on occasions such as the emperor's birthday and accession day, and to the games held in his honour. Leading provincials were enrolled as ministering priests. Officially in Rome itself the emperor was deified only after death, but some of the emperors insisted on asserting their deity in their lifetime, acting out the divine sonship of Jupiter-Zeus which the world recognised in its sovereign head.

As a result of the association of religion and loyalty to the Empire a new kind of high treason was created which destroyed many innocent persons and had the gravest consequences for the early Christians. All disrespect for the emperor was *laesas maiestas*, a capital crime. Suetonius mentions that in the time of Tiberius, 'someone had taken off the head of a statue of

Augustus and put another in its place. . . . The man being put to death, this kind of prosecution for treason was carried so far that it became a capital offence for a man to beat a slave or change his clothes near a statue of Augustus. . . . A person was condemned to death in a colony for allowing honours to be decreed to him on the same day upon which honours had once been decreed to Augustus.'[9]

While there was a widespread recognition of the benefits of Roman rule and the Roman Peace, and everything was done to impress these benefits on the subject peoples and to procure their allegiance, it was not to be concealed that inside the kid glove there was a mailed fist, and that from the Roman viewpoint might and right were interchangeable terms. There was plenty of resentment of Rome's haughty power and assumption that the Romans were a superior race divinely appointed to govern mankind. The representatives of Rome abroad frequently disguised very little, if at all, their contempt for the nations they governed even while they accommodated themselves to their customs and institutions. Rome earned execration as well as encomiums. The imposts which paid the officials and the legions, and kept going all the ramifications of the imperial service and communications, was particularly obnoxious to those who cherished their liberty.

Strong anti-Roman feeling existed; but open expression was difficult and dangerous, and active revolt on any scale almost impossible to promote successfully. It was on the fringe of the Empire and chiefly in Europe that most manifestations of rebellious hostility occurred, and here Rome was sometimes to know defeat as well as victory. Within the Provinces antagonism to Rome normally had to be more circumspect in the methods adopted for its dissemination, the secret meetings of subversive groups, the circulation of literature, oracles and prophecies. Otherwise, and on the surface of affairs, anti-Roman ends were served by invoking the laws and by multifarious political intrigues.

One small people, the Jews, widely scattered throughout

the Empire, had before the inception of that Empire managed to place itself in a unique position in relation to the Romans, procuring privileges while at the same time making it evident that it was not to be integrated in any system of society. Neither under the Empire could it be induced to participate in the imperial cult. In so far as Rome was now a theocracy, that of the Jews was of venerable standing and of a totally different order. For this people the God of Israel was paramount, and there were no gods beside him. As he had been the creator so was he the sole and true ruler of the whole world and the arbiter of its destiny. His laws, his justice, his salvation, were fearlessly to be proclaimed and propagated.

So Rome nourished within its midst what it despised and could not understand, a spirit it could not subdue or bend to its will, which did not scruple to announce the Empire's transience and depict its cataclysmic overthrow. Until provoked in their own homeland the Jews made no resort to arms, when they would have to meet the Romans in the warfare in which Rome excelled. They simply ignored all persuasion that what they stood for could be overcome. Secure in their convictions they were conscious of no competition and rested in a faith they knew to be invincible by any agency however formidable and exalted.

There was a great deal of respect among the Jews for Roman law and order and for the Roman virtues. But once the Empire was committed to a position which violated the sovereignty of the One God it stood self-condemned as the 'Kingdom of Arrogance'.

NOTES AND REFERENCES

1. *The World of Rome* by Michael Grant, p. 63. To this work, published by Weidenfeld & Nicolson (1960), I am much indebted.

2. Virgil, *Eclogue IV*, 'Now is come the last age of the song of Cumae: the great line of the centuries begins anew.' Tr. by H. Rushton Fairclough (Loeb Classical Library).

3. Virgil, *Aenid VI*, tr. by C. Day Lewis.

4. Tacitus, *Hist.* IV. 74, tr. by C. H. Moore.

5. Cicero, *De Div.*, quoted by John J. I. Döllinger, *The Gentile and the Jew*, Vol. II. p. 98.

6. Juvenal, *Satire*, III. 62 ff.

7. Tacitus, *Annals*, XV. 44.

8. Polybius, *Hist.* VI. 56. Adapted by Grant from W. R. Paton.

9. Suetonius, *Tiberius*, LVIII.

2

The Jewish Impact

THE seedbed of Christianity was the Synagogue. Of necessity this was so, since the news conveyed by the early followers of Jesus was that in him the promised Messiah (the Christ) had appeared. The message had to travel over sea and land far from Palestine to reach the widely scattered Jewish communities. The extent of the dispersion may be gathered from the geographer Strabo, who lived at the very beginning of the Christian Era. 'This people', he wrote, 'has already found its way into every city, and it would be difficult to discover any place in the habitable world that has not received this tribe and in which it has not made its presence felt.'[1] Exaggerated as the statement is, it is the fact that by the time of Augustus the Jews gave the appearance of being ubiquitous and strongly influential. In certain countries and great cities they formed no small part of the population. In Egypt alone, largely in Alexandria, there were perhaps a million of them.

This spreading out of Jews had been going on for centuries. An initial cause had been the conquest of the kingdoms of Israel and Judah by the Assyrians and Babylonians respectively, which resulted in deportations of captives and the flight of refugees. But political alliances and the development of international trade had also played their part. So too had policies favourable to the Jews of the Persians, and of Alexander the Great and his successors, who encouraged Jewish settlements in their domains and accorded them special privileges. In many armies that engaged in battle in the cockpit of the Near East there were often Jewish contingents. At least since the middle of the second century B.C. there had been Jewish communities in Italy, at which period there subsisted a formal alliance between the Jews of Palestine and the Romans, renewed for upwards of a century. Rulers found them to be loyal and reliable, contributing to peace and good order.

The organisation of Jewish life abroad in the pre-Christian centuries is something about which all too little is known from available sources. We are immediately interested only in the lands bordering the Mediterranean, and need not go further back in history than the end of the fourth century B.C. Before the triumphs of Alexander the Great the Greeks were not much acquainted with the Jews, who previously had not to any extent settled in their cities. It was otherwise with Syria, Egypt and the North African seaboard. In Egypt there were ancient Jewish settlements which had their own temples and had not greatly been affected by the changes in Jewish religious thought after the Babylonian Exile. The situation was different, of course, in the Hellenic period in Egypt when in the second century Ptolemy Philometor gave permission to the refugee Jewish priest Onias to build a temple at Leontopolis modelled on that of Jerusalem. In other areas nothing is known of the Jews having temples as places of worship. The Jewish expatriates of that time recognised the Temple at Jerusalem as the focal point of their religion, and assembled humbly for prayer and instruction in meeting-house (*synagogue*) and oratory (*proseuche*). Both terms are Greek, and point to an evident feature of Jewish religious life which made it readily distinguishable by their neighbours from their own.

Since Jewish national independence was not fully regained until the close of the second century B.C. there was no cause for the Greeks to be conscious of the Jews except in respect of their way of life. They were taken to be Syrians, a section of that people particularly devoted to philosophy. This is how they appeared to Theophrastus, the famous pupil of Aristotle.[2]

For others, like Clearchus and Megasthenes, the Jews among the Syrians corresponded to the Brahmans among the Hindus.[3] *Judaismos* did not so much appear to Greeks as a distinct religion: it seemed rather to be an oriental philosophy followed by a caste which involved certain attitudes and regulations. It is easy to see how this opinion arose. The synagogues bore no resemblance to temples. They had no images of gods, no altars, no priestly rites. There was no coming and going of devotees and suppliants bringing gifts and offerings and presenting private petitions. These things were the characteristics of a religion. Instead, there was the reading, study and exposition of ancient sacred books, collective chanting and recitations. The philosophy inculcated separatism, the rejection of other religious beliefs, and non-participation in the usual kind of ceremonies. Judaism had curious disciplines, the mutilation of males by circumcision, abstention from various foods and from all work every seventh day, special feasts and ablutions.

For the Greeks, therefore, Judaism was not a *thiasos* (a cult), and it took some time to be appreciated that the Jews among them followed a national cult having its centre in the Temple at Jerusalem. The peculiarities of the Jewish position only emerged gradually as a result of closer contact and political circumstances. In the Hellenic world there were Jews who were citizens in the Greek tribal sense, under the name of Alexandrians or Macedonians; but largely they were metics (sojourners), who yet could have legal privileges and a communal guild type of organisation, being run like miniature states with magistrates and council, the corporate entity vested in the synagogue being able to acquire property according to the means of the community.[4] In many places the Jews obtained special concessions to meet their needs and scruples, which became a cause of offence and ill-will.

In Egypt, later a hotbed of antisemitism, the presence of Jews had not been particularly resented before the large-scale influx of Jewish settlers promoted by Alexander the Great to inhabit his new city of Alexandria. Under the rule of the Greek

Ptolemies the Jewish population further increased, so that in Alexandria alone they occupied two out of the five sections of the city. When reference begins to be made to them at the end of the fourth and early in the third century B.C. by non-Jewish authors, such as Hecataeus, a Greek residing in Egypt, and the Egyptian priest Manetho, it is mainly in relation to historical matters, among others to offer a counterversion to the Jewish story of the Exodus under Moses. Neither writer exhibits any intimate acquaintance with Jews or first-hand knowledge of Jewish literature, and Manetho confesses as much.

Hecataeus, not being an Egyptian, is the more objective, while Manetho's account is strongly nationalistic and somewhat waspish. The exodus of the Jews under Moses is identified with the expulsion of the Hyksos. Two versions are given by Manetho, one supposedly based on ancient records and the other derived from current popular legends. According to Hecataeus all strangers, not only Hebrews, were expelled from Egypt. This was due to a pestilence in that country which was attributed to neglect of the gods. Some of the strangers migrated to Greece led by chieftains such as Danaus and Cadmus, while the greater part under Moses occupied Palestine. Because of the expulsion Moses made laws contrary to those of other nations, which accounts for the Jews having an 'inhospitable and inhuman' way of life.[5] But Hecataeus does pay tribute to the wisdom and courage of Moses, and for some of his statements it appears likely that he had a Hellenised Jew as his informant.

Manetho's second account is akin to that of Hecataeus. An Egyptian Pharaoh Amenophis desiring to behold the gods was told by a priest that this would be granted to him if he cleansed Egypt of all lepers and unclean persons. Accordingly these were assembled to the number of 80,000 and sent to work in the eastern quarries. On their petitioning Amenophis they were granted possession of the city of Avaris as a place of residence. Now this was 'a Typhonian city'. Here under the leadership of Osarsiph they settled and agreed to obey the laws he drew up for them in opposition to the laws and religion of the Egyptians and which provided that 'they would associate with none except their confederates'. Determining to make war on Amenophis, the people of Avaris sent to Jerusalem and enlisted the aid of the Hyksos, who had formerly occupied Egypt, and together they invaded Egypt and occupied it for thirteen years.[6]

In this story there is a fusion of Joseph and Moses. The leader of the outcasts is called Osarsiph by Egyptianising the name Joseph. The Jo (Greek Io) has been taken to represent the Hebrew God-name, and for this the Egyptian Osar (Osiris) has been substituted. Manetho goes further than Hecataeus in stressing Jewish separatism and antagonism to Egyptian customs and beliefs. Intentionally Avaris is stigmatised as a Typhonian city, for in Egyptian mythology Set-Typhon was the archfiend inspired by Apep, the enemy of Ra the sun-god. One of the likenesses of Apep was the Ass,[7] and this animal came to be identified with Typhon.

Writing in the first century A.D., Plutarch tells us: 'Osiris and Isis have, then, changed from good daemons into gods, while as for the dimmed and shattered power of Typhon, though it is at its last gasp and in its final death-throes, the Egyptians still appease and soothe it with certain feasts of offerings. Yet again, every now and then, at certain festivals they humiliate it dreadfully and treat it most despitefully—even to rolling red-skinned men in the mud and driving an ass over a precipice (as the Koptos folk)—because Typhon was born with his skin red and ass-like. While the Busiris folk and Lycopolitans do not use trumpets at all, as they sound like an ass braying. . . .' And further, 'Those who say that Typhon's flight on an ass from the fight (with Horus the sun-god) lasted seven days, and that after reaching a place of safety he begat sons, Hierosolymus and Judaeus, are instantly convicted of dragging Jewish matters into the myth.'[8] Elsewhere Plutarch speaks of the ass as the animal most honoured by the Jews.[9]

Well before Plutarch's time Egyptian hostility to their

Jewish neighbours had become so pronounced that it was accepted by the masses that the Jews were Typhon-worshippers, servants of the dreaded and execrated power of evil, and that the ass was the object of Jewish veneration. This belief was fostered by the Jew-baiting rhetoricians in their writings and harangues, and spread widely through the Roman world. It was already known around 100 B.C., for Poseidonius in a fragment of his *History* quoted by Diodorus mentions that when the Seleucid king Antiochus Epiphanes entered the Temple at Jerusalem he discovered in the innermost shrine 'the statue of a long-bearded man, seated upon an ass and holding a book in his hand'. This figure was presumed to represent Moses.[10] By the time of Augustus the legend was fully-fledged. The mystery of the Holy of Holies, into which only the Jewish high priest entered once a year, was fully explained. The declaration of the Jews that God had no likeness and must not be depicted by a graven image was fraudulent. The truth of the matter was that they were at pains to conceal the fact that in their shrine was a golden ass's head to which their most solemn worship was directed.

The story seems to have originated in antisemitic Alexandria. It was circulated by Damocritus and Apion, and later found its way into the *History* of Tacitus,[11] though the Roman knew better; for referring to the capture of Jerusalem by Pompey in 63 B.C.—when that general entered the Holy of Holies in the Temple—he says, 'It is a well-known fact that he found no image, no statue, no symbolical representation of the deity; the sanctuary was unadorned and simple.'[12]

Inevitably, when the Christians came to accept Jesus, whom they said had ridden into Jerusalem on an ass, as the incarnation of the Jewish Lord of Hosts, the calumny was passed on to them. The North-African Church Father Tertullian addresses the heathen: 'Like many others you have dreamed that an ass's head is our god. But a new version of our god has lately been made public at Rome, ever since a certain hireling convict of a bull-fighter put forth a picture with some such inscription as this, "The god of the Christians ONOKOITES." He was depicted thus—with the ears of an ass, and with one of his feet hoofed, holding in his hand a book, and clothed in a toga.'[13] *Onokoites* (ass-born) can only mean that Jesus was born of the union of a mortal woman with the ass-headed god of the Jews, a jibe at the virgin-birth story.

In 1856 a graffito was found in the Palatine with a variation of this representation. A man with upraised hand adores a crucified figure with an ass's head. The inscription reads *Alexamenos sebete Theon*, 'Alexamenos worships God'. This graffito is preserved in the library of the Collegio Romano. Wunsch, however, does not regard this example as a caricature, but as a genuine relic of the worship of Set-Typhon by the Gnostic sect of Setites or Sethites. He notes that the Y symbol placed on the right side of the head of the ass-Christ is the usual glyph for Typhon on the numerous Roman curse tablets, and he infers that the ass-cult by Christian Gnostics had a foundation in fact.[14] Indeed, the Church Father Epiphanius states that 'the Gnostic Sabaoth has according to some the face of an ass', and he quotes their book *The Genealogy of Mary* as evidence.[15] One Gnostic title for the Supreme Power was Onoel.

Sabaoth, or Iao Sabaoth, was the Greek transliteration of the Hebrew for the Lord of Hosts, the God of the Jews, and Onoel is a combination of the Greek for ass with the Hebrew word for God (El).

We have treated the Graeco-Egyptian anti-Jewish slanders at some length because it is of great importance to consider their cause. One may readily grant that xenophobia was part of it. The Jews stuck together and on account of their religion did not mix with others, refused invitations to dine with Gentiles because of their dietary laws and to avoid countenancing idolatry, absenting themselves also from pagan festivals and ceremonies. They demanded and secured certain privileges, such as having their own meeting-houses, importing special food, refraining from work on Sabbaths and fast days, obtaining on these days immunity from appearing in a court of law, and enjoying liberty to send gold out of the country for the Temple at Jerusalem.[16] It was a grievance that the Jews curried favour with highly placed persons and exerted a political influence without assuming full civic responsibilities. In abundant measure the Jews offered themselves as a target for the 'dislike of the like for the unlike'. Their way of life in the lands of their dispersion, especially in cities where their numbers brought them to special attention, was bound to produce a Jewish problem. Feeling about them could easily be aroused by the ill-disposed.

But when allowance has been made for all such factors, which have been the regular stock-in-trade of antisemitic propagandists down the ages, it has to be remarked that these do not entirely account for the intensification of animus against the Jews which developed in the first century B.C. and led up to the pogroms of the next century. We need to seek for some additional reason why this should have happened. If the opposition and the outbreaks had been confined to Egypt they could be treated as arising from the special circumstances affecting that country. But while they were worse there than elsewhere it is historically evident that there was a widespread strengthening of antagonism in the period indicated. Before we consider what had brought it about we must take a look at the attitude of Roman writers.

Initially, and until Judea was brought under direct Roman government in A.D. 6, official policy could not fail to be broadly favourable to the Jews by virtue of the treaty relationship which had subsisted between Rome and the Maccabaean priest-kings. Consequently when grievances against the Jews were voiced in any of the countries under Roman control the disposition was to uphold the Jews, especially in matters affecting their freedom to be governed by their own laws and follow their native way of life. Josephus cites a number of samples of Roman edicts confirming Jewish privileges and imposing penalties for their infringement.[17] Even when the imperial cult was established and relations with the Jews of Palestine were strained there was exemption in their case from requirements which offended Jewish beliefs. Violations by Roman officials were punishable. The singular attempt of the Emperor Gaius Caligula to have his statue placed in the Temple at Jerusalem as an object of worship was regarded as an act of madness.

The Roman authors frequently scoff at Jewish customs and institutions, but normally in a good-humoured way. We seldom meet with rabid antisemitism. But some of their references betray a sense almost of superstitious fear of Jewish spiritual power and political influence. They seem to suffer from a kind of Jewish Peril complex, which forces them to come out with pointed remarks and allusions. In Italy it is this undercurrent of alarm, a growing unease, which is so striking, and which on rare occasions resulted in action against the Jews at an official level.

It will suffice if we give here two references to Jewish civic pressure, one from Cicero and one from Horace.

The first is in connection with the trial for malpractices while in office of Lucius Flaccus, ex-governor of the Province of Asia. This took place in 59 B.C. and Flaccus was defended by Cicero. Among the charges against Flaccus one dealt with his prohibiting the Jews sending gold to Jerusalem as was their custom. Defending Counsel replied as follows:

'Next comes the malicious accusation about the gold of the Jews. No doubt that is the reason why this case is being tried so near the Aurelian terrace. It is this count in the indictment, Laelius, that has made you pick out this place, and that is responsible for the crowd about us. You know very well how numerous that class is, with what unanimity they act, and what strength they exhibit in the political meetings. But I shall frustrate their purpose. I shall speak in a low tone, just loud enough for the jury to hear. There is no lack of men, as you very well know, to stir these fellows up against me and every patriotic citizen; and I have no intention of making the task of such mischief-makers lighter by any act of mine.

'The facts are these: Every year it has been customary for men representing the Jews to collect sums in gold from Italy and all our Provinces for exportation to Jerusalem. Flaccus in his provincial edict forbade this to be done in Asia.

'Now, gentlemen, is there a man who can honestly refuse commendation to this act? That gold should not be exported is a matter which the Senate has frequently voted, and which it did as recently as my own consulship. Why, it is a proof of Flaccus' vigorous administration that he took active steps against a foreign superstition, as it is an indication of a lofty sense of duty that he dared defy—where the public weal was concerned—the furious mass of Jews that frequently crowd our meetings.'[18]

While Cicero is obviously employing the histrionic arts of the trained advocate to do his best for his guilty client, he could hardly have spoken of Jewish corporate pressure if it was not familiar to his audience. Of course such common action was by no means confined to Jews: it was a feature of the general democratic behaviour, and is so still. But in ancient times it was easier for Jews to stage demonstrations in the midst of non-Jewish communities, even though it made them conspicuous, and that they were able to do so shows that in respect of legal rights they were relatively secure.

One of Horace's allusions to the Jews confirms Cicero's pointed remarks. The poet on a certain occasion was trying to escape from a bore, and spotting his friend Titus Fuscus thought to use him to obtain relief, but in vain.

'Surely,' says Horace, nudging Fuscus, 'you said you had something you wished to speak to me about in private.'

'Yes, yes, I remember,' Fuscus replies, 'but we'll let that go for some more suitable time. Today's the thirtieth Sabbath. Why, man, would you want me to offend the circumcised Jews?'

'I can't say that *I* feel any scruples on that score.'

'But I do. I haven't your strength of mind. I'm only a humble citizen. You'll excuse me. I shall talk over our business at some other time.'[19]

Here the strength of Jewish influence is taken for granted, so that Fuscus is reluctant to discuss any business on the thirtieth Sabbath, an allusion to the Great Sabbath, the annual Jewish fast of the Day of Atonement. So much of commercial and public activity in Rome was brought to a standstill on this day that it could not fail to feature in non-Jewish communications. Thus we find the Emperor Augustus writing to Tiberius, 'There is no Jew, my dear Tiberius, who keeps his fast on the Sabbath as I kept it today.'[20] Similarly the poet Ovid advises that amours may fittingly be started on the Sabbath of Sabbaths since 'it is a day on which other business ought not to be transacted'.[21]

Consciousness of the Jews and their religion had clearly become very strong, and the success of Jewish spiritual propaganda must be considered to be an important additional factor which gave rise to hostility and defensive action.

Historians agree that between 150 B.C. and A.D. 100 especially the Jews did achieve remarkable results in attracting converts from the Gentiles. The obvious reasons are given for this, the high moral standards of the Jews, their pure worship of One Supreme Being without form or substance, the simplicity of their devotions, the possession of venerable sacred writings, and the assurance they offered of immortality for the righteous. But what is not sufficiently admitted by many is that the success of the Jews was largely due to intentional effort. Certain Jewish writers, mindful of the sufferings of their people arising from the conversion methods of the Church, are reluctant to emphasise that Judaism in its first phase was animated by missionary zeal. Some Churchmen, on the other hand, anxious to contrast Christian universalism with Jewish exclusiveness, are unwilling to credit the Jews with a concern for the salvation of mankind equal to that of the Christians.

In the interests of truth we must refuse to be swayed by either of these sensitivities, and address ourselves to clarifying the situation in the light of the records.

We find a useful pointer in the Egyptian references to the

Seleucid monarch Antiochus Epiphanes. As we have seen, the story got around that when Antiochus, aiming to destroy the Jewish religion and convert their Temple into a shrine of Zeus Olympius, penetrated to the heart of the Jewish sanctuary he found there the effigy of a man seated on an ass. It was further told that the Jews sacrificed a foreigner every seventh year, and that Antiochus had released a Greek captive immured in the Temple who would have been the next victim. Antiochus thus appears as an anti-Jewish hero; but the significance of his policy lies in its effect on the Jews themselves.

Until this event there had been a strong inclination to follow the Greek way of life. Ever since Alexander the Great the Jews had come increasingly under Hellenic influences, which particularly affected the cultured and aristocratic families, including many members of the Jewish hierarchy which was the accepted guide in matters of religion. As a result there was a widespread falling away from the strict observance of the Torah, the doctrine of Israel, and a growth of compromise with heathenism. The pious declaimed against this trend and warned of heavy punishment for apostasy, but with no great response until the decrees of Antiochus and the terrible persecution which followed abundantly fulfilled the predictions.

The shock to the nation was tremendous. No such calamity had befallen the Jews since the time of Nebuchadnezzar. The people turned to God in penitence and contrition, and the success of the inspired leadership of the priestly family of the Hasmoneans confirmed them in their new and ardent devotion to their faith. The Jews experienced a religious Reformation. Extremist sects flourished. Loyalty to God and the Torah became paramount, and with this loyalty there was brought to the fore a fresh consideration of what it meant to be the Chosen People. The Law and the Prophets became the subject of acute study to discern the character of the Jewish mission, the circumstances of the Last Times, and the coming of the Messianic Age when all idolatry would be abolished and the nations would be converted to the worship of God.[22] When an independent Jewish state was regained, and Galilee and Idumea were added to it by conquest, the people there were compelled to adopt the Jewish religion.

From this time the Jews became ardently missionary. Many passages of the Scriptures spoke of the illumination of the Gentiles,[23] and these were now seen to impose upon Jews an urgent and positive role in winning the heathen for God. Devout bodies like the Pharisees especially espoused this cause.

It would seem that as early as 139 B.C. there was an expulsion of Jews from Rome by the praetor Hispalus. According to Valerius Maximus, a contemporary of Tiberius, this was due to Jewish attempts 'to contaminate Roman beliefs by foisting upon them the worship of Jupiter Sabazios'.[24] This god-name represents the Jewish Lord of Hosts (*Yahweh Sabaoth*), often transliterated by the Greeks as Iao Sabaoth. We could not have a more definite statement that the Jews were propagating their faith, and Valerius is here supported by Horace. Writing to Maecenas the counsellor of Augustus we find the poet saying, 'You must allow me my scribbling. If you don't, a great crowd of poets will come to help me. We far outnumber you, and like the Jews, will compel you to join our rout.'[25]

Roman imperialism, as we have shown, created the conditions for an influx of foreign cults into the capital eager to make converts, and particularly under the Empire this came to be regarded as both a spiritual and political danger. Maecenas, just mentioned, himself advised the emperor:

'Take part in divine worship, in every way established by our ancestral customs, and compel others to respect religion, but avoid and punish those who attempt to introduce foreign elements into it. Do so not merely as a mark of honour to the gods—although you may be sure that anyone who despises them sets little value upon anything—but because those who introduce new deities are by that very act persuading the masses to observe laws foreign to our own. Hence we have secret gatherings and assemblies of different sorts, all of which are inconsistent with the monarchical principle.'[26]

In other words, the alien faiths were subversive, and that of the Jews was notably so since from the Gentile viewpoint it was atheistic, teaching men everywhere to despise and neglect the gods. In the early Empire very great successes were enjoyed by the devotees of the Lord of Hosts and of Isis, so that the Emperor Tiberius became alarmed.

'He checked the spread of foreign rites, particularly the Egyptian and the Jewish. He compelled those who followed the former superstition to burn their ritual vestments and all their religious paraphernalia. The younger Jews he transferred to Provinces of rigorous climate under the pretence of assigning them to military service. All the rest of that nation, and all who observed its rites, he ordered out of the city under penalty of being permanently enslaved if they disobeyed.'[27]

The measure failed almost completely in its objectives, for very soon the Jews and the others were back, if indeed the expulsion was as wholesale as the Roman historians state. Seneca the philosopher was a youth at the time, and mentions that he himself had been induced to refrain from the flesh of certain animals, and Juvenal writes of those who had come under the Jewish spell, revering the Sabbath, abstaining from swine's flesh, and worshipping the empty sky. 'Soon,' he says, 'they become circumcised. Trained to despise the laws of Rome, they learn, maintain and revere the Law of the Jews, which Moses has transmitted in a mystic volume.'[28] Persius, another poet, speaks of witnessing the Jewish preparations on Friday evenings and of their effect on him: 'You move your lips in silent dread and turn pale at the Sabbath of the circumcised.'[29]

The Jews had ample opportunity to expound their religion to Gentile neighbours, and their synagogues were open to anyone who wished to observe and inquire. But if they were not so blatantly propagandist as other foreign faiths with their public rituals and processions, they were by no means passive, utilising various aids to wean the heathen from idolatry. A favourite medium was literature. Not only did they produce books and tracts of their own; they interpolated the Greek classics with passages which converted their authors into protagonists. 'Orpheus was made to recant his polytheism and proclaim the one true God: Sophocles to foretell the end of the world by fire and the future blessedness of the righteous. All this was merely a forcible entry upon the heritage of the Hellenes; the major premiss underlying it was the genuine conviction that the creed of revelation was in fact older and truer than the wisdom and worship of the Greek.'[30]

The Greek-Oriental prophetic writings, notably the *Sibylline Oracles*, were specially marked down for attention. A collection of these had been acquired by the superstitious Romans, who set great store by the interpretation of their mysterious pronouncements. Many spurious Oracles came into circulation, frequently of Jewish composition, which so impressed the credulous, rather like the prophecies attributed to Nostradamus, that what people were believing on such mystical authority could not help being regarded as a threat to the Empire. When Augustus became Pontifex Maximus he had a quantity of spurious Oracles burnt, and his successor Tiberius also instituted a purification of the collection because of a popular prophecy that the end of the Empire was at hand.[31] After the failure of the Jewish revolt in A.D. 66–70 the anti-Roman aspect of the oracular and apocalyptic propaganda was intensified and reached a peak around the close of the century.

The subject of Jewish evangelism and its prophetic message to the nations is of the utmost importance in considering the character of Christianity. We must therefore deal with it more fully in the following pages. What we have illustrated is that the Jewish impact on the Graeco-Roman world was extensive, and after 150 B.C. increasingly influential. The antisemitic manifestations which accompanied this development were not wholly due to resentment of Jewish privileges and social insularity: they were due in large measure to the clash between monotheism and polytheism. This collision arose not only because through the Jewish dispersion the opposing ideologies were thrown together, but because the Jews had now become zealously missionary.

NOTES AND REFERENCES

1. Strabo, quoted by Josephus, *Antiq.* XIV. vii. 2.

2. Theophrastus of Lesbos: 'inasmuch as they are philosophers by race, they (the Syrians who are Jews) discuss the nature of the Deity among themselves, and spend the night in observing the stars....' Quoted by Porphyrius, c. A.D. 275.

3. Radin, *The Jews among the Greeks and Romans*, p. 85 ff.

4. Radin, *op. cit.*, p. 115, citing *Greek Papyri of the British Museum*, iii. 183.

5. Radin, *op. cit.*, p. 92 ff.

6. Manetho, quoted by Josephus, *Against Apion*, I. 26.

7. Ani the Scribe in a hymn to Ra prays: 'May I smite the Ass; may I crush the Evil One; may I destroy Apep in his hour' (*Papyrus of Ani*, i. 14).

8. Plutarch, *Concerning Isis and Osiris*, xxx.

9. Ibid., *Moralia*, ii. 813.

10. Poseidonius, quoted by Diodorus, *Eclogae*, 34.

11. Tacitus, *History*, v. 4: 'They consecrated the figure of an ass in their inner shrine.'

12. Tacitus, *Hist.* v. 9.

13. Tertullian, *Apologia*, xvi.

14. Wunsch, *Sethianische Verfluchungstafeln aus Rom*, p. 112.

15. Epiphanius, *Panarion*, xxvi. 12: 'The cause assigned for the death of Zacharias the son of Barachias is, that going into the Temple he beheld standing within the sanctuary a man with the face of an ass; and when he was rushing out to cry to the people, "Woe unto you! Whom do you worship?" he was struck dumb by the apparition.' See further *Jewish Encyclopaedia*, article Ass-Worship.

16. Hardy, *Studies in Roman History*, p. 18, and Josephus, *Antiq.* XIV. x.

17. Josephus, *Antiq.* XIV. x.

18. Cicero, *Pro Flacco*, 66–9, for the full text.

19. Horace, quoted by Radin, *The Jews among the Greeks and Romans*, p. 246.

20. Suetonius, *Augustus*, LXXVI.

21. Ovid, *Ars Amatoria*, i. 413.

22. See Schonfield, *The Passover Plot*, Part I, ch. i. and Part II, ch. i.

23. E.g. Isa. xi. 9 (Hab. ii. 14); Isa. xlix. 6; Mic. iv. 1–3; Zech. xiv. 16.

24. Valerius Maximus, I. iii. 2. See Hardy, *Studies in Roman History*, p. 15.

25. Horace, *Satires*, I. iv. 18.

26. See *Dio Cassius*, xxxvi. 6.

27. Suetonius, *Tiberius*, XXXVI. Tacitus refers to the same expulsion (*Annals*, ii. 85), and mentions that 4,000 freedmen of military age were consigned to Sardinia to crush brigandage there. But these men apparently were not Jews but 'tainted with this superstition'.

28. Seneca, *Epistles to Lucilius*, 108, 22; Juvenal, *Satires*, xiv. 96.

29. Persius, *Satires*, v. 176.

30. H. N. Bate, *The Sibylline Oracles*, p. 18.

31. Suetonius, *Augustus*, XXXI; *Dio Cassius*, lvii. 18.

3
Messianic Explosion

THE Jewish spiritual revival which followed the experiences of the nation in the time of Antiochus and his successors brought into prominence a renewed sense of Israel's destiny and mission. The prophetic vision of the ultimate Brotherhood of Man under the rule of the One God and Father of all men was seen to be associated with a Divine Plan for its realisation. 'According to this plan God had chosen and set apart one nation among the nations of the world, neither numerous nor powerful, to be the recipient of his laws, and by observing them to offer a universal example. The theocracy of Israel would be the persuasive illustration of a world theocracy: it would be "a kingdom of priests and a holy nation" witnessing to all nations.'[1]

The revival therefore stimulated an outburst of Messianic and apocalyptic fervour. The tracts for those times, of which the Book of Daniel is a Biblical specimen, spelled out the doom of the heathen empires and foretold the speedy advent of the Kingdom of God governed by the saints of the Most High depicted in the likeness of a Son of Man. But the earlier part of this book is a challenge to heathenism in the persons of Daniel and his three companions. They refuse to touch the pagan king's food and drink, and thrive on pulse and water. The supremacy of the One God over the worship of idols is demonstrated by the salvation of the Holy Children when condemned to the flames, and of Daniel himself when thrown into a den of lions. The second book of Maccabees in the Apocrypha has its own story to tell of brave martyrdom out of loyalty to God and his commandments under pressure of blandishments and the most extreme torture.[2] A whole new fortifying and prognostic literature came into being.

It is curious to reflect how history might have been changed if Antiochus Epiphanes had not embarked on the subordination of Judaism to Hellenism in such a drastic manner. Before this the influence of Greek culture on the Jews had been very marked, ever since the benign ideas of Alexander the Great had made such a favourable impression. His dream of world unity had seemed to catch the spirit of the Hebrew Prophets in a different way. Plutarch tells us that 'Alexander desired to render all upon earth subject to one law of reason and one form of government and to reveal all men as one people, and to this purpose he made himself conform. And if the deity that sent down Alexander's soul into this world of ours had not recalled him quickly, one law would govern all mankind, and they would look toward one rule of justice as though toward a common source of light.'[3]

Antiochus may have thought that he was contributing to the fulfilment of this ideal. But his actions, so far as the Jews were concerned, had exactly the opposite effect. There was a revulsion against Hellenism and its enticing culture. A stern mood set in, and the Jewish rulers, including members of the high priestly families, who continued to follow Greek manners, were denounced as apostates and sinners.

The strictest morality was enjoined by new eclectic groups. Religiosity flourished. We find this attitude of mind, with its rigidities, its fault-finding, its horror of lust, fully reflected in the pseudepigraphic literature of the Essenes and Pharisees and in the Gospels.[4] What has not been sufficiently understood is why this absorption with perfectionism was so strongly in evidence at the time, why there was this striving and sweating to conform to the last jot and tittle of the Torah. It is totally lacking in insight to talk of Jewish legalism. What was manifesting itself was a penitent contrition for former waywardness. A whole nation was in the grip of a revivalist urge to get right with God. This is what brought men to scrupulous observance, to prayer and fasting. This is what brought the crowds flocking to Jordan to wash in its waters at the bidding of a John the Baptist. Belial and all his works were to be renounced; and the pious proclaimed that he ruled in the seats of government. Resistance movements accordingly found eager supporters. Petitions were poured out for God's intervention in sending the Messiah as the righteous king who would smite the wicked with the sword of his mouth and eradicate all idolatry.

It is a well-known fact that revivalism is a great stimulus to missionary enterprise. It followed naturally, therefore, under these conditions, that Judaism should pass from the defensive to the offensive. Throughout the Graeco-Roman world an ideological warfare was launched to hasten the coming of the Kingdom of God by an all-out campaign to witness to and convert the heathen. In areas remote from the pressures in Judea it was not conducted with the same intensity; but it was still powerful enough to have a very considerable impact and success, alarming the pagan populace as antisemitic orators played on their fears and forcing the fairly complacent Roman government to take occasional heavy-handed action in the interests of the safety of the state.

We have mentioned that at an intellectual level Jewish propaganda concentrated on indoctrination through literature, by interpolating the Greek classics and by publishing books in Greek expounding the Jewish philosophy. Not only was idolatry and all unrighteousness assailed, there was also built up in the minds of the heathen the idea of the special character and mission of the Jews as God's Holy Nation. To the Gentile world this was a novel and extremely influential idea which appears in a variety of propaganda documents such as *The Letter of Aristeas*, the *Wisdom of Solomon* and the *Sibylline Oracles*. A quotation from each of these sources will illustrate this teaching.

In *Aristeas* the Jewish high priest Eleazar discourses about the Mosaic code and explains its regulations and proceeds: 'Hence it comes that the priests who rule the Egyptians, and have closely investigated many things and been conversant with literature, call us "Men of God", a designation which does not belong to the rest of mankind, but to him only who reverences the True God: but they are men of meat and drink and raiment, for their whole nature finds its solace in these things.[5] But with our countrymen these things are counted of no worth, but their reflections throughout their whole life concern the sovereignty of God. To the intent, then, that we should not become perverted through joining in the pollutions of any, or consorting with base persons, he fenced us round on all sides with laws of purification in matters of meat and drink and handling and hearing and seeing.[6] For, speaking generally, all these, if viewed in the light of their inward meaning, are alike, being directed by a Single Power, and in every detail there is a profound reason for the things which we abstain from using and those of which we make use.'[7]

'Great are thy judgments,' declares the *Wisdom of Solomon*, 'and hard to describe; therefore uninstructed souls have gone astray. For when lawless men supposed that they held the Holy Nation in their power, they themselves lay as captives of darkness and prisoners of long night, shut in under their roofs, exiles from Eternal Providence.'[8]

The *Sibylline Oracles* speak of the Jews as 'a holy race of godfearing men', 'a royal tribe', and 'the people of the great God . . . they who are to be the guides of life to all mankind'.[9]

There is a clear indication in this last statement of the universality of the Jewish mission. The apostle Paul alludes to it in his letter to the Romans. Apostrophising the Jew, he declares, 'You rely on law and boast in God. You are acquainted with his will, and can make clear distinctions, being instructed from the Law. You are convinced that you are a guide to the blind, a light to those in darkness, a tutor of the backward, a teacher of infants, because in the Law you have the whole corpus of knowledge and truth.'[10] Similarly Josephus points out: 'The masses have long since shown a keen desire to adopt our religious observances; and there is not one city, Greek or barbarian, nor a single nation, to which our custom of abstaining from work on the seventh day has not spread, and where the fasts and the lighting of lamps and many of our prohibitions in the matter of food are not observed. . . . The greatest miracle of all is that our Law holds out no bait of sensual pleasure, but has exercised this influence through its own inherent merits; and, as God permeates the universe, so the Law has found its way among all mankind.'[11]

The Jewish message could not fail to be universalistic, and spread by missionary effort as well as by example, since it proclaimed the existence of one universal God, and directed itself to emancipating the heathen from idolatry and immorality. It announced a coming Day of Wrath and Judgment for the whole earth, and the setting up of the Kingdom of God embracing all mankind. There was no syncretism, no advocating of one cult alongside others, no endeavour to make all men Jews. Instead, and far more potently, there was a prophetic and dynamic call to all nations, while remaining distinct nations, to enter into the relationship of the righteous by yielding allegiance to God and to the Divine laws applicable to all humanity.

Unlike so much of religious thought at the time Judaism was not given to philosophising on the nature of deity, neither did it concern itself unduly with the individual self. Its creed was a creed of revelation, of the Eternal and Invisible God who had made himself known to his creation, and had made known his will for the world he had created, mediated through a people of his choice. This revelation was the evidence of God's love and care for his creatures. To a society speculating on the lot of men and the influences of Fate and Fortune the Jews proclaimed with a startling positiveness and authority the existence of a Divine Plan working itself out over the Ages with an ultimate goal and objective of the highest good for mankind, a plan which called for the active participation of men for its furtherance. The revelation had been made. The fulfilment of the plan was inevitable, and the means of fulfilment predesignated and progressively made known: but a choice was given to everyone to work with the plan or against it, to obey or disobey its requirements. There would be reward for the just and punishment for the unjust when the time for Judgment came; but men should serve God from love and not from fear, and keep his commandments with joy and not out of hope of reward.

What the Jews asserted not only carried conviction to many, backed up as it was by a venerable collection of sacred writings, it was quite distinctive in its outlook and in its demands, though having some kinship with the teaching of the magians. There was posited, as we have seen, that among the nations of the world God had appointed a priestly nation to bless the others and minister to them in spiritual things. A whole people was performing the office of a priestly caste. This people was therefore a holy people, and the ordinances governing it constituted the peculiar discipline of its priesthood, setting it apart from all peoples of the world. It was not a comfortable idea to grasp or to live with, and by no means easy to credit, since Jews were engaged like their neighbours in trade and commerce, litigation and agitation. There were bad and unpleasant Jews. Their peculiarities could be taken by Gentiles to be a mark of aversion to the rest of mankind rather than one of benevolence. They repelled as well as attracted.

Again, unlike other faiths, the Jews were not for the most part seeking to make complete converts. It was possible to become a Jew and cease to be a Gentile. Such a new Israelite underwent a rebirth. His personal past and associations were expunged and washed away in the waters of baptism. He was a proselyte of righteousness, new born, new named, henceforth subject to all the restrictions and penalties affecting the natural Jew. He was divorced totally from his former life, from family and friends. He could neither eat with them nor have fellowship with them.

The major aim of Jewish evangelism was not so far-reaching. Its intention was not to create more Jews but an ever-expanding multitude of Godfearing Gentiles. It was not part of the Divine Plan that all men should be Jews. The Prophets had revealed that even in the Messianic Age the world would consist of many nations; but they would know and worship the One God, practice justice and mercy, and abolish war. All Gentiles who now responded to the message would be a kind of first-fruits of the nations, assured of participation in the felicities of the approaching new order, the World to Come. It was not needful for them to enter the covenant with Abraham by circumcision or the covenant with Moses by taking upon themselves the yoke of the Law. It sufficed that they govern their lives by the Primeval Laws given to Noah, and principally to abjure the three major sins of idolatry, fornication and murder.[12] Such semi-proselytes (*ger-toshab*) did not cease to be Gentiles, but were to be accepted as entitled to all the care and privileges of 'the stranger within the gates'.

This cause of enlightening the Gentiles as foretold by the Prophets was particularly dear to the Pharisees, who not only had a strong Messianic consciousness but also a strong social sense. It was from his Pharisaic background that Paul derived his deep desire to become a missionary to the Gentiles, so that when he had a vision of Jesus as the Messiah the mandate he received reflected what was already in his heart.

The Pharisees, indeed, saw their task as twofold in accordance with the words of Isaiah, to bring Israel fully back to God, and to be the instrument of God's salvation to the ends of the earth.[13] To achieve the first they interpreted the Torah so as to assure the sanctification of every part of Jewish life, while for the second they employed every persuasion they could bring to bear through their propaganda.

We cannot rightly assess the character of Christian beginnings unless we give full weight to the circumstances in which they were grounded. We have to be aware of the mounting excitement and fervour which took possession of the Jewish people as they were warned by the pious that the climax of the Ages was fast approaching with its terrors, its judgments, and its promise of deliverance for the faithful at the advent of the Messiah. Knowledge that the time was short lent an urgency to Jewish evangelism as it no less inspired an extremity of zeal for the observance of the Torah. While some more puritanical sections might retire to the wilderness to isolate themselves from evil and temptation, others went forth to battle as a Church militant to take the Kingdom of Heaven by storm.

In Palestine it was felt acutely that the Holy Land should be contaminated by alien rulers following heathen ways. During the long reign of Herod the Great, client-king of the Jews sponsored by Rome and a lover of Greek culture, resentment and antagonism had grown, so that it was only by converting the country into a police state that open rebellion, largely having a spiritual sanction, was averted. The king was a professing Jew, but of Idumean origin and strong Graeco-Roman sympathies, and his flaunting of unJewish manners caused the name of Edom, Israel's traditional foe, to become a synonym for the power of unrighteousness embodied in the Roman Empire. Henceforth Rome was the arch-enemy in the eyes of the populace of Palestine whose feelings were readily aroused by religious hotheads and revolutionaries, whose slogan was 'No ruler but God'. All Jews in the homeland who supported the Roman rule, whether in high places or low, were scorned and despised.

Incident after incident is reported by Josephus, which reveals the undercurrent of emotional hostility coming to the surface whenever something happened that caused its release. To purify the land from every taint of heathenism became a fetish and affected all public relations. For the Zealots it meant driving out the Romans and destroying their minions as the ultimate aim; but for so long as this was not practicable every act of government was to be watched in case it should involve violation of some principle to be upheld at all costs, or some invasion of sacred liberty to be resisted. The tension of this apocalyptic atmosphere was terrific, built up by the extraordinary awareness of the Messianic import of the times until it finally burst out in open war. But for many years previously peace had been taken away, so that in many cases family harmony was destroyed. Brother looked on brother with a jaundiced eye, and bigotry and intolerance were rampant. We meet with much evidence of the state of affairs in Jewish literature relating to the time and in the Gospels. But we do not have clearly defined for us what lay behind these manifestations and have to turn to other sources like the histories of Josephus for their explanation.

We read, for example, that while Herod was dying pious youths incited by their teachers pulled down and hacked to pieces the golden eagle which the king had set up over the great gate of the Temple. We learn of the outbreaks of violence following his death, of the exploits of Judas the Zealot leader in Galilee, of Simon in Perea, of Athrongeus and others elsewhere, of bloody battle with the Romans in the Temple courts, of the later opposition to the imposition of the Roman tribute when Judea was incorporated in the Province of Syria, of the massive demonstration against Pontius Pilate when as governor he sent troops with their effigy-adorned ensigns into the holy city. These and many other incidents testify to the acute spiritual sensitivity of the Jewish people at a period when they believed the hour of Divine Destiny was about to strike, and which engendered a mood of extreme self-criticism joined with a reckless disregard of personal safety. 'Whoever would preserve his life would lose it.'[14]

The harsh prophecies of the Zealots spread out from Palestine mingling with the universal Jewish call to the nations to repent of their vice and idolatry. The bogus *Sibylline Oracles* became boldly seditious in their predictions of the fate of Rome, now associated with the Great Judgment preceding the advent of the Kingdom of God.

God's revelation of great wrath to come
In the last time upon a faithless world,
I make known, prophesying to all men . . .
On thee some day shall come, O haughty Rome,
A fitting stroke from heaven, and thou the first
Shall bend the neck, be levelled to the earth,
And fire shall utterly consume thee, bent
Upon thy pavements. Thy wealth shall perish,
And on thy site shall wolves and foxes dwell,
And then shalt thou become all desolate
As though thou hadst not been. . . .
Near at hand
Is the end of the world, and the last day,
And judgment of immortal God for such
As are both called and chosen. First of all
Inexorable wrath shall fall on Rome:
A time of blood and wretched life shall come.
Woe, woe to thee, O land of Italy,
Great barbarous nation . . .
And no more under slavish yoke to thee
Will either Greek or Syrian put his neck,
Barbarian or any other nation.
Thou shalt be plundered and shalt be destroyed
For what thou didst, and wailing aloud in fear
Thou shalt give until thou shalt all repay.[15]

Another Oracle proclaims: 'But when Rome shall rule over Egypt, though still delaying, then shall the great kingdom of the immortal King appear among men, and a holy king (i.e. the Messiah) shall come who shall rule over the whole earth for all ages of the course of time. Then shall implacable wrath fall upon the men of Latium. . . . Ah, wretched me, when shall that day come, and the judgment of immortal God, the great King? Yet still be ye builded, ye cities, and all adorned with temples and theatres, with market squares and images of gold, silver and stone, that so ye may come to the day of bitterness.

For it shall come, when the smell of brimstone shall pass upon all men.'[16]

No wonder that Augustus and Tiberius in alarm took action to purge the Sibylline collection and to restrict the activities of eastern astrologers and soothsayers. Prognostications of the doom of Rome, readily credited by subject peoples, could stimulate a spirit of revolt, encouraging on such mystic authority the conviction that Rome was not as invincible and invulnerable as she would have the world believe. The fateful pronouncements were in the highest degree unsettling and could well become positively dangerous. It is to be noted, as in the first passage quoted, that the Jewish oracle-makers cleverly played on the hostile sentiments which were rife among the peoples subservient to Rome. Greeks, Syrians and barbarians are advised that the day is at hand when they will no longer be enslaved. The Sibyl cries again: 'For all the wealth that Rome has taken from tributary Asia, three times as much shall Asia take from Rome, requiting upon her her cursed arrogance: and for all the men who were taken from Asia to go and dwell in Italy, twenty times so many of Italy shall serve in Asia as penniless slaves, and a thousand-fold shall be the requital.'[17] The Slaves' Revolt under Spartacus was still remembered, and Roman affluence still greatly depended on the substantial slave population.

In the first century of the Christian Era the Jewish missionary enterprise, laudable in its original designs, was being increasingly taken over and directed by Zealot extremists bent on promoting and seeking allies for a universal disruption of the Empire by subversive propaganda. Their agents visited the Jewish communities of the Dispersion sowing disaffection and trying to win support for risings and civil strife which would go hand in hand with a revolt in Palestine, distracting and weakening Rome's military might to such an extent by the widespread diffusion of insurrections that victory would be won despite all the odds against it. In most places these activities proved abortive, and the Jewish communities under

Roman protection remained loyal. The incitement, however, did score some successes, appealing as it did to patriotic and religious emotions which had been greatly stimulated by Messianism. The conscription by Tiberius of Roman Jews and their Gentile supporters of military age, whom he dispatched to Sardinia to put down brigandage, may be regarded as a counter-measure, like the later expulsion of foreign Jews from Rome in the reign of Claudius, which Suetonius specifically ascribes to Messianic agitation.[18]

At this juncture there was a fresh development which complicated the situation still further. A second wave from the Jewish Messianic explosion came flooding over the Empire. The Jewish propaganda had been putting it about that a king of their race was expected who would govern the world in place of Caesar on behalf of God. Now new emissaries from the Holy Land began to arrive in the cities of the Empire dramatically announcing that the promised king had appeared, that the Romans had crucified him in Jerusalem, but that he had thwarted his enemies by conquering death and ascending to the skies, from whence he would speedily return with the legions of heaven at his back to execute judgment and take his throne.

The synagogues of the Empire became a battleground of conflicting opinions as hope contended with suspicion, incredulity and fear of fraud. Was this another move by the Jewish militants to gain adherents for the cause of revolt? Was it a sectarian folly of yet another duped and deluded body of fanatics? Whatever was behind it, Rome was alerted to an additional peril, the conversion of a vague anticipation into a concrete threat, however fantastic was the story being circulated. The eastern king identified in the *Oracles* with the downfall of Rome now bore a name, that of a man, a Jewish rebel who had been executed in Judea in the governorship of Pontius Pilate at the close of the reign of Tiberius. But his death signified little if it was believed that like the dead Caesars he had winged his way to heaven in a manner corresponding to their apotheosis.[19]

The effect of an insubstantial being, who could not be touched, was a graver matter than that of any leader in the physical world. The name Jesus coupled with the mysterious title Christus, employed among the Jews with reference to the world ruler they foretold, meant that a superstition had arisen which if allowed to grow unchecked might undermine the whole structure of Roman security. The most heartening indication was that outside the Province of Syria the Jews themselves seemed most reluctant to accept the doctrine of the Christian agents. The chief danger spots, nevertheless, were Rome itself and Alexandria with their large Jewish populations. Temporarily the Emperor Claudius closed certain synagogues in Rome and expelled a number of the foreign Jews.[20] He also wrote to the Jews of Alexandria warning them not to entertain itinerant Jews from Syria if they did not wish to be treated as abettors of 'a pest which threatens the whole world'.[21]

NOTES AND REFERENCES

1. See Schonfield, *The Passover Plot*, p. 24 ff.

2. *II. Macc.* vi–vii.

3. Plutarch, *Moralia*, tr. by F. C. Babbitt (Loeb Classical Library), p. 405.

4. See for example the admonitions in the *Testaments of the XII Patriarchs* and in the Sermon on the Mount in Matthew's Gospel.

5. Cp. Mt. vi. 31–2.

6. Cp. Col. ii. 21.

7. *Letter of Aristeas*, tr. by H. St. J. Thackeray, 140–2.

8. Wisdom of Solomon, xvii. 1–2 (The Apocrypha, R.S.V.). The preceding chapters xiii–xvi deal with the folly of idolatry. Similarly *Aristeas* (130–9) speaks of the One God and attacks idolatry.

9. *Sibylline Oracles*, Bk. III, tr. by H. N. Bate.

10. Rom. ii. 17–20.

11. Josephus, *Against Apion*, II. 39, tr. by H. St. J. Thackeray (Loeb Classical Library).

12. 'Any sins denounced by the Law may be committed by a man if his life is threatened, except the sins of idolatry, fornication and murder' (Talmud, *Sanh.* 64a). On the Laws of Noah see Schonfield, *The Jew of Tarsus*, ch. iii, and below ch. v.

13. Cp. Isa. xlix. 5–7. 'And now, saith the Lord that formed me from the womb to be his servant, to bring Jacob again to him, that Israel may be gathered to him. . . . It is a light thing that thou shouldest be my servant to raise up the tribes of Jacob, and to restore the preserved of Israel: I will also give thee for a light to the Gentiles, that thou mayest be my salvation unto the ends of the earth.' The pious in Israel saw themselves in the Messianic role of the Suffering Servant, who yet is the instrument of the salvation of mankind.

14. Cp. Mk. viii. 34–5. 'Whoever will follow me must be utterly reckless and ready for execution in joining me; for whoever will preserve his life will lose it. . . .'

15. *Sibylline Oracles*, Bk. VIII, 1–3, 37–42, 91–5, 121–9, tr. by M. S. Terry.

16. *Sibylline Oracles*, Bk. III. 45–60, tr. by H. N. Bate.

17. *Ibid.*, 350 ff.

18. Suetonius, *Claudius*, XXV.

19. The Romans were fully familiar with apotheosis in respect of their rulers, who continued their existence by ascension to heaven. A comet had given evidence of the assumption of Julius Caesar, and the same was signalised at the death of Augustus when an eagle was seen flying out of his funeral pyre. Even women of the imperial family, like Drusilla, were given divine honours and their asumption was recorded on evidence held to be reliable. Seneca caricatured the current belief in his *Apocolocyntosis*: 'You demand evidence? Right. Ask the man who saw Drusilla *en route* for heaven. He will tell you that he saw Claudius going up too, cloppety-cloppety in his usual fashion. That man just can't help seeing what goes on in the sky.' See J. P. V. D. Balsdon, *The Romans*, p. 257 f.

20. Dio Cassius, lx. 6, and Suetonius.

21. *Letter of Claudius to the Alexandrians*, tr. by H. Idris Bell, *Jews and Christians in Egypt*.

4

The Door of Faith

IN its origins the movement which gave rise to Christianity was wholly Jewish. It was a direct product of those circumstances which we have outlined, and could not have come into existence without their stress on the advent of the Last Times and the concomitant expectation of the coming of the Messiah. Since this development has been fully traced in the author's previous volume *The Passover Plot* it is not needful to elaborate here how the Galilean Jew Jesus, a descendant of David, came to see himself as the God-sent king of Israel, that anointed one, the Messiah (Christ), who was destined to inaugurate the Kingdom of God on earth and rule the nations in righteousness for the duration of time. Kingly this man was, a powerful personality, so sublime in his convictions, so assured, so purposive in his actions, as to make it impossible for his followers to see him otherwise than as the fulfilment of Israel's hopes. There had been the difficulty that he had been rejected by the forces of the present evil age, and crucified by the Romans and their minions as a rebel against Caesar. But this could not obliterate the confidence Jesus had inspired, and his own words had conveyed that his adversities were part of the pattern of the Messianic programme, the essential prelude to his being revealed in all the majesty of his more comprehensive and immortal sovereignty.

Jesus had not doubted at all his future role. The sceptic may regard his convictions as a mental aberration, or as a fantasy induced by the prevailing Messianic emotional atmosphere. But for Jesus his faith was of that order which can remove mountains, and therefore he could plan so far as this was humanly possible for his triumph over death, for his availability in the land of the living for that transformation which would signalise God's exaltation of him to the throne of a world to be newly born to the accompaniment of the thunders and lightnings of heavenly judgment.

The dividing line between the two phases was an empty tomb from which the Messiah's body had mysteriously disappeared. The immediate conclusion of the close associates of Jesus was that human hands had been responsible. But presently the faith of Jesus himself was driving doubt into a far corner of consciousness, and one and another were convinced that they had seen and spoken with someone who by some miracle must be the Master risen from the dead. To the same conclusion, it was found, certain Scriptures which could be applied to the Messiah seemed inescapably to point. 'Thou wilt not leave my soul in hell; neither wilt thou suffer thine holy one to see corruption. Thou wilt shew me the path of life. . . .'[1] No rational explanation of what had transpired, once faith had taken hold, was therefore to be sought for or entertained.[2] The whole temper of the time, as it appeared to these devout Jews excited by Messianic fervour, was against it. In these Last Days miracles and prodigies were in order, as they were when of old Moses led Israel out of bondage to the Egyptians.

In those Closing Days, God says,
I will pour out my Spirit on all flesh,
And your sons and daughters will prophesy:
Your young men shall see visions,
And your old men dream dreams.
Even on my menservants and maidservants,
Will I pour out my Spirit,
And they will prophesy.
I will show portents in the skies above,

And signs on the earth beneath,
Blood and fire and fumes of smoke.
The sun will be turned to darkness,
And the moon will become blood red,
Ere that great and awful Day of the Lord comes,
Then all who invoke the Lord's name will be saved.[3]

The opening chapters of the Acts of the Apostles, which report briefly, selectively, and to an extent imaginatively the inception of the Christian movement, correctly convey the atmosphere of the period. The histories, Roman and Jewish, similarly make much of supernatural signs and portents presaging startling events and calamities. It was an epoch which particularly had caught the fever of an otherworldly witness and warning to men and nations, and its story cannot omit the general credence placed in strange and fantastic occurrences and their significance. In these respects the isolation of the New Testament, in the minds of Christians, from the literature of the ancient world familiar to scholars, puts a false value, in point of what are regarded as Divine interventions, on what is apprehended as being of the order of the miraculous. We have to accept that miracles and wonders were part and parcel of contemporary beliefs, whether credited to the gods or to the powers of sage and holy men. The accounts are so widespread and often circumstantial in narration that it is fruitless to argue whether they are true or untrue. What is relevant is that men's minds were attuned to the reception of such reports as accurate and in accordance with their understanding of the ordering of things.

Words are not to be wasted, therefore, on disputing about the veracity of recorded happenings of a seemingly inexplicable nature. These establish nothing so far as any faith is concerned which determines the status of those to whom they relate or under what control they acted. They cannot be employed to prove that anyone, man or woman, was Divine or divinely influenced, any more than that he or she, as opponents would have it, owed their powers to demons and evil spirits. There is not ruled out by any means that certain events and experiences could have extra-human causes; but it betrays an immature mentality if conclusions are reached without due regard for the historical and scientific, including psychological, processes of investigation. It is all too easy to confuse issues, and miss perceiving what is really consequential, because we are greatly attracted by the mysterious.

While it is not appropriate at this stage to concern ourselves with Christian theology, as it developed, we can, for example, see great *a priori* improbability in the doctrine of the deity of Jesus Christ by reason of the fact that Christianity began as a Jewish movement. The doctrine is diametrically opposed to the Jewish concept of God at the time Jesus lived, and no one being a Jew, subscribing to the Hebrew Scriptures, and seeking acceptance by Jews, would be likely to present himself in such a contrary character. Taken with the evidence that the doctrine was agreeable to current heathen notions the obvious inference is that it was an intrusion from Gentile sources and not fundamental. Since the doctrine was also resisted by the main body of Jewish believers in Jesus as Messiah[4] this tends to confirm that it was alien in its derivation and that Jesus himself could not have entertained it. Early Gospel material shows him exercising all the extreme care of the devout Jew in guarding the name of God from profanation and representing him as the sole Being to be worshipped and described as good.[5] The author of the Acts of the Apostles appears to have been aware that the deity of Jesus was no part of the teaching of the earliest Christians. Consequently, when he offers some glimpses of the movement in Judea in those days and makes Peter and others refer to Jesus in suitable speeches, there is no trace of the idea of the Incarnation. Jesus is 'a man proved to be from God'. This man, the Messiah, God raised from the dead and exalted him to his right hand. God 'has honoured his servant Jesus' and sent him to bless Israel first. Prayer is addressed to God 'the Lord of the universe, maker of heaven and earth' and

Jesus is mentioned as 'thy devoted servant, whom thou didst anoint'. Even the hellenistic Jew Stephen, in his vision, sees Jesus as the Son of Man standing at God's right hand.[6]

The importance of apprehending the beginnings of Christianity as wholly Jewish cannot be exaggerated. Only to the extent that we are able to do this by priming ourselves with information about Jewish life, thought and faith at the time do we become capable of understanding Jesus and the original character of Christianity. We have to divest ourselves—no easy task for anyone nurtured in the creed and traditional views of the Church—of every consideration that what Jesus and his immediate followers represented was anything other than Jewish. In other words, the Christian must become a Jew in comprehension, sympathy and spirit before he is qualified to address himself to matters Christian. Scholarship is not enough, because it does not necessarily involve commitment and identification with the Jewish soul. While there lingers any sense of what is Jewish being alien, and still worse hostile or opposed, there is not the slightest possibility of getting Christianity in correct perspective. Hence the unusual lead-in of the opening chapters to a book about the rise of Christianity, especially in the consideration of Judaism abroad, in the world to which the Gospel message was directed.

The inauguration of the Christian movement is ascribed in the Acts to a meeting of the disciples and family of Jesus in Jerusalem at the festival of Pentecost (Feast of Weeks), second of the three Jewish pilgrim festivals, associated with the offering of the first fruits of the wheat harvest and commemorating the giving of the Law to Moses on Sinai. These connections may well have some bearing on what is related. The story tells how on this occasion the Spirit of the Lord, which Jesus held had descended upon himself to inaugurate his Messiahship in fulfilment of prophecy, now came upon his followers. The manifestation, physically answering to the wind called by the Arabs *khamsin*, could be said to be a fulfilment of Psalm xxix where such a wind is called the voice of the Lord 'which divides the flames of fire'. The effect on those concerned was that they became ecstatic and began to speak in various tongues.

The story as it stands is quasi-legendary; but evidently something happened which gave rise to it and which was interpreted as the outpouring of the Holy Spirit. Certainly it is clear from the letters of the apostle Paul that psychic phenomena were a feature of Christian gatherings. They were held to betoken the spiritual presence of Jesus, and were gifts from above that heralded and certified to the recipients the powers of the Messianic Age to come. Such 'possession' and mediumship conveys to us something of the emotional intensity and fanaticism of the members of the movement, and also, as we learn from the sources, that these members initially were largely recruited from the orders of society among whom phenomena of this type are of more frequent occurrence. Women and artisans, freedmen and slaves, were the chief ingredients of the early Christian communities.

There was nothing at first to suggest that a new religion was being born. The Christians, better known to Jews as Nazoreans (*Notsrim*), appeared as one more Jewish sect brought into existence by the spiritual excitement of the times. Its central feature was the conviction that in Jesus of Galilee the Messiah had been revealed, and besides this it had attributes, some distinctive, others similar to those of such groups as were assured they were the predestined Elect of Israel.

Inevitably, the Glad Tidings (the Gospel) that the Messiah had come, and was now in heaven waiting for the fateful moment when his enemies would be made his footstool, assured the movement of a success in winning adherents which other sects without that pregnant and electrifying message could not emulate, though those who held John the Baptist to have been the Messiah also secured considerable support. But, over and above, Christianity flourished abroad because it obtained ardent advocates like the brilliant Saul (Paul) of Tarsus, because it extended its constituency to Gentiles in addition to

Jews, and because it took up and gave greater emphasis to the propaganda which the Jews had busied themselves with circulating among the nations. At one stroke the visions were translated into realities, the dreams into actions. All the imperatives of the prophecies of impending change and judgment were accentuated, since now they were linked with the name of the man who would shortly bring them to pass. The Great Secret was out. The forces of the World to Come were being openly displayed in the New Society already being created. The door of faith was flung wide open to admit all who were ready and foreordained to enter.

Not a new religion, then, but the Jewish Gospel made concrete was the first effect of the fresh Messianic explosion. Those who conveyed the message, and were on that account called apostles or envoys, were the emissaries of that now exalted Jewish king who had been foretold as the world ruler, before whom at his glorious return the idols would vanish and the haughty Roman in common with all other kings of the earth would bend the knee in homage.[7]

Such a message, bursting upon a world held together by an awe of naked power and military might and already rife with rumours that the sway of Caesar was doomed, was as startling as it was dangerously subversive. The missionaries who were Zealots were aware of this. But mystics like Paul, and those who followed his lead, were almost completely oblivious of the social and political repercussions of their activities. They 'moved in the spirit', on another plane of consciousness. They were prone to misinterpret the opposition they encountered, attributing it to the machinations of the Evil One who dominated the present world instead of to the natural reactions of those whose peace and security was threatened.

Neither was everything on a spiritual plane among Christians who were previously Gentiles. It came as a terrible shock to Paul when the communities he founded often proved to be extremely earthly, rife with vice, corruption, faction and disaffection, a breeding ground for revolutionaries and a refuge for wastrels. Some of the converts gave themselves airs as privileged persons who had been relieved of the burdens of an honest day's toil and to whom laws whether human or divine no longer applied. The salvation they had obtained they had got for nothing, without cost or effort or ordeal of a strenuous ritual of initiation. They did not see why they should make any contribution for the benefit of others. They even accused Paul of feathering his own nest under pretext of collecting for the poor. The man who believed that he had once been caught up into paradise was forced to descend into hell, to rebuke, denounce and castigate, driven almost to despair.

To a very large extent, and quite unwittingly, Paul himself was responsible for the state of affairs which speedily developed as a result of his peculiar teaching. His own Jewish morality was so strict, and his principles were so strong, with his Pharisee upbringing, that it did not occur to him that the Gentiles he claimed for Christ could be other than what he was. Before very long the Christians of the Empire were getting a bad name, and became more readily distinguishable from the Jews by their behaviour, as well as by their special customs and organisation. This did not apply, of course, to the stricter Nazoreans, who were predominantly Jewish and were as devoted to the laws of Moses every bit as zealously as other eclectic groups in Israel.

So far as Paul was concerned, what he was doing was making faith in Jesus as the Christ the single qualification for membership of the people of Israel, though naturally with Gentiles this faith also implied their acceptance of Israel's God and the abandonment of idolatry. Where Jews had faith in Jesus they were included in the Holy Nation, the Israel of God, but not otherwise.

Paul claimed that he was the recipient of a special revelation. According to this it was no longer essential for Jews to observe the Law as a means of atoning for sins and attaining a state of righteousness, as the Messiah by his perfection and by offering up his life had provided a sacrifice wholly and finally acceptable to God. All who put their faith in Christ were therefore exonerated, not because of anything worthy they might do, but because they were looked upon with favour by God as 'in the Messiah' and his merits pertained to them and covered them. They were freed from guilt in Messiah's sinlessness. The Gentile who trusted in the atoning work of Christ had no requirement, therefore, to place himself under the Law, and if he did so he was denying the efficacy of the atonement. The only difference marking the approach of the Gentile, compared with that of the Jew, was that the former did change his religion.[8] As a convert he became an Israelite, a fellow-citizen with the saints, and an heir of the promises God had made of old to his people.

According to Paul, the community of believers in Christ now constituted that nation whom God had redeemed from Egypt and to whom he had revealed himself throughout past history. We are so used to the term Church as the designation of the collectivity of Christians that its national connotation is obscured in our minds. We may speak about God's people, sometimes with the qualification 'heavenly' to distinguish between Christians and Jews; but we are not commonly aware that 'heavenly', in the Pauline view, has only an appropriateness in relation to the derivation of Jesus and his temporary absence from the earthly scene. Functionally the Church is Israel loyal to its Messianic lord, and its components have no other nationality than that which is in descent from the Hebrew patriarchs Abraham, Isaac and Jacob. The Greek word *ekklesia*, to which we owe the word Church, and which for Greeks was employed in respect of the assembly of citizens in ancient times, was already before Christianity used to translate the Hebrew *kehillah* in the Greek version of the Old Testament (as in Deut. xxxi. 30; Ps. xxii. 22, I. Ki. viii. 14, etc.) as relating to the body of the people of Israel, the Hebrew community.

Thus the nationality of all Christians is Israelite. They are resident aliens in the lands of their dispersion. As the author of the anonymous *Epistle to Diognetus* expressed it: 'They dwell in their own countries, but only as sojourners. . . . Every foreign country is a fatherland to them, and every fatherland is foreign.'

Despite changes of emphasis in the presentation of Christianity the assertion of independent Christian nationhood was still being made in the fourth century. 'It is evident', wrote the ecclesiastical historian Eusebius at this period, 'that but a short time after the appearance of our Saviour Jesus Christ had been made known to all men, a new nation suddenly came into existence, a nation confessedly neither small nor weak, nor situated in a remote corner of the earth, but the most populous and religious of all, and so much the more indestructible and invincible as it has always had the power of God as its support. This nation, appearing at the time appointed by inscrutable wisdom, is that which among all is honoured with the name of Christ.'[9]

It was argued by the early Church Fathers that because the Jews had rejected Jesus as the Messiah they had forfeited their position as the people of God. Accordingly, the promises made of old to Israel had ceased to apply to the Jews and now belonged to the Christians. In keeping with this view the Gospel of Matthew makes Jesus say to the chief priests and Pharisees, 'Therefore I tell you, the Kingdom of God will be taken from you and given to a nation which yields its fruits.'[10] This was not the view of the Nazoreans, or indeed of Paul, but the saying does at least reinforce that the character of the Church was once understood to be that of a nation, a religious nation like the Jews, and not of the order of a purely religious institution.

Jesus had seen the immediate function of the Messiah as one of calling all Israel to repentance, since it was through Israel that the nations of the world would be enlightened and the Kingdom of God established. To this end he appointed twelve Apostles as missionaries to the twelve tribes of Israel, and instructed them to keep away from Gentile centres and

Samaritan towns, and to go instead to the lost sheep of the house of Israel. As he told a Syro-Phoenician woman on another occasion, 'I have only been sent to the lost sheep of the house of Israel.' The Apostles were promised that in the Messianic Age they would occupy twelve thrones judging the twelve tribes.

It was perhaps natural that many of Paul's converts from the Gentiles should have misunderstood his teaching about freedom from the Law in Christ and jumped to the conclusion that they had no connection with the Jews. But it was a misunderstanding as Paul was at great pains to explain. What he was contending was not that the Church was another people of God, but in fact the True Israel, faithful Israel, in direct succession to the Hebrew patriarchs and prophets and all the people who had been loyal to God. The people of God had not been changed. That was impossible. Only some of them had stumbled and had become unfaithful, and this had created the opportunity for believing Gentiles to become Israelites. 'I ask, therefore, has God rejected his people? God forbid! I too am an Israelite, of the seed of Abraham, the tribe of Benjamin. God has not rejected his people whom he knew of old.... I would not have you ignorant of this secret, brothers, in case you should "give yourselves airs", that partial immobility has come to Israel until the full complement of Gentiles has come in, and so all Israel will be saved.' The whole argument is set forth in Romans x–xi. Paul's special concern was to establish not that Christians were other than Israelites but that Gentile converts, without coming under the Law, were genuine Israelites and therefore heirs to the promises.

Obviously the nature of the Church as conceived by Paul and also by his opponents is vital to any consideration of Christianity and will have to be more fully explored as we proceed. But it affords an important insight into the subject that Christianity appeared on the world scene in a national guise and not as a new religion.

It is by no means easy to penetrate to and expose the original ingredients of Christianity because the activities and teaching of Paul bulk so largely in the Biblical story of Christian beginnings that they completely overshadow and almost exclude the contribution of the direct inheritors of the doctrine of Jesus. We are permitted by the New Testament, dominated by Pauline material, only brief and totally inadequate glimpses of the very substantial Nazorean movement to which the Apostles appointed by Jesus in his lifetime belonged. But because we have Paul's thinking so fully stated in his own words, and because this became later the mainspring of subsequent Christian doctrine, we are not to treat it as reflecting original Christian positions held in common by the followers of Jesus. In many matters Paulinism was in conflict with native Christianity, and ultimately got the upper hand through its greater appeal to Gentiles and because political conditions made it increasingly difficult for the legitimate Church to exercise an effective corrective influence. In the end the relationships were reversed. Pauline heresy served as the basis for Christian orthodoxy, and the legitimate Church was outlawed as heretical.

It would, however, be an injustice to Paul to suppose that he was wholly responsible for the character of Christian theology as it afterwards came to be formulated. For all his hellenistic associations he remained consistently a Jew, a Jew of a mystical type, who was impatient of all criticism of doctrine which he believed he had received by a Divine revelation peculiarly vouchsafed to himself. A Jewish occultist could understand him much more readily than his non-Jewish adherents could and did. They misinterpreted elements of his recondite philosophy and arrived at conclusions alien to his meaning and intention.[11]

The evolution of Paul's ideas, founded as they were on his early experiences and training as one who had explored to the limit the Jewish mysteries,[12] was governed primarily by the nature of what he regarded as his foreordained mission. This required that the converts from the Gentiles should clearly apprehend on what firm grounds they were entitled to Israelite status without becoming Jews. Their convictions on this score must be reinforced by the recognition of a comprehensive scheme of things Divine now for the first time fully revealed to the saints, and in which the relationship between Christ and the Church was set forth, so that the faith of believers would be stabilised. They would be immune to the cogent arguments of those who insisted that Gentiles to become Israelites must accept the yoke of the Torah, and weaned from that scandalous behaviour which gave so much justification to the representations of the Church's central authority at Jerusalem. You belong to Christ, Paul insisted, you are the very organs of his body, and Christ belongs to God and derives from God. Are we therefore to make the organs of Christ the organs of a prostitute? As Jesus was the temple in which the Spirit of God took up its abode, so are you that same temple. You are Christ's slaves, obedient to him, bought at a high price, Christ's precious blood. You are not your own masters.

By many metaphors Paul strove to remedy a situation which horrified him as much as it did the Jewish believers. It was the greatest weakness in his case for redemption by faith alone, and he was very conscious of it. While his converts continued to practice the abominations of the Gentiles and gave no evidence of being an Israel which was 'a kingdom of priests and a holy nation' they supplied ammunition to his adversaries. Yet pertinaciously he stuck to his guns and would not admit himself to be in the wrong. The credit of his revelation was at stake.

Paul was a remarkable individual and something of a religious genius, so that it came to be assumed that he had the mind of his master as he claimed in addressing his converts. Yet this was not the opinion of those who had known Jesus personally, and they did not hesitate to say so. For this Apostolic Church much that Paul taught was grievous error and not at all in accord with the mind and message of the Messiah. The original Apostles could urge that the truth was known only to them. Paul had never companied with Jesus or heard what he said day after day, and Paul's visions were the delusions of his own misguided mind. No doubt, as Paul's statements indicate, they spoke out strongly and sometimes bitterly, and he hit back in kind. The exaltation of Jesus had inaugurated a new era. 'Even if we have known Christ in the physical sense, we do so now no longer. Consequently, if anyone is in Christ he is a new creation. The old relationships have gone, replaced by the new.'[13] Paul challenges the Corinthians, who had taken sides against him: 'If someone who comes along can proclaim another Jesus whom I did not proclaim, or you can receive a different Spirit than you did receive, or a different gospel than you accepted, you can well put up with me. For I reckon myself in no way inferior to such super-envoys.'[14]

What the native Church's emissaries contended was so logical, however, and so convincing, that before Paul's death Paulinism was defeated over a wide area, and many of his converts were won over to become full proselytes so that their standing and assurance of participation in the felicities of the Messianic Age should be in no doubt. Decades elapsed before the teaching of Paul was reinstated and his letters treated as inspired.[15] The writing of the Acts of the Apostles was a contribution to this rehabilitation.[16] By this time the original Apostles had long been dead, and the churches of the West, now predominantly non-Jewish in composition, were almost entirely out of contact with the Nazoreans as an outcome of the Jewish war with Rome.

NOTES AND REFERENCES

1. Ps. xvi. 10–11.

2. See Schonfield, *The Passover Plot*, where the accounts of the Resurrection are examined.

3. Acts ii. 17–21, quoting Joel ii. 28–32. The passage from Joel figures in the Jewish service for Passover eve.

4. The Jewish Christian communities during the centuries they continued

to exist consistently rejected the deity of Jesus (Justin, *Dialogue with Trypho*, xlviii; Irenaeus, *Against Heresies*, I. xxvi. 2, etc.).

5. See Mk. x. 17–18 and compare the circumlocutions Heaven and Power in the expressions 'Kingdom of Heaven' and 'right hand of Power'. In the temptation in the wilderness Jesus quotes Deut. vi. 13, 'Thou shalt worship the Lord thy God, and him only shalt thou serve.'

6. Acts i. 22, iii. 13, iii. 26, iv. 30, vii. 55. The A.V. (King James Version) incorrectly renders the Greek *pais* as Son as applied to Jesus. The New English Bible rightly substitutes Servant.

7. Paul writes: 'By him—Jesus of the line of David—I have obtained favour and envoyship to procure loyal submission to his authority on the part of all nations, among whom you [of Rome] are summoned by Jesus Christ' (Rom. i. 5–6). See also Phil. ii. 9–11.

8. In Rom. iii. 30 Paul differentiates between the Jews, who since they already believed in God are exonerated *by* (*ek*) faith in Jesus, and the Gentiles, who since they have to acquire this belief are exonerated *through* (*dia*) faith. See also I. Cor. xii. 2 and I. Thess. i. 9.

9. Euseb., *Eccl. Hist.*, I. iv.

10. Mt. xxi. 43.

11. II. Pet. iii. 15-16. See *The Christology of Paul* at the end of this volume.

12. Cp. Gal. i. 14, 'How I advanced in Judaism far beyond many students of my own age: for none was more keenly enthusiastic than I to master the traditions of my ancestors.' Also I. Cor. xiii. 2, 'Even if I possess the power of prophecy and know all mysteries and secret lore . . .'

13. II. Cor. v. 16–17.

14. II. Cor. xi. 4–5.

15. II. Pet. iii. 16.

16. According to tradition the Lukan writings represent the gospel which Paul preached. They make a strong bid to give the Christianity of the beginning of the second century the support of a Hebraic foundation, which both served as a substitute for the relationship with Palestinian Christianity which had ceased to exist and at the same time idealised the past and greatly toned down its conflicts. In the Acts the early history of the Church introduces and is connected with the life and work of Paul, who there stands not unfavourably with the Apostles and Elders at Jerusalem who are persuaded to sanction his mission.

5

Odd Man Out

PAUL figures so prominently in the New Testament and his writings occupy so much of it that he has often been described as the real founder of Christianity. There is considerable justification for this view, for the Christian Faith as we know it would not have existed if it had not been for his contribution to its development.

The Christian movement was in its infancy when this powerful personality dramatically became one of its adherents, a circumstance which was as unexpected as it was disturbing to the initial body of believers. Not only had he been persecuting them unmercifully as an agent of the hostile hierarchy which had condemned the Messiah: he was of such a different type and calibre that his association was an acute embarrassment. It was at first considered by some that his profession of faith was a trick to disrupt and destroy the movement, and he started his discipleship under a cloud of suspicion which only deepened as a result of his subsequent activities. There could not have been a more inauspicious beginning of a career marked by the highest courage and devotion.

Paul, whose Jewish name was Saul, was a native of the important city of Tarsus in Cilicia, where Hellenic culture had been superimposed on an oriental one going back to the ancient Hittites. His family adhered to the Pharisees, which meant that he had been brought up very strictly in his religion; but he also inherited the privilege of Roman citizenship. As a youth he was sent to Jerusalem to study under the Jewish sage Gamaliel, grandson of the great Hillel. In his autobiographical references he reveals himself as an eager scholar, but one who like his royal namesake suffered from moods of resentment and depression.[1] He was afflicted by some physical disability of an unpleasant nature which at times overcame him, and it has been suggested that in common with other men of genius, including Julius Caesar, he was a victim of the falling sickness, an epileptic. This would be consistent with his character, abilities and mysticism. It is clear that he had grandiose ideas related to the conviction that he had been chosen of God for an exalted mission, and anxious to establish his worthiness he plunged in excess into recondite spiritual studies outstripping many of his contemporaries. These intensified his asceticism and gave him an almost morbid and fanatical sense of sin.

From Paul's writings it can be deduced by those acquainted with such matters that as a young man he devoted himself to a particular branch of Jewish occultism with all its attendant risks, physical and mental,[2] and a strong case can be made out that his violent and beserk antagonism to the followers of Jesus arose in no small part from his secret belief that he himself was the Messiah destined to be 'a light to the nations'.[3] The Acts fails to clarify the reason for his frenzied opposition, but the cause of it comes out in an analysis of all the available information taken in conjunction with eclectic Pharisaic ideas.

After Paul's psychic experience, perhaps due to an epileptic seizure,[4] as a result of which he gave allegiance to Jesus as the Messiah, he went into retreat in northern Arabia to wrestle with his problems and there he had 'an excess of revelations'. He had not been wrong in his youthful belief that he was a chosen vessel to bring the knowledge of God to the Gentiles. The voice that had spoken to him had confirmed what was in his heart. But he could see now where he stood: he was appointed of God as the personal agent and deputy of the exalted Messiah, to carry out his mighty work in the world until Jesus should return in glory to inaugurate the reign of righteousness on earth. Henceforth he would live and move and speak at the bidding of the heavenly Messiah who was his master. He thought of his status as that of a trusted slave, so intimate with his owner, so fully in his confidence, as to be in effect his *alter ego*. He was the *eikon* (image) of Messiah, as Messiah was the *eikon* of God. He was convinced that in the mercy of God he had been judged and sentenced to assume a new identity as the reflection of Christ's presence. As he expressed it: 'In law I have died in the legal sense. I have shared Christ's crucifixion. I am alive, it is true, but strictly speaking it is not I who live, but Christ who lives in me. . . . From now on let no one deal me any more blows, for I carry the scars of Jesus on my body.'[5]

Paul's Christology brought him an inward peace and a tremendous joy. The nightmares of his youth could never return. He was released from the incubus of a guilt-laden conscience, able to throw himself energetically and enthusiastically into the work which he believed had been entrusted to him as envoy to the nations. He could brave all dangers and hardships. Yet effectively to manifest a Christ who was no longer on earth created fresh problems. Paul dramatises his Christ-concept. He is acting, not always successfully, the part of Jesus as he proclaims him, perpetually endeavouring to transform himself into a likeness which is alien to his true self. He sees himself in a special sense as the one who makes Jesus visible in the flesh. In his battered and uncomely body the marks and mien of the Crucified are paraded and displayed through the cities of Asia and Europe.

But though the effort is genuine, and Paul labours and sweats to make the identification as consistent as he can, the performance frequently does not come up to standard or is overdone. He had been denied personal experience of the human Jesus and could not therefore hope to reflect the man Jesus had been. Jesus 'according to the flesh' had consequently to be left out of account, and Jesus 'according to the spirit' substituted, so that the nature and mind of the Messiah as revealed to Paul could be communicated to believers and transplanted into their hearts. He is very conscious of the difficulty of representing in any way adequately such an idealised figure, of his own unperfected character and traits breaking through. In vain he declares that he is nothing, for plainly he is something in his own right: he will not boast, but he does boast.

It was not only the teaching and activities of Paul which made him obnoxious to the Christian leaders; but their awareness that he set his revelations above their authority and claimed an intimacy with the mind of Jesus greater than that of those who had companied with him on earth and had been chosen by him. To them he was a presumptuous upstart. It was an abomination, especially as his ideas were so contrary to what they knew of Jesus, that he should pose as the embodiment of Messiah's will and dare to instruct them as if he were Jesus himself. They may not have guessed Paul's Messianic secret; but they did realise that he held himself to be uniquely and independently inspired, and they appreciated the power of his personality, his persuasive force, his mystical erudition, and his cultural and intellectual superiority. Physically insignificant, unlike King Saul of old, he yet—as that monarch had done in stature—stood head and shoulders above his fellows. It became imperative to cut him down to size.

The Saul of today, who used the Roman name of Paul, was seen as the demon-driven enemy of the new David. When eventually he became a prisoner of the Romans the Christians neither of Jerusalem nor Rome lifted a finger to aid him.[6] None of Paul's efforts, including raising funds for the poor saints of Judea, had mitigated opposition to him. For the more intransigent of the legitimate Church Paul was a dangerous and disruptive influence, bent on enlisting a large following from among the Gentiles in order to provide himself with a numerical superiority with the support of which he could set at defiance the Elders at Jerusalem. Paul had been the enemy from the beginning, and because he had failed in his former open hostility he had craftily insinuated himself into the fold to destroy it from within. This he was doing by setting aside the sacred Torah and recruiting anyone willing to join him on the merest profession of belief. He should never have been received; but there were those who were so innocent and unsuspicious that they had not realised what he was up to. And see to what a state of affairs their misplaced confidence had led! The whole Nazorean cause, the cause of Messiah himself, was in jeopardy of being utterly discredited in Israel. Because Paul seemed to be one of its chief spokesmen and was announcing that the Torah was invalid as a means of salvation it would be believed by pious Jews that the followers of Jesus were the worst kind of renegades.

Since it is the Pauline viewpoint which is given in the New Testament we are obliged to search out and put forward how the situation appeared to those who have been scorned as Judaisers. There was much more to their attitude than is generally realised. Naturally it was the principal plank in Paul's platform which was attacked because here his position was most vulnerable. But it was his pretensions which rankled. Two rival authorities among the Nazoreans, two presentations of Jesus as the Messiah, two inspirations, two gospels, could not be tolerated. It stood to reason that no revelation which was of God could possibly contradict that which had been given by God to Israel, and what was so well known of Jesus and his doctrine. The very novelty of Paul's teaching, therefore, condemned his revelations as fraudulent.

It was at Antioch in Syria, which Paul had made the base for his missionary operations and where for some time he had been a teacher of a Christian community numbering many converts from the Gentiles, that matters came to a head. Unfortunately we only have one side of the story in two versions, a compromising account in the Acts and an uncompromising one in Paul's letter to the Galatians. We have to do the best we can to overcome both the bias and the discrepancies.

According to Paul's account Peter had come to Antioch and had made no difficulty about accepting the converts from the

Gentiles as brethren. 'Before certain persons came from James he had eaten with Gentiles. But after their arrival he drew back and separated himself out of fear of those of the Circumcision. The other Jews played up to him, so that even Barnabas was carried away by their hypocrisy.' Paul says that he publicly challenged Peter: 'If you a born Jew live like a Gentile, why do you force the Gentiles to keep Jewish ways?' The Acts omits this episode and makes no reference to the presence of Peter at Antioch. It simply declares that 'certain persons came down from Judea and instructed the brothers, "Unless you are circumcised in accordance with the Mosaic ordinance you cannot be saved." ' An important point in Paul's statement, much older than the Acts, is that the visitors from Jerusalem represented an official delegation from the Christian government whose president was the brother of Jesus. This suggests that information about Paul's first missionary journey, perhaps communicated by Mark, and the terms on which he was admitting Gentiles to membership, had got back to Jerusalem and had caused considerable alarm and dismay.

The Commission, as we may judge, did not question the right of Gentiles to be admitted into the family of Israel of which the Messiah was the head; but it pointed out that this involved implicit obedience to the covenant made by God with Israel. The people of Israel stood in a different relationship than did other nations, since they were sanctified to God by commandments, so that they might be qualified to carry out his will in the world. Jesus the true Israelite was himself obedient to the covenant and upheld the Law by his teaching and example. It was incumbent, therefore, on all those wishing to be joined with him and who aimed at likeness to him to follow in his steps and to exhibit, by circumcision and the practice of God's precepts, the outward signs of the inward grace.

The decision was taken, not at all to the liking of Paul, to refer the issue back to the Apostles and Elders at Jerusalem. Indeed, it would seem as if Paul and Barnabas were summoned to appear before the highest Christian court, and had no option but to obey. Paul naturally does not admit this in his letter to the Galatians. He makes a virtue of necessity. 'I went up to Jerusalem by a revelation and reported to them the terms of the gospel I preach to the Gentiles. This was privately to those of repute, in case I should strive or had been striving to no purpose. But there was no forcing of Titus, who accompanied me, to be circumcised, Greek though he was, despite the infiltrated false brothers who had crept in to spy out the liberty we enjoyed in Christ Jesus in order to enslave us. Not for an instant did we strike our colours, so that the true character of the gospel might be preserved to you.'

Paul could see very well that appearing before the Christian leaders would put him at a double disadvantage: he would seem to be subservient to their authority, whereas he claimed a superior and independent status, and his very small minority could easily be overawed and outvoted. If he failed to make good his case he would be completely discredited. His work and influence would be destroyed, and he could no longer claim to speak in the name of the Messianic Community which had rejected and cast him off. The split would be irrevocable, and what then became of his mission? Paul was no schismatic: he could not conceive of a Church which was not an integral part of the Nazorean body politic, and which did not look to Jerusalem as its organic spiritual centre. At least this was his view at the time. The risk of an adverse decision was for him, therefore, very grave.

Paul's astute mind conceived a plan for extricating himself. He would not wait for the plenary session of the Nazorean Council, but first tackle the leaders privately, submitting his cause in suitable terms and emphasising the nature, scope and success of his mission, with Titus as living confirmation. The leaders could not deny the operation of the Holy Spirit, and would then be bound to support him in the assembly. As a helpful gesture he consented to the circumcision of Titus.

We receive the impression from Paul's record of the event that the plan worked reasonably well. The issue was really settled out of court. The subsequent meeting of the assembly was fully under control. The Acts understandably makes no reference to the private meeting, and proceeds with what followed. After an initial period permitted for the indictment of Paul, the moderate Peter took over. Paul and Barnabas then recited their experiences, and James the president summed up and gave his ruling. His findings were adopted and the meeting was over. Paul does not mention the proceedings of the assembly or its conclusions, since these did not bear out that he had scored a complete victory. He only gives in a breezy and offhanded manner his version of what took place at the private session with the leaders. 'As for those of repute—whatever they were makes no difference to me: God takes no one at face value—they imposed on me nothing additional. Quite the contrary. When they saw that I had been entrusted with the gospel for the Uncircumcised, as Peter for the Circumcised . . . and when they realised the privilege that had been granted me, then James, Cephas (Peter) and John, the reputed "Pillars of the Faith", extended to myself and Barnabas the right hand of fellowship. We were to go to the Gentiles, they to the Circumcised. Oh yes, they did add one more thing, we were to remember the poor, which personally I was only too ready to do.'

If we are to credit the Acts what Paul says here is no more than a half-truth. The outcome was not as he represents it. A compromise solution had been found, but this did impose on Paul and his supporters certain conditions. There was no agreement at all about separate spheres of influence, and the Nazorean leaders did not relinquish their right to make converts among the Gentiles. What they consented to simply regularised the position of those Gentile converts who did not become full Jews.

Paul's concern was to secure that his converts from the Gentiles should be recognised as part of Israel. If he had been founding a new religion this would not have been vital to him. But he was doing nothing of the kind: he was building upon the foundation of the Prophets and Apostles, proclaiming only what was predicted by the Scriptures, extending Israelite citizenship to believing non-Jews. All who believed in Jesus should therefore be acknowledged as rightfully belonging to Israel which Jesus had died to redeem.

The Nazorean leaders had their own problem. They could not repudiate that the Holy Spirit had come on Gentiles as well as Jews. On the other hand, if no distinction was made between Israel and the Gentiles, so that non-Jewish believers were not required to surrender their Gentile state, then the revealed will of God would be nullified.

There was this common ground. Both parties agreed that the Israel of God, the Messianic Community as it then existed, was only a fraction of the whole. Part of the lineal Israel had temporarily been sundered because of unbelief. The envoys of the Messiah were entrusted with the responsibility of giving opportunity—by allegiance to him—for these lost sheep to be brought again within the fold. But the ideal number of the people of God would be made up by the inclusion of multitudes not of Jewish origin. The ideal number is symbolically given by the seer of the Revelation as consisting of twelve thousand of each of the twelve tribes plus ten thousand times ten thousand from all nations, tribes, peoples and tongues.[7]

Prophetic Judaism brought the doctrine of the Faithful Remnant strongly to the fore, and this was bound to raise the question of how the prediction to Abraham would be fulfilled, when he was told (Gen. xv. 5–6), 'Look now toward heaven, and tell the stars, if thou be able to number them: and God said unto him, So shall thy seed be. And he believed in the Lord; and he counted it to him for righteousness.' A late Nazorean source, the *Clementine Recognitions*, explains: 'Inasmuch as it was necessary that Gentiles should be called into the room of those who remained unbelieving, so that the number might be filled up which had been shown by God to Abraham, the preaching of the blessed Kingdom of God is sent into all the world.' Dealing with the same question in Romans, Paul quotes Hosea to the effect that God would call those his people, who previously were not his people, and Isaiah that 'though the number of the children of Israel is as the sand of the sea, only a remnant will be saved. For the Lord will make a full and summary settlement on earth.'[8] Paul argued that the promise to Abraham had stated that in him and his seed should all nations be blessed. The word seed is singular, implying not a number but one, namely the Messiah descended from Abraham. 'Those who have been identified with Christ by baptism have assumed Christ's personality. It is impossible for there to be Jew or Greek, slave or freeman, male or female, for in Jesus Christ you are all one and the same person. If you are in Christ you are "the Seed of Abraham", heirs in accordance with the promise.'[9] The nations are to be blessed in the Christians, of whatever origin, since by faith these are now Israelites.

But on what basis were the believing Gentiles to be included in the people of God? Paul said, by faith in Christ alone. If Abraham was accounted righteous because he believed God, in that case it was his faith which was rewarded and not his deeds; and the Law had not yet been given. If then faith alone was sufficient for Abraham our father, why should more be required of those who had never been under the Law, and who also believed God? What was more, was the promise made to Abraham when he was circumcised, or while he was still uncircumcised? Undoubtedly, before he was circumcised. Therefore the promise had nothing to do with circumcision, and believers from the Gentiles could share in it without circumcision or observing the Law.

A contrary view is expressed in the letter of James. 'Can you not realise, you dunce, that faith without deeds is unproductive? Was not our father Abraham vindicated by his deeds when he offered his son Isaac upon the altar? Can you not see how faith assisted his deeds, and by his deeds his faith was perfected? And so the Scripture was fulfilled which states, Abraham believed God, and it was credited to him as rectitude, and he was called the friend of God. You see, then, that a man is vindicated by his deeds, and not simply by faith.'[10] The whole history of the choice of Israel was against the opinion that obedience to God's commandments was superfluous.

The decision taken at Jerusalem was that so far as the Jewish followers of Jesus were concerned there could be no doubt about their obligation to keep the commandments of God. But let the Gentile believers be granted a status equal to that which Abraham had before he entered into the covenant by circumcision. But they must still demonstrate their belief by obeying the Primeval Laws applicable to all the sons of Noah from whom the nations derived. The court would not go beyond the regulations laid down for Gentile Godfearers attaching themselves to Jewish communities throughout the Dispersion. Those who formally renounced idolatry and took upon themselves the Primeval Laws were to be regarded not as members of the house of Israel, but as equal participants in the felicities of the World to Come.

The brother of Jesus as president announced the findings to be in accordance with Scripture. He chose the Prophet Amos as offering the necessary guidance.

It was written that God would destroy 'the sinful kingdom' (currently understood as Rome) from the face of the earth. Israel would be dispersed among the nations. The faithful among them would survive; but the rest would die by the sword. So ran the prophecy (Amos. ix. 8–10). But it continued, that in those days God would restore the Messianic Community ('re-erect the fallen tent of David') and repair its breaches, and that 'a remnant of Edom' (Rome) should be saved. Here James exegetically substituted *Adam* for *Edom*, as the Greek Septuagint had done, to signify the rest of mankind, all the Gentiles 'upon whom the name of the Lord would be called' (11–12).

'My verdict is, therefore,' said James, 'that those of the Gentiles who turn to God be not molested, but that we write to them to abstain from whatever is polluted by idols, from sexual impurity, from eating strangled animals, and from blood.'[11] If they wished to go further the synagogues were there, where the Laws of Moses were read and taught every Sabbath. The verdict was a compromise. It was not to be insisted upon that believing Gentiles should become Jews as a condition of recognition as brethren; but neither was Paul's contention allowed that such brethren were to be regarded as Israelites.

The assembly agreed to this ruling and Paul had to bow to it at the time. But he repudiated it later on when relations had worsened.

To prevent any misinterpretation of the decision, it was agreed that it should be delivered in writing, with two prominent Nazoreans, Judas bar-Sabas and Silas (Silvanus) to confirm and explain it verbally. These men would return with Paul and Barnabas to Antioch.

The text of the letter as given in the Acts reads as follows:

> The Apostles and Elders, your brothers, present their compliments to the brothers from the Gentiles in Antioch, Syria and Cilicia.
>
> Since it has come to our attention that some of our number, to whom we gave no such instructions, have been confusing you with their statements, unsettling your minds, it was unanimously resolved to send you special delegates along with our good friends Barnabas and Paul who have so devoted themselves to the cause of our Lord Jesus Christ. Accordingly, we have commissioned Judas and Silas, who will confirm our decision verbally.
>
> It was resolved by the Holy Spirit and ourselves to impose upon you no greater burden than these essential things, to abstain from what is dedicated to idols, from blood, from eating strangled animals, and from sexual impurity. If you keep strictly to this you will be quite in order.
>
> Farewell.

How far this letter is authentic it is now impossible to judge;

but it bears many of the marks of genuineness. We should note that the Gentile believers are still considered to be Gentiles though addressed as brethren, and that the name of Barnabas precedes that of Paul as he was one of the Jerusalem Elders. The imposed restrictions, with one exception, represent what the Jews regarded as the minimal requirements for human society under God. The exception is the dietary law concerning animals killed for food by strangulation. This is actually omitted in the Western text of the Acts, but an alternative prohibition of eating flesh cut from a living animal is found in the rabbinical lists of the so-called Laws of Noah. The other three prohibitions are possibly related to the rabbinical primary crimes of Idolatry, Adultery and Murder. The same three figure in the Sermon on the Mount, Murder (Mt. v. 21), Adultery (27), and Idolatry (33) where the commandment against oaths involves idolatry in speech. Similarly in the Revelation (xxi. 8, xxii. 15) 'whoremongers, murderers and idolaters' are grouped together among those who are excluded from the Tree of Life and the City of God, and meet their fate in the lake of fire.

Paul does not make any direct reference to the decretal letter; but he may be referring to it incidentally when he lists among 'deeds of the flesh' these and other sins, and warns the Galatians (v. 19–21) that those who are guilty of them will not inherit the Kingdom of God. On the whole, in obtaining such a document, Paul had come off very well. He had secured official recognition of his work, and his Gentile converts were not compelled to become Jews. They were received as brethren but could not be accorded status as Israelites unless they became full-proselytes by obedience to the Law. They had full freedom of choice. Hands were clasped across the wall of partition; but the wall still stood.

The great importance of this first crisis in Christian affairs is that it plainly establishes that the Nazorean Council at Jerusalem, consisting of the Apostles and Elders under the presidency of the brother of Jesus, was functioning in the character of a

Jewish Sanhedrin as the *de facto* government of Israel loyal to the Messiah and exercising the same kind of powers. Its existence was an open and rebellious repudiation of the authority of the *de jure* Jewish Sanhedrin now regarded by Jewish Zealots as pro-Roman and apostate.

NOTES AND REFERENCES

1. 'I myself was once lacking in sense, ungovernable, erratic, a slave to various passions and pleasures, spending my time in resentment and jealousy, gloomy, hating others' (Tit. iii. 3).

2. See *The Christology of Paul* at the end of this volume.

3. Schonfield, *The Jew of Tarsus*, ch. vi.

4. See J. Klausner, *From Jesus to Paul*, pp. 324–30. Paul's experience was wholly consistent with an epileptic attack. Klausner quotes a letter from the mystic Rabbi Moses Luzzatto (dated 1730) describing revelations made to him by a 'messenger from heaven'. 'I saw nothing of him,' he wrote, 'but I heard his voice speaking out of my own mouth.'

5. Gal. ii. 19–20, vi. 17.

6. When Paul was a prisoner at Caesarea there is no mention in the Acts of any Christian defending him or testifying in his favour (Acts xxiv–xxvi). As regards the Christians at Rome Paul wrote, 'At the first hearing of my defence no one supported me: everyone deserted me. May it not be counted against them!' (II. Tim. iv. 16).

7. Rev. vii. 4, 9.

8. Rom. ix. 25–8.

9. Gal. iii. 27–9.

10. Jas. ii. 20–4.

11. Acts xv. 19–20.

6

Signs and Portents

The decision taken by the Christian Council at Jerusalem was a victory for the moderates, all the more striking since militancy and fanaticism was fast gaining the upper hand in Jewish affairs. Such a decision would probably have been impossible ten years later as events moved rapidly towards a climax in the relations between the Jews and the Romans. Like many compromises, however, the decision failed to satisfy extreme opinion, and it was not surprising in all the circumstances that antagonistic attitudes should speedily gain the upper hand.

The influence of the spiritual struggle which raged within the Church in the fifties of the first century is heavily impressed on the letters of Paul. Not only can we find in them abundant evidence of the bitterness of the conflict, we can also trace its effects on the development of Pauline teaching. Some of his thinking, not as a rule related in our minds to this strife, ideas of a striking and elevated character the products of his genius, proves on careful examination to be a defensive response to opposition challenges. The Pauline version of Christianity did in fact lay the foundations of a new religion in many respects alien to that of Jesus and his Apostles. Christian scholars who reached this conclusion in the nineteenth century were in the right, but because the Church ultimately built its teaching on Paulinism in its development outside Palestine it was difficult at any earlier period to make this clear. Theologically, the Church is still compelled to take its stand on the judgment that Paul had the true light and to consider Jesus in terms of his Christology. Yet in the interests of truth the historian is now forced to oust the theologian from his dominance, so that judgment is brought into line with the factors which have operated at the human level to produce changes and divergences. Ignorance of these factors can no longer be allowed to obstruct the intelligent assessment of the validity of beliefs.

Before we are entitled to appraise Pauline doctrine we have to reconstruct the conditions which gave rise to it as well as take account of the kind of man Paul was. We have to appreciate what were the imperatives governing the attitudes both of himself and those who had the ordering of early Christian affairs, the friends and family of Jesus and those associated with them. We have to realise what was going on, affecting the Jewish people and the Nazorean movement.

Readers of the author's former works and his most recent volume *The Passover Plot* will now be conversant with that feverish excitement which had gripped the Jews, particularly in their homeland, in what was regarded as the Last Times. Account has been furnished of the religious fervour engendered by these convictions of the imminent advent of the Kingdom of God, the multiplication of curious sects and parties, the emergence of prophets, teachers and messianic figures. The political aspects of the situation have been described, which manifested themselves in patriotic revolutionary activities directed against Rome and its Jewish collaborators. Yet at risk of some repetition we must review the circumstances which were shaping the course of Christian history, which initially was closely linked with Jewish fortunes and concerns.

The follies of the Roman governor Pontius Pilate, at the close of whose administration Jesus had been executed as a rebel against Rome and pretender to the Jewish throne, were as nothing compared with what followed. While the direct action methods of the militants were frowned upon by the more spiritual, who believed that the intervention of God must be patiently awaited and solicited by prayer, fasting and charity, events conspired to give more and more encouragement to the Zealots. Within thirty years of the death of Tiberius in A.D. 37 the Zealots were able to mount a full-scale rebellion against Rome and force many of the moderates to go along with them. The Council of Jerusalem which pronounced on the status of Gentile believers in Jesus took place about midway through this period and must be viewed in the context of the steadly deteriorating conditions.

A startling Sign of the Times was provided by the madness of the Emperor Gaius Caligula, who believed he was already a god. To this obsession Lucius Vitellius, legate of Syria, had contributed, when, returning to Rome at the end of his term of office, he adored the emperor, and would only appear before him with his head veiled.[1] Caligula's dementia offered a golden opportunity to the antisemitic Alexandrians to indict the Jews as the only people which refused to acknowledge his godhead. In spite of the petitions of a Jewish embassy led by the philosopher Philo nothing would content Gaius but insistence that his statue as Jupiter incarnate should now be set up in the Temple at Jerusalem. Petronius, the new legate of Syria, was instructed to employ force if necessary. The legate obeyed, and arrived with two legions at Ptolemais; but thousands of Jews begged him there and at Tiberias not to proceed with the design. Faced with this fanatical determination to resist, Petronius wavered, and finally agreed to write to the emperor to abandon the project. Gaius had now reluctantly decided to do so on the representations of his Jewish friend Herod Agrippa; but learning from Petronius that the Jews were ready to revolt, and that his legate was unwilling to proceed with the war, he ordered him to commit suicide as an example to others who might think to disobey him. The letter was delayed in transit, and only reached Petronius after news had come to hand that Gaius had been assassinated. In this way the Jews were saved, and received fresh justification for holding that God was on their side. The 'abomination that maketh desolate' had not at this time stood in the holy place as had happened when Antiochus Epiphanes had persecuted the people of God.

The effect of the threat had been none the less electrifying, and in Nazorean and kindred circles it had intensified the conviction that the Woes of Messiah had commenced. Temporarily the threat had been removed, but it helped to bring into renewed prominence a personification of the enemy of the saints, an anti-God and anti-Messiah (Antichrist), the Lawless Man (son of Beliar), 'the Doomed One who opposes and elevates himself above everything regarded as a god or as an object of worship, so that he himself sits in God's Temple claiming to be God.'[2] What was more, that apocalyptic figure assumed with increasing clarity the aspect of a Roman emperor. For Nazoreans and Zealots Rome was the power hostile to God, and the knowledge was a common bond between them.

The Jewish authorities at Jerusalem responsible to Rome could only regard both these movements as manifestations of the same spirit of revolt. Which was the worse form of the evil it was hard for them to say, whether it was those who acted violently or those whose visions and denunciations incited to violence. On the whole, official opinion inclined to regard the latter, who included the Nazoreans, as the more dangerous, those whom Josephus calls 'another body of villains, with purer hands but more impious intentions, who no less than the assassins ruined the peace of the city'. These were 'deceivers and impostors, under the pretence of Divine inspiration fostering revolutionary changes'.[3] The situation subsequently reached such a pitch that, as the same historian records, 'the impostors and brigands, banding together, incited numbers to revolt, exhorting them to assert their independence, and threatening to kill any who submitted to Roman domination and forcibly to suppress those who voluntarily accepted servitude'.[4]

When Claudius succeeded Gaius as emperor, Herod

Agrippa, who boasted on his coins of being 'friend of Caesar and the Romans', was made king of Judea, and a member of the detested Herodian family briefly replaced the even more detested Roman governor. To the extremists the change made very little difference, and Agrippa found himself with this sharp thorn in his side for the period of his short reign (A.D. 41–4). Many moderates swung over to the side of the king as at least a Jewish sovereign; but the testimony of the Acts indicates that the Nazoreans, for whom Jesus was the God-ordained king of Israel, remained hostile. Agrippa arrested and executed James the son of Zebedee, one of the two firebrand brothers who had been close companions of Jesus. He then proceeded to apprehend the chief apostle Peter. So notable was the prisoner that trouble was feared, and a strict guard was kept. Not only was Peter chained to two soldiers, but two others were also on duty, the four being changed for each three-hour watch. In addition there were the prison warders. Such precautions would be superfluous for a harmless religious enthusiast, but appropriate for one who was regarded as the ringleader of seditionists. Yet in spite of them the prisoner's escape was contrived. The canonical record speaks of a miracle; but it was rather one of careful planning by drugging the custodians. The escape clearly alarmed Agrippa, since he had the warders put to death and himself left Jerusalem hastily for the safety of Gentile Caesarea, the residential seat of the Roman governors. There he died not long after, punished by God, as it was said, for failing to rebuke Gentile flatterers who hailed him as a god.[5]

The Signs were multiplying that the Day of Judgment was at hand, and they included a great famine predicted by the Nazorean prophet Agab. A Jewish seer recalls the portentous period which ensued.

'For that time will arise which brings affliction; for it will come and pass by with quick vehemence, and it will be turbulent coming in the heat of indignation. . . . And there will be many rumours and tidings not a few, and the works of portents will be shown, and promises not a few will be recounted, and some of them will prove idle, and some of them will be confirmed. . . . And whilst they are meditating these things, then zeal will arise in those of whom they thought not, and passion will seize him who is peaceful, and many will be roused in anger to injure many, and they will rouse up armies in order to shed blood. . . . And it will come to pass at the self-same time, that a change of times will manifestly appear to every man, by reason of which in all those times they were polluted and practised oppression, and walked every man in his own works, and remembered not the Law of the Mighty One. Therefore a fire will consume their thoughts, and in flame will the meditations of their reins be tried; for the Judge will come and will not tarry.'[6]

All this Jesus himself had prophesied, as the Nazoreans related, and in heaven he was now awaiting the signal for his return to earth in triumph and judgment, according to the psalmist's words: 'The Lord said unto my lord [i.e. the king], Sit thou at my right hand until I make thine enemies thy footstool. The Lord shall send the rod of thy strength out of Zion; rule thou in the midst of thine enemies. Thy people shall be willing in the day of thy power. . . . The Lord at thy right hand shall strike through kings in the day of his wrath. He shall judge among the heathen, he shall fill the places with the dead bodies: he shall wound the head over many countries.'[7]

This was the early Christian belief, shared by Paul, as when he wrote to the Thessalonians: Your trials 'are a proof of God's strict justice, in having treated you as worthy of the Kingdom of God, for which indeed you suffer. For that being so, it becomes just on God's part to repay affliction to those who afflict you, and to give you who are afflicted relief with us when the Lord Jesus is revealed from heaven with his mighty angels in flaming fire, inflicting retribution on those who do not acknowledge God [i.e. the heathen] and do not respond to the gospel of our Lord Jesus'.[8]

Having such convictions, we cannot dissociate primitive

Christianity from apocalyptic Judaism. We are dealing with one and the same phenomenon, which demanded an excited observation of every indication that the Day was at hand, and by no means excluded involvement in activities which were regarded as contributing to the encouragement of political unrest and disaffection. The Christians were classed with the anti-Roman revolutionaries. They and the Zealots stood in the same condemnation: they were different sides of the same coin.

We have quoted from one of Paul's letters to the Thessalonian believers, and we have to note that it was at Thessalonica that he and Silas were held by the local Roman-protected Jews to be Zealot agitators. They raided the house of one Jason where the apostles had been staying, and failing to find them brought him and others before the city prefects, clamouring that 'these subverters of the Empire have now reached here, and Jason has harboured them. All of them are violators of Caesar's decrees, and declare there is another emperor, Jesus'.[9] Some years later, at Caesarea in Palestine, Paul was indicted before the Roman governor Felix in these terms: 'We have found this man a plague-carrier, a fomentor of revolt among all the Jews of the Empire, a ringleader of the Nazorean sect.'[10] Not only did this happen to the politically inoffensive and unworldly Paul, himself a Roman citizen; it reveals that for a considerable time the Nazoreans, as the Christians were called in Judea, had been listed as known enemies of the regime. There is explained a great deal that we encounter in early Church history, and the presence among the Christians of Jerusalem of many with Zealot affiliations, who had reason to regard Paul as a traitor and not at all as one of their champions.

With such Jews, no different as adherents of the Messiah, patriotism and religion had ever gone hand in hand; and in these evil and critical times both were intensified. For Israel to continue loyal to God in face of the gigantic array of inimical powers rigorous security measures had to be adopted. There could be no pandering to heathenism in any shape or form, for the slightest weakness might be perilous. Every devout Jew must redouble his vigilance and use the utmost circumspection in his external relations. Every Gentile proselyte received must sever completely his former ties and wholly identify himself with his adopted people and faith, otherwise he might prove to be a liability rather than an asset, and even a danger as a spy for the Romans. The royal house of Adiabene converted to Judaism at this time was highly praised for its exemplary support of the Jewish cause. The Last Days complex inevitably bred bigotry and fanaticism, but the hostile attitude of the Roman rulers undoubtedly stimulated it. It is reported of the Zealot-Essenes, 'Some of these observe a still more rigid practice in not handling or looking at a coin which bears an image, nor will they even enter a city at the gates of which statues are erected. Others again threaten to slay any Gentile taking part in a discourse about God and his Law if he refuses to be circumcised. From this they were called Zealots by some, Sicarii (i.e. dagger-men) by others. Others again will call no man lord, except God, even though they may be tortured and killed.'[11] There is a certain confusion of identities in this report; but it could be made because there was some affinity of outlook.

After the death of King Agrippa when Cuspius Fadus was sent to be governor of Judea, he found a situation similar to that which had prevailed on the death of Herod the Great, when Zealots and disaffected elements had gone on the warpath. Now there were attacks by a body of Jews in Perea across the Jordan on the natives of Philadelphia, the modern Amman. A 'brigand chief', Tolmai, was raiding Idumeans and Arabians in the south, and there were other outbreaks elsewhere, which Josephus passes over except to say that Fadus cleared Judea of brigandage. The governor also informed the Sanhedrin at the command of the emperor that the high priest's robes in which he officiated in the Temple on solemn festivals must once more be returned to the custody of the Roman garrison at Fort Antonia overlooking the sacred precincts to be given out on each occasion. By this measure the Romans were determined to show they were the masters. But so keenly were they aware of public hostility that Cassius Longinus, now legate of Syria, arrived at Jerusalem, 'and had brought a great army with him, out of fear that the injunctions of Fadus should force the Jews to rebel'.[12] The Sanhedrin asked leave to send an embassy to Claudius, and on the petition of Agrippa son of the late king, the decree was rescinded. But the emperor thought it politic to put a pro-Roman Jew, Tiberius Alexander, son of the Alexandrian Alabarch, in control of Jewish affairs with Fadus.

A ruthless suppression of the nationalists was now attempted. Nazoreans, Zealots, and all fanatics were dealt with in the 'pacification' carried out by Fadus and Alexander. Among the victims was the prophet Theudas, who had invited the people to follow him to the Jordan, where the river would miraculously be divided to give them passage. Fearing what this design might portend Fadus sent out cavalry to cut the people down, and the prophet was captured and beheaded. Other victims were two of the sons of the former patriot leader Judas of Galilee, whom Alexander ordered to be crucified. Another well-known leader, Eleazar bar Dinai, only escaped with difficulty.

The necessity for many of the Zealots and Nazoreans to fly the country, while some were banished from it, helped to spread the revolutionary propaganda to other lands. Certain of the refugees would act on their own, while others were apostles sent out as part of a plan to promote an uprising of Jews throughout the Empire. Roman harshness and brutality in Judea not only failed to achieve its objective in suppressing elements hostile to Rome, it actually contributed to enlarging the area of hostility. As we have seen, Paul and Silas were taken to be two of such agitators, and we have the records of the attempts of Claudius to combat Messianic sedition. From this period around A.D. 50 is dated the great missionary activity of the Nazoreans to which the ecclesiastical historian Eusebius refers when he relates that 'the rest of the apostles, who were harassed in innumerable ways with a view to destroy them, and driven from the land of Judea, had gone forth to preach the gospel to all nations, relying on the aid of Christ, when he said, Go ye, teach all nations in my name'.[13] What Eusebius, writing some three centuries later, did not perceive was the connection between the spread of the gospel and the political circumstances. It is probable that the first written accounts of Jesus demonstrating that he was the Messiah were prepared at this time for the service of the evangelists.[14] While these are now lost, except in so far as they may underlie the existing Gospels, it is to be remarked that tradition makes Peter arrive in Rome in the reign of Claudius, and some manuscripts of the first three Gospels are inaccurately subscribed as having been written in the same reign.

We see, therefore, that the ruling of the Council at Jerusalem on the subject of Gentile converts had been made in the midst of events calculated to have the strongest emotional effect on the Nazorean community. Paul had been fortunate in the verdict he obtained. If the Zealots had had their way he would have fared very differently, and he was fully conscious of their antagonism. But his faith in his revelations and his passionate sense of the mission with which he had been entrusted did not permit him to apprehend what were the considerations which made his opponents so strenuous in their determination to undermine his influence and compass his downfall. For them he was the enemy of the Messiah and of Israel, raised up by Satan to falsify the truth, a notable sign in these Last Times of which Jesus had given warning that there would arise false prophets to deceive even the very Elect. Accordingly, it was essential that Paul's converts should be informed of their danger and wherever possible extricated from his clutches. The Holy War was on, and apostles from Jerusalem made it their business to visit as many as possible of the Christian communities Paul had founded.

Paul found himself forced to retort in kind to the assaults on his character which impugned the veracity of his doctrines and the authenticity of his revelations, still not realising what was at stake for those who attacked him. 'Should I, or an angel from heaven, proclaim to you anything different to what I did proclaim to you,' he wrote to the Galatians, 'cursed be he! Having said that, I am going to repeat it. If anyone proclaims to you anything different to what you received, cursed be he! ... You were running so well. Who brought you to a halt by making you lose confidence in the truth? ... He who is confusing you must bear the blame, whoever he may be. And what of me, brothers? If I am still preaching circumcision, why am I still being persecuted? So much for the "abolition of the obstacle of the cross"! It would be a good thing if those who unsettle you over circumcision would cut themselves off as well!' He tells the Corinthians that 'such people are false envoys, deceitful agents, masquerading as envoys of Christ. And no wonder, when Satan himself masquerades as an angel of light! So it is hardly surprising if his ministers masquerade as ministers of religion, whose fate will correspond to their actions.'[15]

All Paul's brilliance of intellect and imagination was enlisted to overturn the cogent arguments of his traducers. There was nothing of which they could boast in which he was not their equal, and if it came to that their superior, as he felt compelled to stress in no uncertain terms. He 'magnified his office' as apostle to the Gentiles. Their Israelite status apart from the Law of Moses became for him a fetish. Even Jewish believers were not exempted from his ruling that salvation could be procured solely by faith in the virtue of the Messiah's atoning death. Therefore if his adversaries relied on loyalty to the Law they were rejecting the grace of God.

Paul's teaching took on more and more the character of counter-propaganda, and the finest flights of his oratory, as we shall presently illustrate, were directed to meeting the challenges to which he was being subjected. These ideas of his were to become through his treasured letters the chief ingredients of the new religion of Christianity which subsequently developed, and the basis of its theology. So enticingly acceptable did they prove, united with the passionate sincerity of their author, his command of language, and his capacity for producing a remarkably elevated and coherent christological scheme, that in the absence of the voices which had spoken authoritatively in contradiction it was difficult to suppose them to be alien to the mind of Jesus whose status Paul had so exalted. The illusion was fostered by the injection into the evangelical records of Jesus of sayings and comments which confirmed and accorded with what Paul had postulated. Thus readers of the Christian Scriptures had little to go on to persuade them that what they were offered was the *tour de force* of a wayward religious genius rather than the legitimate expression of the Gospel.

For the Nazoreans the cross of which Paul made so much was evidence of the hostility of the world ruled by Rome towards God and his Messiah, an instrument of redemption only in the sense that the Messiah had accepted this suffering at the hands of his enemies as a means of persuading his people to repent and thus advancing the day of deliverance. To present the crucifixion as a saving mystery was pandering to heathen notions such as those of the devotees of Dionysus, Adonis and Mithras. The merits and sufferings of the Messiah could indeed be pleaded by the repentant in turning back to God, in so far as Jesus had exemplified complete obedience to the Law and had performed the will of God in fulfilment of the words of the Prophets; but they could be no substitute for the keeping of God's commandments which had never been abrogated. The Laws of Noah sufficed no doubt for Gentiles who did not stand within the covenants, and their observance assured them of a place with the righteous in the World to Come. But to belong to the people of God demanded a total commitment to the laws divinely ordained for this people. If Gentiles were deluded into believing that a mere act of faith on their part was a passport to membership of the house of Israel this was positively criminal, preventing such Gentiles facing up to their responsibilities. If proof was needed, it was supplied by the intemperate and licentious behaviour of many of Paul's converts. What he was urging was tantamount to saying, 'Let us do evil that good may come of it.'[16]

While faith certainly operated to change the lives of many, as it often would do no matter what was its spiritual focal point, Paul was very conscious that the conduct of numerous converts played directly into the hands of his adversaries. The literalness with which they interpreted 'freedom from the law' was scandalous and vexed his soul beyond measure. From the Law of Moses they might be free, but they were now under the law to Christ. He chided, exhorted and denounced in passage after passage in his letters. The space he devoted to this one subject speaks eloquently of the problem created by his soteriology. He himself had had a morbid obsession with sin, as he reveals in Romans, and he found it hard to grasp that what in his experience had removed a weight of guilt could be employed as a justification for casting off all restraint of the passions. He stuck, however, to the validity of his contentions, which were the principal plank in his platform, refusing to abate by one iota his proposition that faith in the atoning death of Christ alone conferred absolution. His thoughts found ever fresh arguments to support it. But he saw need to ally with these a resurrection doctrine, which insisted that the believer having died to sin by Christ's death must go on to be raised with him to newness of life. He must put off the old man, and put on the new. The following extract from the letter to the Romans is typical.

'What are we to say then? Are we to continue in sin that mercy may be magnified? God forbid! We who have died so far as sin is concerned, how can we still live in it? Can you be ignorant that those who have become associated with Christ by immersion, have become associated by it with his death? . . . We are thus united with him in burial, so that as Christ was raised from the dead by means of the Father's glory, we too should conduct ourselves in newness of life. For if we have become identified with the manner of his death, surely we should be with his resurrection also, knowing this, that our former self has been associated in crucifixion to dispose completely of the sinful body, that we should no longer be enslaved to sin; for the dead has met all the claims of sin upon him. . . . As Christ died, he died permanently so far as sin is concerned, but as alive again, he lives to God. And so you no less can count yourselves dead so far as sin is concerned, but alive to God in Christ Jesus. Therefore do not let sin rule your mortal body by obeying its lusts, nor offer your organs as instruments of iniquity. . . . Rather offer yourselves to God as alive from the dead, and your organs as instruments of rectitude to God. Sin shall not have dominion over you, for you are not under law but under mercy.'[17]

Some of Paul's teaching, as we can see here, was profoundly influenced by the solution he had found to his own personal problems, and which had come to him as a revelation. But if we study his ideas carefully we can appreciate how the hostile pressures upon him contributed to their development and how they came to be employed to wean his converts away from all sense of dependence on those who could rightly claim to have known by personal association all about Jesus and his actual instruction. The converts had to be shown that they could confidently turn their backs on any earthly authority and stand resolutely on their own feet, since all that was past had been superseded and they were now controlled by what was revealed by the Spirit.

With the ascension of Jesus on high a new era had commenced, the era of the New Covenant, and secrets were being spiritually revealed which previously could not be known. All who were in Christ were the children of the Kingdom Age, and the revelations conveyed to them were an earnest of the knowledge and conditions of the World to Come. Consequently the Apostles and Elders in Palestine had ceased to be the effective authority for believers, and there was no call to pay attention to their instructions and the institutions they represented which belonged to the age which was passing away. What they gave out as binding because of what Jesus had said and done when on earth was largely irrelevant, and it has often been remarked upon how little direct use Paul makes of the sayings and actions of Christ. 'From now on,' as he said, 'we know no one in the physical sense. Even if we have known Christ in the physical sense, we do so now no longer. If anyone is in Christ he is a new creation. The old relationships have gone, replaced by the new.'[18]

The effective authority for Christians is the Christ in heaven, who had existed from the beginning of the creation of the universe,[19] and had been manifested on earth essentially for the salvation of men by his death, having temporarily subjected himself to the conditions of humanity. But that work was finished, and in the glorified body of Jesus the Christ was again in heaven, no longer subject to limitations and able to communicate what could not previously be revealed. 'Our form of government originates in heaven', not in Judea, and it is not the Jerusalem below but the Jerusalem above which is our mother.[20] Yet all Christians are truly Israelites, the seed of Abraham and heirs of the Messianic promises, no matter whether they were formerly Gentiles, since the seed of Abraham is Christ in person, and himself comprehends Israel.[21] To become an Israelite it is therefore enough to be 'in Christ' and it is a rejection of the grace of God to enter the Jewish community by following the way of the Law. We know now from the Dead Sea Scrolls how much the Essenes emphasised the Way of the Law, and they certainly did not encourage the admission of Gentiles.

Paul elaborated a new doctrine of the Church as the body of which the Christ in heaven was the invisible head. It was a striking conception, but partly aimed like much else at establishing that his converts were totally released from allegiance to any visible head of the Church, the Council of the Apostles and Elders presided over by the still living brother of Jesus. The Papacy in Roman Catholicism would not have appealed to Paul at all.

Thus out of the bitter struggle between the apostle to the Gentiles and those who were the direct inheritors of the teaching and convictions of Jesus there emerged a whole new system of Christian thought, presented with all the curious logic and reasoning of Paul's rabinically trained mind and acquaintance with hellenic culture. Once the Church was deprived by circumstances of the arguments and personal influence of those who had been intimately associated with Jesus, and once it had become predominantly gentilised, the profundities and Gentile-directed contentions of Paulinism were hailed as divinely inspired as their author had claimed they were. The Church took Paul as its spiritual guide, thereby becoming involved down the centuries in conflicts and schisms, enmity, persecution and bloodshed, as Christians wrestled with the implications and interpretation of Pauline doctrines, the nature of Christ, revelation by the Holy Spirit, adoption, predestination and justification by faith, doctrines which could never be rightly understood without knowledge of Paul's background and training.

The asserted higher instruction of the Christ in heaven, communicated through Paul as the medium, did not prevail, however, as long as it could be effectively challenged by the legitimate Church. Paul's own letters reveal that the evidence produced by his opponents powerfully influenced his converts against him and his teaching, despite the affection as well as the arguments which he poured out. The pathos of his language is often deeply moving. He fought hard and desperately; but lost the battle in his lifetime though never his faith and courage, so that at the end he had to write to his devoted disciple Timothy, 'You are well aware that all the Asiatic believers have turned from me.'[22] He seems at times not to have been without qualms of conscience about what he was doing in standing up against the Apostles and Elders. Whenever he can he tries to assert his identification with them and their tradition. He presses upon his churches the collection of funds for the poor saints of Judea, and accepts the risks of personally conveying their bounty to Jerusalem.

The down-to-earthness of Jesus and those who followed him in Palestine, their accent on the social significance of religious belief, their vision of the Kingdom of God as the manifestation of the operation of his laws in the world, made sense to ordinary people where Paul's occultism went right over their heads. Paul realised this, and attempted to make himself intelligible; but in this respect he could not emulate convincingly the Messiah of whom the Apostles told. The sincerity of Paul is transparent, but his difficulties are equally so, as in the following passage from one of his letters to the Corinthians.

'There is a wisdom we employ with the initiated; but it is a wisdom which has nothing to do with this world, or with the transient forces governing this world. It is the Hidden Wisdom of God contained in a Mystery, which God formulated of old to be our glory before the Ages began; for had they known it they would never have crucified the Lord of glory. But as it is stated,

> What eye has never seen, nor ear heard,
> What never entered the mind of man,
> God has prepared for those who love him.

'Yet God has revealed it to us by the Spirit; for the Spirit delves into everything, even into the profundities of God. For who among men knows a man's ideas except the human spirit which is in him? So too none can know God's ideas except the Divine Spirit. Now what we have received is not the spirit of the created world, but the Spirit that emanates from God. So that we may know what God graciously grants us to know. Those are the things we speak of, not in the language that human wisdom provides, but in the fashion of spiritual instruction, bringing spiritually-equipped people into touch with spiritual realities. The materialist cannot entertain the ideas of the Divine Spirit: to him they are nonsense, and he cannot grasp them, because they have to be discerned spiritually. But the spiritually-equipped person discerns all these things, though they are to be discerned by no one unaided, for "who has ever known the mind of the Lord, that he should teach him?" But we have Christ's mind.

'It was impossible however, brothers, for me to speak to you as spiritually-equipped people, only as physically-equipped, as infants in Christ. I had to feed you with milk rather than solid food, for you were not equal to it. Neither are you equal to it yet, for you are still at the physical stage.'[23]

Paul stands out in the first period of Christian history unique in his qualities and in the novelties he introduced, a man who —in the name of a Jesus Christ who was largely of his own creation—departed so radically from the Jesus who had walked in Galilee that he left behind him a puzzle on which Christians have expended all the resources of erudition in a vain endeavour to find a solution that satisfactorily harmonises the incompatible representations. To the Corinthians, said Paul, there had been proclaimed 'another Jesus whom I did not proclaim'. A great question mark still overhangs those pregnant words, since that other Jesus was surely the Jesus of history, the real Jesus of whom so little is still known positively and whom Paul no longer found it profitable to know.

NOTES AND REFERENCES

1. Suetonius, *Vitellius*, II.
2. II. Thess. ii, 3–4.
3. Josephus, *War*, II. xiii. 4.
4. Josephus, *War*, II. xiii. 6.
5. Josephus, *Antiq.* XIX. viii. 2 and Acts xii. 22–3.
6. *Apocalypse of Baruch*, xlviii. 31–9, tr. by Dr. Charles. Cp. Jas. v. 1–9.
7. Psalm cx.
8. II. Thess. i. 7–8.
9. Acts xvii. 6–7.
10. Acts xxiv. 5.
11. Hippolytus, *Philosophumena*, Bk. IX, xxvi. This information probably derives from Josephus.

12. Josephus, *Antiq.*, XX. i. 1.
13. Eusebius, *Eccl. Hist.* III. v.
14. See Schonfield, *The Passover Plot*, Part Two, ch. iv.
15. Gal. i. 8–9, v. 7–12; II. Cor. xi. 13–15.
16. Rom. iii. 8.
17. Rom. vi. 1–14.
18. II. Cor. v. 16–17.
19. Col. i. 15–18; Eph. iv. 7–16.
20. Phil. iii. 20; Gal. iv. 25–6.
21. Gal. iii. 7–9, 26–9; Eph. ii. 11–22. According to Justin Martyr, 'Israel was Christ's name from the beginning, to which he altered the name of the blessed Jacob when he blessed him with his own name, proclaiming that all who through Christ have fled for refuge to the Father constitute the blessed Israel' (*Dial.* cxxv).
22. II. Tim. i. 15.
23. I. Cor. ii. 6–16.

7

The Storm Breaks

PAULINISM created a new and peculiar expression of the Christian message, an individual interpretation which represented a radical departure from the Messianism of Jesus as espoused and propagated by the original Christians.

Paul was the first to speak of Jesus Christ as Son of God and Saviour in a sense which, however, drawing on the resources of Jewish occultism,[1] made contact with religious thinking current in the pagan world. Salvation by identification with risen Saviours was an established teaching. So was the *post mortem* deification of world rulers and their ascension to heaven. Paul produced an amalgamation of ideas which, however unintentionally, did give rise to a new religion. He did not actually ascribe deity to Christ. As a Jew he could not go as far as this. But his cosmology and the language he employed did allow it to be inferred by Gentiles that this is what he intended to convey; and without question the Jesus Christ he proclaimed was ruler in the heavenly spheres, all Powers under God being subject to him.

For the present the earth and its inhabitants were not yet in subjection, and the purposes of God could not be fulfilled until this took place. An eschatology, doctrine of the Last Things, was therefore essential to Paul's scheme. Jesus Christ had to emerge once more from heaven, and that very soon. The event would be sudden and unexpected and attended by supernatural manifestations. Christ would return for the judgment of all who had not acknowledged God and accepted the gospel: even the followers of Christ would be tried for their conduct, and to this end, that they might appear before his judgment seat, the dead in Christ would be raised and take their stand beside the Christians living at the moment, whose mortal bodies would be instantaneously immortalised by being changed to new bodies not subject to corruption. The saints past and present would be immune to death, but their behaviour since they became Christians might exclude them from the felicities of the millennial reign or involve other punishments. Apart from these initial judgments, of the nations and separately of believers, the object of Christ's return would be to reign over the earth until it was as subordinated to the will of God as were the heavenly spheres. After this, all dead humanity, excluded from the first resurrection relating only to believers, would be raised for judgment. Many might be condemned to destruction; but after this death would be abolished. Heaven and earth would be in harmony. The function entrusted by God to Christ being thus successfully completed, Christ would abdicate his authority, so that henceforth God alone without intermediary would be patently supreme, the one and sole Ruler of the Universe.

Such a programme of the passage from time into eternity, consistent enough in its bold outlines and majestic progression, raised questions which did not always produce coherent and satisfactory answers. Christians are still wrangling about many aspects of eschatology, and have had more cause to do so since the Church asserted the deity of Christ and transferred the eternal home of believers from earth to heaven. If Christ is God and his habitat is heaven, why should he leave it for a second time to come to earth? Paul's grandiose vision of the exalted Christ who had pre-existed from the beginning of creation, and the doctrine of the single incarnation for purposes of the atonement, would seem to make a second advent totally unnecessary. He should not come again to us, and we—the believers—should go to him. And why to enjoy the heavenly state should we have to wait on the realisation of an extraordinary series of events in the earthly sphere?. Why should we not be finally united with Christ at death? Is there any requirement of bodily resurrection at some future time? What is the Judgment, and where will it take place? What is going to happen to all who are not Christians? The Church enmeshed in the confusion of its contradictory speculations cannot even today furnish the measure of straightforwardness offered by Paul and the early Christian teachers. It can employ their language while fighting shy of clear definition, taking refuge in the plea, God is merciful: his love is infinite, which will also demonstrate his justice.

Christian shifting away from the hope of the terrestrial Kingdom of God did not prevail until the second century. The first generation of believers, especially Paul's Gentile converts, were far more inclined to dwell too much on the delights of the coming Age which their faith in Christ entitled them to enjoy. Many of them were slaves, many of them poor people living wretchedly in horrible slum conditions. These had eagerly embraced what they understood Paul was offering, a free pardon for sins, a free salvation, the overthrow of the existing oppressive government, the end of laws, taxes, lordship, harshness and misery, a new era in which the downtrodden would be the privileged and have abundance of everything. Eagerly they looked forward to the Day, the Day of Emancipation, savouring its pleasures in anticipation and no less the retribution which would overtake the wealthy and the high and mighty. The cry was raised, 'When is the Day coming? How long must we wait?' Multitudes started to comport themselves as if the Day had already arrived. They downed tools, strutted about and gave themselves airs, insulted officials, bickered and quarrelled, and put no restraint on their passions. On all sides the Christians were looked at askance as outside the pale of decent law-abiding society, and by the authorities they were further regarded as dangerous seditionists.

The state of affairs comes clearly through to us when we

read the letters of Paul with attention, not as sacred literature but as human documents reflecting pressing problems and a rapidly deteriorating situation. It is all too easy to provide confirmatory quotations in Paul's warnings and exhortations, and we need furnish only a few examples.

'I beg you, brothers, as regards the coming of our Lord Jesus Christ . . . not to take speedy leave of your senses or become agitated . . . under the impression that the Day of the Lord has begun. Let no one deceive you in any way whatever; for it will not begin before the Defection has first taken place and the Lawless Man has been revealed. . . . Do you not recall that this is what I told you while I was still with you? . . . I bid you shun every brother who behaves as a shirker, and not in accordance with the tradition you have received from me. . . . That is why when I was with you I gave you this order, "He who will not work, neither shall he eat". For I hear that there are some among you behaving as shirkers, not busy but busybodies. I order and exhort such as these, that going quietly about their work they eat their own bread.'[2]

'If you bite and devour each other, take care that you do not exterminate one another. I say, therefore, conduct yourselves spiritually, and do not allow your physical passions to have their way. . . . You are not free to do as you please. Yet if you are spiritually guided you are not under law. Now the deeds of the physical nature are obvious: they are adultery, impurity, sensuality, idolatry, sorcery, enmity, quarrelling, envy, passions, intrigues, dissensions, factions, malice, heavy drinking, revelling, and everything of the same description about which I have warned you, just as I am warning you now, that those who act in this way will not inherit the Kingdom of God.'[3]

'Already you are glutted! Already you have grown rich! Already you have occupied the throne! And I only wish you had taken the throne, so that we too could reign with you. As it seems to me, God has kept us envoys for the end of the show, like those doomed to death; for we have become a spectacle for the universe, for angels and men. . . . I am reliably informed that there is immorality among you, immorality such as has no parallel among the Gentiles, that one should have his brother's wife. And you are full of elation, instead of grieving. . . . There is no justification for your boasting. Are you not aware that "a little leaven leavens the whole lump"? Get rid of the old leaven that you may be a new lump, once more in the unleavened state, for our passover—Christ—has been sacrificed. Consequently, let us observe the festival, not with the old leaven, nor with the leaven of vice and immorality, but with the unleavened bread of purity and sincerity. . . . I am writing to you now not to keep company at all with anyone bearing the name of brother if he is immoral, or a usurer, or foul-mouthed, or a drunkard. You are not even to take meals with such people. Is it for you to judge those outside when you do not judge those inside? Leave God to judge those outside, while you "put away the wicked from among you". . . . But here is news I do not appreciate, that when you assemble it is not for the better but for the worse. I learn first of all that when you hold your meetings there are divisions among you, and to a certain extent I believe it. . . . But is not your coming together for the common purpose of eating the supper that is specifically the Master's? In partaking of this it is for each of you to have had his own supper beforehand. Yet one is famished and another is consumed with thirst. Have you no homes in which to eat and drink? Or do you mean to treat God's Community with contempt, and humiliate those who have no homes?'[4]

'Let every individual be subject to the responsible authorities; for there is no authority except from God, and those who are constituted hold their appointment from God. Whoever, therefore, opposes the authority sets himself against the Divine order and those who resist it will duly receive punishment. . . . Of necessity you must be subject to the laws, not merely from considerations of punishment, but also of conscience, which applies equally to your payment of taxes. Those who levy them are God's officials regularly employed for this very purpose. Render to everyone their dues, tribute to whoever is entitled to it, tax to whoever is entitled to it, respect to whoever is entitled to it, honour to whoever is entitled to it. . . . This further, because I know the time, it is high time for you to awaken from sleep; for our deliverance is now much nearer than when we believed. The night is far advanced, the day is at hand. Let us therefore lay aside what belongs to the darkness and put on the habits of the light. Let us conduct ourselves with daytime decorum, not in revels and carousals, not in sexual intimacy and licentiousness, not in wrangling and rivalry. Rather, invest yourselves with the Lord Jesus Christ, and make no provision for the fulfilment of physical desires.'[5]

Paul is always so careful to avoid if he can hurting anyone's feelings, so eager to praise and speak well of his communities, that what he says in passages like these is all the more telling, and an understatement of the circumstances rather than the reverse.

Viewing the course of Jewish and Christian history under the Emperor Nero (A.D. 54–68) we can readily perceive that from the Roman standpoint stronger measures were found to be demanded to combat a challenge from the East far more difficult to meet than that of armed force. This was an assault that penetrated by stealth like a pestilence, insidious, destructive, creeping forward, spreading out, wherever conditions were favourable. It penetrated the meanest hovel and could find its way as easily into Caesar's palace. Its effects were subversive; but it was not always possible to tell who had been influenced and who were immediately responsible. Agents of the enemy mysteriously came and went. Those who brought themselves or were brought to official notice by inflammatory language, disorderly behaviour, or denunciation by informers, were not usually persons of consequence. There were leaders, but no single ringleader to be seized, since the man in whose name the Christians acted had long been dead, and the world ruler whom the Jewish agitators expected was nameless and had not yet appeared.

What was popularly reported about the Christians, their hatred of humanity, their gross and criminal activities in secret, was doubtless greatly exaggerated, though having some foundation in fact as Paul's letters convey. What was certainly known about them, that like the Jews they avoided social engagements outside their own fellowship and would not participate in the general religious rites and observances as was proper with loyal subjects, marked them down as misanthropic and atheistic. The authorities were aware that Christianity had a relationship with the Jews, but where Christians were not Jews and had separate meetings it made their conduct all the more suspect and reprehensible. It would hardly have escaped attention that Christians were anticipating the overthrow of the Roman Empire, even if they were not directly engaged in seeking to accomplish it by militant action. Therein lay the most serious menace of the growing and expanding superstition.

It would be underestimating the security consciousness of the Romans to imagine that they thought of the Christian movement as either negligible or harmless. The later New Testament documents are concerned to give this impression, and to blame the Jews rather than the Romans for hostility to Christianity. But this was because they were written with an apologetic interest when Jewish fortunes were at a low ebb after the defeat of their revolt. The Christians liked to represent themselves to others as enveloped in an aura of sanctity, and no one can blame them for wanting to do so. They had numbers of good and spiritually-minded people among them; but as a whole they were not a body of innocents. There is ample evidence in Christian, Roman and Jewish sources that the emphatic Messianism which gave Christianity its name was very quickly recognised as politically pernicious, and that measures were taken to cope with it.

Messianism was born and bred in Palestine. It could not, therefore, be tackled effectively anywhere else. It was not to be neglected to combat manifestations of the disease in other places, especially in Rome itself and in Alexandria with its substantial Jewish population. But it could only be dealt with conclusively at the source. According to Sulpicius Severus, this was fully appreciated by Titus, son of the Emperor Vespasian. Before the final assault on Jerusalem in A.D. 70 Titus as Roman commander-in-chief is said to have held a war-council to deliberate on whether the world-famous Temple should be spared or destroyed. The decision was taken that it should be destroyed in order to stamp out both Judaism and Christianity; 'for these religions, though opposed to each other, none the less had the same origin. The Christians derived from the Jews, and when the root was torn up the stem would more readily perish.'[6]

The statement of Severus cannot wholly be relied on, but it is thought to have been based on a lost portion of the fifth book of Tacitus' *History*. The underlying truth appears to be that it was Jewish and Christian Messianism which the Romans were seeking to eradicate. Eusebius seems to confirm this when he relates 'that Vespasian, after the capture of Jerusalem, commanded all who were of the family of David to be sought, that no one might be left among the Jews who was of the royal stock'.[7]

The historical question has therefore to be considered, whether in order to eliminate the threat of Messianism, both Jewish and Christian, it had not been Roman policy for some years previously to provoke a Jewish revolt in Palestine? Such a policy would have great advantages for the Romans. They were highly superstitious, and gravely concerned at the widespread circulation of propaganda foretelling the imminent destruction of Rome and the downfall of the Empire. They were ill-equipped for a war of nerves, for a struggle with forces which did not employ physical weapons, which were here, there and everywhere and seldom came out into the open. With armed insurrections and the assembly of crowds swayed by some prophet or agitator it was different. Troops could quickly be sent if needed to quell such disturbances. These were now of frequent and increasing occurrence in Judea, the hotbed of Messianism. If the Jews could be induced to commit themselves to a full-scale rebellion the problem confronting the Romans might be solved once and for all. The issue would be settled if it could be dealt with by Roman might.

If the Romans had such a policy, to strike at the roots of Messianism by deliberate incitement, it was one which could not be publicised. Of course there would have been no call for it if the Roman governors of Judea and the Jewish authorities loyal or at least subservient to Rome had succeeded in getting the upper hand and suppressing the disaffected elements. But though in the reign of Claudius there had been many arrests and executions, and ruthless punitive action had been taken, these measures had failed. The movement, both in its Jewish and Christian aspects, continued to gain ground. As Tacitus puts it, by the execution of Christ 'the sect of which he was the founder received a blow, which for a time checked the growth of a dangerous superstition; but it broke out again, and spread with increased vigour, not only in Judea, the soil that gave it birth, but even in the city of Rome'.[8] If we look at developments in the reign of Nero it does not seem at all far-fetched that there were concealed intentions underlying Roman behaviour.

Josephus the historian, who was a young man in Judea at the time, has quite extraordinary things to say about the later Roman governors, Albinus and Florus. He describes them as tyrannical and inordinately rapacious; but also accuses them of being hand-in-glove with the Jewish militants, the sworn enemies of Rome, and of sharing the spoils of their depredations. Such conduct would be fantastic in Caesar's official representatives if it were not prompted by a secret design of which they had cognisance and which could not be disclosed. We may quote Josephus' own words.

'Festus, who succeeded Felix as procurator, proceeded to attack the principal plague of the country: he captured large numbers of the brigands (i.e. the militant nationalists) and put not a few to death. The administration of Albinus, who followed Festus, was of another order; there was no form of villainy which he omitted to practice. Not only did he, in his official capacity, steal and plunder private property and burden the whole nation with extraordinary taxes, but he accepted ransoms from their relatives on behalf of those who had been imprisoned for robbery by the local councils or by former procurators. . . . Now, too, the audacity of the revolutionary party in Jerusalem was stimulated; the influential men among their number secured from Albinus, by means of bribes, immunity for their seditious practices; while of the populace all who were dissatisfied with peace joined hands with the governor's accomplices. . . .

'Such was the character of Albinus, but his successor, Gessius Florus, made him appear by comparison a paragon of virtue. The crimes of Albinus were, for the most part, perpetrated in secret and with dissimulation: Gessius, on the contrary, ostentatiously paraded his outrages upon the nation, and, as though he had been sent as hangman of condemned criminals, abstained from no form of robbery or violence. . . . He stripped whole cities, ruined entire populations, and almost went the length of proclaiming throughout the country that all were at liberty to practise brigandage, on condition that he received his share of the spoils.'[9]

The conclusion reached by Josephus was, that Florus wanted war as 'his only hope of covering up his enormities. For, if the peace were kept, he expected to have the Jews accusing him before Caesar; whereas, could he bring about their revolt, he hoped that this larger crime would divert inquiry into less serious offences. In order, therefore, to produce an outbreak of the nation, he daily added to their sufferings.' While Josephus here charges Florus with personal responsibility for promoting the war to save his own skin, the historian may have been getting nearer the truth than he knew. It cannot be excluded that the governors were lending themselves to the carrying out of a Roman endeavour to goad the

Jewish people, multitudes of whom were non-militant, into open war with Rome, so as to be able by force to put an effective end to the menace of Messianism in all its manifestations, and by an awful example and warning deter all individuals and subject nations who might be imagining that the doom of Rome was at hand.

The seventh decade of the first century was a period of abnormal emotional excitement and political unrest. The Romans with the monstrous Nero at their head were in a mood to credit that anything could happen and to devise any scheme that would enable them to hit out desperately at the mysterious as well as the comprehensible forces ranged against them. The year A.D. 68 camc as a kind of climax with the suicide of the abandoned emperor and the unique phenomenon of three contenders for the purple, Galba, Otho and Vitellius.

The atmosphere of the time has often been represented by students of Roman literature. Long ago Dean Farrar depicted it in eloquent language.

'Men seemed to be tormented and terrified with catastrophes and portents. "Besides the manifold changes and chances of human affairs," says Tacitus, "there were prodigies in heaven and on earth, the warnings of lightnings, and the presages of the future, now joyous, now gloomy, now obscure, new unmistakable. For never was it rendered certain by clearer indications, or by more deadly massacres of the Roman people, that the gods care nothing for our happiness, but do care for our retribution." In Rome a pestilence had carried off tens of thousands of the citizens. A disastrous inundation of the Tiber had impeded the march of Otho's troops, and encumbered roads with ruins. In Lydia an encroachment of the seas had wrought fearful havoc. In Asia city after city had been shattered to the dust by earthquakes. "The world itself is being shaken to pieces," says Seneca, "and there is universal consternation." Comets, eclipses, meteors, parhelions, terrified the ignorant, and were themselves the pretexts for imperial cruelties. Auroras tinged the sky with blood. Volcanos seemed, like Vesuvius, to be waking to new fury. . . . The whole Empire was in a state of agitation. That the sacred sun of the Julii should set in a sea of blood seemed an event frightfully ominous, while, owing to the obscurity which hung about the death of Nero, and the very small number who had seen his corpse . . . not only was there a universal belief that he would return, but as early as the end of A.D. 68 a false Nero gained many adherents, and caused widespread alarm.'[10]

In A.D. 64 someone had significantly remarked to Nero, 'When I am dead let fire devour the world.' To which the emperor is said to have replied, 'Nay, let it be while I am living.'[11] Suetonius, who reports this, alleges that Nero acted accordingly and set fire to Rome. He thus literally fulfilled the Jewish and Christian predictions that Rome would go up in flames. After the fire had done its worst for days on end only four of the fourteen sections into which the city was divided remained intact. Tacitus agrees that there was some doubt as to whether Nero was responsible, though probabilities pointed to him. What is not in doubt is that he put the blame on the Christians. Here we follow Tacitus.

'Nero proceeded with his usual artifice. He found a set of profligate and abandoned wretches, who were induced to confess themselves guilty, and on the evidence of such men a number of Christians were convicted, not indeed, upon clear evidence of their having set the city on fire, but rather on account of their sullen hatred of the human race. They were put to death with exquisite cruelty, and to their sufferings Nero added mockery and derision. . . . At length the cruelty of these proceedings filled every breast with compassion. Humanity relented in favour of the Christians. The manners of that people were, no doubt, of a pernicious tendency, and their crimes called for the hand of justice: but it was evident that they fell a sacrifice, not for the public good, but to glut the rage and cruelty of one man only.'[12]

Again we must ask, was there a policy behind the event? Was the emperor's action as conceived in his perverted mind akin to that of his governors, Albinus and Florus, in Judea? The Messianists were foretelling the doom of Rome by fire. Very well, let us have the fire on which they insist and charge them with it. Let us use the prophecy as a means of destroying them. The Roman historians writing a considerable time after the event do not spell this out in so many words; but Tacitus does list the modes of executing the condemned Christians, tearing by beasts, converting them into living torches by putting them on crosses and covering them with inflammable material, and these agree with the Roman penalties prescribed for those who practise sorcery and magic.[13] The punishment fitted the crime of ill-wishing Rome and the Empire.

Turning once more to Judea, we learn of an endeavour in A.D. 62 to deprive the Christians of their leadership. The principal sanhedrists, linked in their fortunes with the Roman government and abominated by the pious and the Jewish populace, seized an opportunity to dispose of the inoffensive and non-militant James the brother of Jesus. Before the arrival of Albinus to take over the governorship he was seized on the orders of the high priest, accused of law-breaking with certain others unnamed and summarily executed.[14]

Horrified Pharisees protested and even sent a delegation to Albinus. But the time when moderate counsels could prevail was nearly ended.

For the followers of Jesus the judicial murder of his brother, their venerated head, was a great blow: it was as if Jesus had died again. Hegesippus, writing in the second century, tells of his virtues which earned him the name of Zaddik (the Just) and 'Bastion of the People'. He reports that the last words of James were the prayer, 'I beseech thee, O Lord God and Father, forgive them, for they know not what they do',[15] words which in Luke's Gospel alone are attributed to Jesus himself.

The signs were indeed multiplying that the End was approaching. One of the most alarming Signs of the Times, according to Josephus, who may be accepted as speaking here from personal knowledge, occurred on the Feast of Tabernacles in the very year James was martyred. 'One Jesus son of Ananias, a rude peasant, standing in the Temple, suddenly began to cry out, "A voice from the east, a voice from the west, a voice against Jerusalem and the Sanctuary, a voice against the bridegroom and the bride, a voice against all the people." Day after day he went about all the alleys with this cry on his lips. Some of the leading citizens, incensed at these ill-omened words, arrested the fellow and severely chastised him. But he, without a word on his own behalf or for the private ear of those who smote him, only continued his cries as before. Thereupon the magistrates, supposing, as was indeed the case, that the man was under some supernatural impulse, brought him before the Roman governor; there, although flayed to the bone with scourges, he neither sued for mercy nor shed a tear, but, merely introducing the most mournful of variations into his ejaculation, responded to each stroke with "Woe to Jerusalem!" When Albinus, the governor, asked him who and whence he was, and why he uttered these cries, he answered him never a word, but unceasingly reiterated his dirge over the city, until Albinus pronounced him a maniac and let him go.'[16]

It may be considered that this account of another Jesus has left its traces in John's Gospel, where Jesus of Nazareth is represented as crying aloud in the Temple on the Feast of Tabernacles, and when he is brought before Pilate, and the governor asks him, 'Whence art thou?' he makes no reply.[17]

With the death of James, and in face of the signs, the moderate Nazoreans took the decision to leave Jerusalem. Eusebius reports that they obeyed the command of an oracle given by revelation to men of approved piety before the war. Epiphanius variously says that the warning was delivered by Christ and by an angel. There would appear to be some connection with the prophecies of Jesus about the Time of the End incorporated in the Gospels, often called the Little Apocalypse.[18] The Nazoreans are stated to have migrated across the Jordan to Pella; but precisely when they left

Jerusalem is uncertain, whether before the war broke out in 66 or later after hostilities had fully developed. The traditions are not clear.

Events, as we have seen, now went from bad to worse in Judea until, as a consequence of Roman oppression and in the fanatical conviction that the hour of deliverance was approaching, the Jewish people spurred on by the Zealots rose in revolt. Even when Jerusalem was in ruins and the Temple was destroyed a remnant fought on, holding out at the mountain fortress of Masada until A.D. 73. The triumphant Romans joyfully paraded the spoilts of the Temple through the streets of their capital and struck coins with the legend *Judea Capta*; but what they had killed was the body, not the soul, as they were soon to discover.

The first phase of Christianity was ended by this tragic yet heroic chapter in Jewish history. The great figures of that phase had passed away, James in Jerusalem, Paul and possibly Peter at Rome. The voices of controversy were temporarily stilled. In retrospect the seer of the Revelation declares that there was silence in heaven for the space of about half an hour. Such were the horrors of that dread time that even the angels, who praise God day and night, ceased their singing.[19]

NOTES AND REFERENCES

1. See *The Christology of Paul* at the end of this volume.
2. II. Thess. ii. 1–5, iii. 6–12.
3. Gal. v. 15–21.
4. I. Cor. iv. 7–9, v. 1–13, xi. 17–22.
5. Rom. xiii. 1–7, 11–14.
6. Severus, *Chron.* II. xxx. 6.
7. Euseb., *Eccl. Hist.* III. xi, probably based on Hegesippus.
8. Tacit., *Annals*, XV. xliv.
9. Josephus, *War*, II. xiv. 1–2.
10. Frederic W. Farrar, *The Early Days of Christianity*, pp. 425–6.
11. Suetonius, *Nero*, XXXVIII.
12. Tacit., *Annals*, XV. xliv.

13. Paulus, *Sent*, v, quoted by E. G. Hardy, *Studies in Roman History*, First Series, pp. 53–4.

14. Jos., *Antiq*. XX. ix. 1.

15. Hegesippus, *Memoirs*, Bk. V, quoted by Euseb., *Eccl. Hist*. II. xxiii.

16. Jos., *War*, VI. v. 3.

17. Jn. vii. 37; xix. 9.

18. Euseb., *Eccl. Hist*. III. v. 2–3; Epiphanius, *Adv. Haeres*. xxix. 7 and *De Mens. et Pond*. xv; Mk. xiii and parallels.

19. Rev. viii. 1.

8

Post-War Reconstruction

THE Roman general charged with putting down the Jewish revolt had in the course of the war become emperor of the Romans. The Julian dynasty was ended and in its place the Flavian was installed. The bluff Vespasian (Titus Flavianus Vespasianus Augustus) entered the capital of the Empire invested with an aura of mystical fervour inspired by legend and prediction eagerly accepted by a country which had been rent and torn by civil strife. He was hailed as *restitutor orbis*, 'restorer of the world'. To him, it was being said, and not to any Jewish king, had the mysterious prophecies of the Hebrews pointed as the predestined world ruler. In keeping with this relief-bringing interpretation Vespasian while at Alexandria had healed a lame man and given sight to the blind.[1] For the Romans the truth was now manifest, and the power of Jupiter was confirmed, when Titus the emperor's son, left in command in Judea, had taken Jerusalem and destroyed the temple of the Jewish God.

The reading of events meant one thing to Roman imperialism and quite another to the Jewish Messianists. To the followers of Jesus in the East, when they looked back on what had transpired, it seemed as though a new phase of the Last Times had then commenced, with the Evil One, the Primeval Dragon, playing his master-stroke by resurrecting the Beast, the Imperial regime, and conferring upon it fresh power and prestige. The Beast had re-emerged cured of his deadly wound to awe the world with a false Messianism and blasphemous parody of the Kingdom of God. He was permitted to make war with the saints and to overcome them, and given authority over every race and people, tongue and nation. 'The whole earth was in awe of the Beast, and worshipped the Dragon because he conferred authority on the Beast. They even worshipped the Beast, saying, "Who is like the Beast? Who can fight with him?" '[2]

It cannot be over-emphasised that the effects of the war, both for Judaism and Christianity, were profound. Throughout the land of Israel there had been devastation and disruption, heavy loss of life, loss of records, impairment of memory through misery, malnutrition and shock. But over and above there was acute consciousness of the magnitude of the disaster in terms of change. Suddenly the earthly focal point of Jewish and Christian faith had been eliminated. Many had anticipated that this would be the outcome of the war; but when it happened it did not dull the ache of the void created or diminish the sense of bereavement. Joined with these feelings there was anger, and horror and foreboding as to what trials might still be in store.

As it transpired, it was in the area in and around the scene of the conflict that recovery was speediest. For the Pharisees and the Nazoreans there were links with the past which had not been completely severed and a form of organisation which could be reactivated to meet the new conditions. Both parties had in a measure been prepared for the result of the war and had adequate leadership to cope with the state of emergency. The Pharisees had Jochanan son of Zakkai and the Nazoreans had Simeon son of Cleophas.

The Pharisees had long been opponents of the Sadducean hierarchy and had centred their religious activites on the synagogues as much as on the Temple. With the Sadducees they had participated in certain functions of government through the Jewish Council, the Sanhedrin, but they were not nearly to the same extent affected by the cessation of the

Temple ritual and worship. Thus it was possible for them to make the Torah (the body of Jewish doctrine as they interpreted it) the central feature of Jewish faith in place of the Temple, though they did not abandon belief in its restoration. They could reconvene a Sanhedrin of sorts, charged with making and administering decisions with the guidance of a college of experts, and transfer some of the features of the Temple worship to the liturgy of the synagogues. In this way there could develop in rabbinical Judaism a new orthodoxy in place of the former varieties of Jewish spiritual expression, a workable and coherent system suited to the post-war conditions.

One of the chief architects of the new order was Jochanan son of Zakkai. He may have been of Galilean origin, and he lived to a great age. He is credited with the gift of prophecy and was deeply versed in mystical lore. He is said to have warned the Galileans that they would come under the sway of the Zealots, and when the door of the Temple mysteriously opened of its own accord not long before the revolt he foretold the fate of the Sanctuary. 'O Temple, Temple,' he exclaimed, 'why dost thou frighten thyself? I know that thou shalt be destroyed. Zechariah son of Iddo [Zech. xi. 1] has already prophesied concerning thee, "Open thy doors, O Lebanon, that the fire may devour thy cedars".' He too, like Josephus, announced that Vespasian would become emperor.

Jochanan had been a leader of the moderate Pharisees in Jerusalem, and had done his best to restrain the extremists from going to war with the Romans. During the partisan struggle inside the city, when it was already besieged, he contrived to escape by feigning death, and having himself carried out in a coffin by his disciples. Thereafter he asked permission of the Romans to settle at Jabneh (Jamnia) in the coastal region, where his school became the centre for the new Judaism. His Council took over many of the attributes and functions of the former Sanhedrin, and he was its first president.[3]

In many ways comparable to Jochanan was the Nazorean leader Simeon son of Cleophas. He was a Galilean, and according to tradition reached the very advanced age of one hundred and twenty years when he was executed by the Romans in the reign of Trajan after being denounced as a descendant of David and a Christian.

It was around the person of Simeon that the Nazoreans regrouped. Eusebius relates, on information derived from the second-century author Hegesippus, that, 'After the martyrdom of James (brother of Jesus), and the capture of Jerusalem which immediately followed, the report is that those of the apostles and disciples of the Lord that were yet surviving came together from all parts with those that were related to the Lord according to the flesh; for the greater part of them were still living. These consulted together to determine whom it was proper to pronounce worthy of being the successor of James. They all unanimously declared Simeon son of Cleophas (of whom mention is made in the sacred volume Lk. xxxiv. 18) as worthy of the episcopal seat there. They say he was a cousin of the Saviour, for Hegesippus asserts that Cleophas was the brother of Joseph.'[4]

Prior to the war it is clear from the Christian records that the Nazoreans had established in Jerusalem a Council for the government of all the followers of Jesus, which was in fact an opposition Sanhedrin, consisting of the Apostles and Elders under the presidency of James. The Nazoreans saw themselves as loyal Israel which gave allegiance to Jesus as the rightful Jewish king. They were therefore justified, pending the return of Jesus to take the throne, to create a government exercising supreme authority and jurisdiction over all believers at home and abroad. Thus the Council had a political as well as spiritual significance, being set up in express rejection of the governmental body which had taken action against Jesus and which owned Caesar as lord. The appointment of James to the presidency had been in no small measure a political appointment, since he was of the blood royal and brother next in age of the absent monarch. This explains why he rather than Peter had been chosen.

Our knowledge of the Jewish Sanhedrin, as it functioned in the first century, is not very exact, since later descriptions in the rabbinical literature are coloured by idealisation after the war with Rome. It was, however, the agency entrusted with so much of Jewish autonomous administration as had been permitted by the Romans. At one time, of course, it had been the very real and supreme government of the nation. It consisted of seventy Elders, apparently elected by their fellows and not by the people and chiefly from prominent and representative families, together with a president and vice-president. There are some indications that the Sanhedrin had an inner committee or cabinet of ten. There was also, if this was distinct from the committee, a religious Council which was convened and presided over as in the case of the full Sanhedrin by the reigning high priest, or by his official deputy.[5]

Among the activities of the Sanhedrin which concern us were the levying of the Temple tax, the sending out of apostles and delegates to assure the proper religious conduct of the Jewish communities abroad, and the final determination of all questions affecting the due observance of the Torah.

From what we learn of the Nazorean Sanhedrin it was similarly constructed and had similar functions. The ruling body consisted of seventy Elders. It is said that Jesus appointed these after the twelve Apostles; but in the actual Council it would seem that the twelve were part of the seventy, or at any rate also ranked as Elders, though they formed the inner cabinet. In the same way as the president of the Sanhedrin was the high priest, so James, according to tradition, was invested with the high priestly office, and had Peter and John as his deputies, the three constituting 'the pillars' referred to by Paul in Galatians. Later Nazorean records style James 'the supreme Overseer, who rules Jerusalem, the holy Community of the Hebrews, and the communities everywhere excellently founded by the providence of God'.[6] He was of the line of David, being the son of Joseph, 'and moreover we have found that he officiated after the manner of the ancient priesthood. . . . Furthermore, he was empowered to wear upon his head the high priestly diadem.'[7]

In the Acts we find the Nazorean Council acting exactly like the Sanhedrin. They send out officers to supervise new communities of believers, Peter and John to Samaria, Barnabas to Antioch. They dispatch, with the president's commission, a delegation to Antioch to investigate the terms of admission of Gentile converts, and when there is a dispute on this matter the case is referred back to Jerusalem for final decision, and James the president gives judgment. The verdict is conveyed by letter by envoys of the Council, and is binding on all Christian communities. The interference with his work and teaching which Paul so much resented was action mandated to its official representatives by the Christian Sanhedrin in accordance with its supreme authority and in due performance of its obligations. This was no unauthorised action by Judaisers. Further, in the Acts and Pauline writings, we find a practice of collecting funds among the communities and transmitting them to Jerusalem, comparable to the payment of the Temple tax by Jews of the Dispersion.[8]

A great deal that is obscure is illuminated for us when we have appreciated that before the war in the formative years of the Christian movement a Nazorean Sanhedrin had functioned, and that this Council exercised sovereign powers over the entire body of believers throughout the world. It was in fact the national government of Israel loyal to the Messiah.

The reconstitution of a Sanhedrin in such form as was practicable after the war was thus a matter of the utmost consequence for the Pharisees and the Nazoreans equally. Without a Sanhedrin, however denied by the Romans any political recognition, not only would spiritual coherence be jeopardised, but the prospect of continuing as a distinct people with all that this meant of hope for the future would have been seriously imperilled in the great despondency and dislocation following the national catastrophe. Hence the independent action taken by the leaders of the two Jewish bodies.

The Romans, for their part, were determined to stamp out Jewish nationalism in every shape and form, though they did not seek to destroy the Jewish religion. They had been made acutely aware of the threat of Messianism to the security of the Empire. There had been far more to the war than the revolt of a subject people. Two opposing concepts of world government, two mutually exclusive theocratic systems, were in collision. Roman fears of the subversive effects of Jewish and Christian propaganda were related to the sense of an ever-present peril from the East, which had arisen not only from the power of the Parthians and the strongly independent attitude of client rulers in Asia Minor, but from recollection of the Roman rivalries which had set East against West in the conflicts between Pompey and Julius Caesar and between Mark Antony and Octavian. The Jewish Messianic movement had accentuated these fears, and after the war continued to play upon them, enlisting in the cause the legend that Nero of the old Julian dynasty had not perished but had fled to the East, whence he would very soon return to wreak vengeance on Rome.

So, when Vesuvius erupted in A.D. 79 and destroyed Pompeii and Herculaneum, this was seized upon by the Jewish Sibyl to announce:

> But when from a cleft in the earth, in the land of Italy,
> a flame of fire shoots out its light to the broad heaven,
> to burn up many cities and slay their men,
> and a great cloud of fiery ashes shall fill the air,
> and sparks fiery red shall fall from heaven,
> then should men know the wrath of the God of heaven,
> because they destroyed the blameless people of the godly.
> Then shall come to the West the strife of war stirred up,
> and the exiled man of Rome, lifting up a mighty sword,
> crossing the Euphrates with many tens of thousands.[9]

Roman measures against a recrudescence of Jewish nationalism were as comprehensive as possible. One mark of sovereignty which might have been revived was the collection from all Jews of the former Temple tax. Accordingly it was decreed that in place of this tax there should be a Jewish tax paid into the Roman exchequer as a tribute to the temple of the Roman patron god Jupiter Capitolinus.[10] The miserable Jews were forced to bear the insult of appearing to pay homage to the deity of their masters to remind them continually of their fallen condition. We have already mentioned how the Roman counter-propaganda had seized upon the fact that Vespasian had been proclaimed emperor in Judea as a stick to beat the Messianists.

The Christians in particular, as a superstition owning Jesus as the Messiah and predestined world ruler, were denied licence of assembly. Vespasian, it is said, ordered all descendants of David to be sought for and arrested, that no one belonging to the ancient Jewish royal house should be left at liberty.[11] But, as we have noted, some of the family of Jesus succeeded in evading capture, and Simeon his first cousin was elected present head of all the Christians by the surviving Apostles and Elders of the old Nazorean administration. By this time few of them could have been much less than seventy years of age. Thus defiantly, but as far as Christians in the rest of the world were concerned not very effectually, by appointing again not an apostle but a kinsman of Jesus they showed their determination to re-establish a government in readiness for the return of King Jesus.

In the revived Nazorean administration the relations of Jesus had a specially honoured place. They were known as the Heirs. 'There are those', wrote Hegesippus, 'who take the lead of the whole Church as witnesses, even the kindred of the Lord, and when profound peace was established throughout the Church they continued to the time of Trajan Caesar.'[12] It is unfortunate that we know so little of the activities of this body and its leaders owing to the loss of records. Such Christian sources as we possess are very one-sided, and we cannot exclude that documentation giving the other side of the story was destroyed or suppressed.[13] But certain statements, like that just quoted, have been preserved, and both Eusebius the ecclesiastical historian and Epiphanius bear witness that the Nazoreans, harried and persecuted as they were, flourished in the East in the years after the war and that numbers of Jews joined them.[14] From Julius Africanus we learn that the Heirs took pride in their Davidic descent and circulated the genealogy which now stands at the head of Matthew's Gospel. It has been noted by Lukyn Williams that this genealogy is in mnemonic form, consisting of three groups of fourteen names covering the periods from Abraham to David, from Solomon to the Babylonian Exile, and from the Exile to Jesus, answering to the three letters of the name David (DVD) in Hebrew, the numerical value of which is fourteen.[15] Actually in the Greek text of Matthew there are only thirteen names in the third division; but the present writer has been able to restore the missing name from an old Hebrew manuscript of the Gospel. The name is that of Abner, which had dropped out between Abiud and Eliakim by a scribal error due to a likeness in Hebrew of Abner (Abiner) to Abiud (Abiur).[16]

Catholic Christianity had good reason to seek to discredit the Nazoreans and to brand them as heretical. For one thing it was fatal to the doctrine of the deity of Jesus that his own Apostles and the Christian members of his family had held that he was no more than man, and had been anointed by the Spirit of God at his baptism, thus becoming the Messiah (the Christ). The true apostolic tradition had to be fiercely denied and controverted; but in the late second century when a movement arose urging the Church to return to what came to be called the Adoptionist view, that Christ had been received into sonship of God when he was baptised in terms of Psalm ii. 6–7, its advocates could still point out that this view had been held 'by all the first Christians and by the Apostles themselves'.[17] The evidence available establishes that they were right.

This evidence comes to us only to a slight but nevertheless telling extent from the books of the New Testament, since these in the main reflect Pauline concepts and those of the Church at large in its new thinking. It was not possible to eliminate in historical passages all indications of the original Christian beliefs; but we should not expect the New Testament to be the medium for their plain expression, and we do not possess any Christian pre-war Hebrew texts. What counts for so much is the witness of the ecclesiastical historians that the original Apostles and Elders and relations of Jesus were the spokesmen of the Jewish Christianity with jurisdiction over the whole Church. This Christianity in its teaching about Jesus continued in the tradition it had directly inherited, and could justifiably regard Pauline and catholic Christianity as heretical. It was not, as its opponents alleged, Jewish Christianity which debased the person of Jesus, but the Church in general which was misled into deifying him.

To understand how this came about we have to appreciate the difficulties of the Nazoreans. The Simeonite government, although it was the legitimate Christian authority, was not in a position effectively to exercise control of Christian affairs. By reason of its Davidic leadership and strong Messianic convictions the Nazorean Council was marked down as anti-Roman, and could only exist and function somewhat precariously in the East. This created a vacuum fatal to Christian coherence under the post-war conditions, which had to be filled if Christianity in other parts of the Empire was to survive.

Here it is needful to look at the position of the Jews of the Dispersion. Essentially for the synagogues throughout the Empire little had been changed by the war. It had been a war which many of the Jewish communities, secure under Roman protection, had not at all favoured when it was launched by the militant Zealots. To challenge the might of Rome seemed an act of madness, and it could well imperil the safety of tens of thousands of Jews depending on Rome to preserve them from the worst consequences of Greek and Egyptian anti-semitism. There was mourning for Zion, shock at the destruction of the Temple, and the Jews of Rome in particular had had to bear the humiliation of the sacred vessels of the Sanctuary being borne in triumph through the streets of the capital. There was acute questioning and anxiety; but many Jews of the Empire were not too distressed that the Romans had conquered, since the Jewish religion remained and could be openly practised, and the Roman government had acted promptly in suppressing Greek attempts to turn on their Jewish neighbours by instigating pogroms. The new Jewish Tax paid to the temple of Jupiter Capitolinus was paid with qualms, but was not resisted. For the Romans, the eradication of Messianism was one thing: the way of life of peaceful and friendly Jews was quite another.

The position with Christian communities in the West was different. It behoved them to exercise the greatest circumspection because they were the objects of the gravest official suspicion and had no authorisation to meet for worship. They were not at this time being actively persecuted, since it was felt that the Roman victory had dealt their Messianic hopes a death-blow, but they had need to give as little opportunity as possible for hostile tongues to wag. The destruction of Jerusalem and the Temple could be deemed a great sign that the return of Christ was at hand; but militancy had not paid off, and the Zealot element was reduced to silence. Commonsense directed that the vital thing for Christianity was to remain in being for what was left of the time of waiting and to this end to re-appraise the situation.

Deprived of sufficient guidance from the apostolic body in the East, and perhaps rather fearful of it in view of Roman hostility to political Messianism, the Church in Rome, the capital of the Empire, appears to have considered itself called upon to exercise special responsibilities in the post-war period which gradually acquired the character of an assumption of the mantle of Christian leadership. The process took time and necessarily involved the employment and preparation of propaganda material to substantiate the claims put forward and to denigrate the authority of the legitimate apostolic succession. In the end, though there was a spirited but belated endeavour by the Nazoreans to hit back with counter-propaganda,[18] Roman catholicism could not be unseated. The response, when it could be made, came much too late, since by the end of the second century most of the churches subscribed to the new orthodoxy and the documents which had aided its establishment were widely regarded as divinely inspired.

According to the view which prevailed the Catholic Church of the new orthodoxy was the inheritor of the true tradition of the Apostles, an assertion which illustrates the power of a lie if it is a thumping big one. This tradition, according to Irenaeus the opponent of all heretics, was handed down in that great, ancient and universally known church founded and established at Rome by the two most glorious apostles Peter and Paul, 'and for this reason every other church and all the faithful everywhere ought to agree with that church'.[19]

The supremacy of the Roman Church became a fact, but its entitlement to it was a cleverly cultivated myth on which it is possible to throw fresh light by investigating both the historical and documentary evidence.

The Roman Church was certainly not founded by Paul, since it was already in existence when he wrote his epistle to the Romans and before he had been to Rome. Neither is there any convincing evidence that it was founded by Peter, who according to a rather legendary tale circulating in the second century went to Rome in the reign of Claudius to undo the harm done there by the teaching of Simon Magus. The Jewish Christians afterwards used this story to convey Peter's opposition to Paul, who is thinly veiled in their account by the figure of this enemy of Christianity.[20] That Peter did visit Rome and was martyred there under Nero is quite possible, though surprisingly Paul makes no reference to knowledge of his presence in Rome, neither does the Acts make any allusion to it.

The church in Rome prior to the war had largely been composed of Jews and proselytes, who followed the teaching of the Apostles and Elders of Jerusalem, strongly characterised by zeal for the Law and a positive Messianism. The Roman writers speak of the Messianic agitation in the city in the reign of Claudius in which the Christians appear to have been involved, and which caused the emperor temporarily to close the synagogues and expel the foreign Jews. At Corinth Paul had become intimate with Aquila, a native of Pontus in Asia Minor, and his wife Priscilla, followers of Jesus who had been banished from Rome at the time. Paul's epistle to the Roman believers was not calculated to endear him to the community in the capital, and when he reached Rome as a prisoner in chains awaiting the hearing of his appeal to Caesar he found many opponents during the two years or so he had liberty to teach those who visited him. Writing from Rome to the Colossians he speaks of having only three Jewish Christian associates, Aristarchus, Mark and Jesus Justus, and he tells the Philippians of the divisions created by his teaching, and refers to those who proclaimed Christ 'in a factious spirit, trying deliberately to make trouble for me in my fettered state'.[21] In II. Timothy there is again mention of opposition and isolation: 'Alexander the blacksmith has shown himself very ill-disposed towards me. The Lord will requite him in accordance with his actions. Watch out for him yourself, for he is strongly opposed to our views. At the first hearing of my defence no one supported me: everyone deserted me. May it not be counted against them!'[22]

In A.D. 64 the Christian community at Rome was largely wiped out, barbarously put to death on the accusation of implication in the Great Fire. About this time both Paul and Peter had perished. Then had come the Jewish revolt against Rome, to end in political disaster for the Jewish people and an agonising consideration of what this implied in terms of the Messianic Hope.

The church in Rome after the war was probably much less

Jewish in composition. At any rate the situation was calculated to cow and dispirit the Zealot element. The circumstances were conducive to paying much more attention to Pauline doctrine. Paul had been a Roman citizen and had also favoured a mystical soteriology in substitution for the efficacy of the Mosaic Law. His viewpoint had been non-political and he had recommended recognition of Roman hegemony and obedience to its officials and mandates.[23] The apostolic body previously centred at Jerusalem no longer existed as a functioning authority as far as anyone in the West knew. Its members were dead or scattered. The Christians in many lands were on their own, deprived of authoritative leadership, forced to adjust to the completely changed and highly uncertain conditions. To carry on until Christ should return first consideration had to be given to survival, to finding a way to maintain coherence.

The mood of the Roman Church demanded an open repudiation of militant Messianism and placation of the government. Opinion swung over to espouse the Pauline spiritual gospel divorced from Judaism, which previously had been attacked and largely rejected. We may hold on the evidence that before long Paul became the hero of post-war Christianity in the West, and that to this development the initiative of the Roman Christians made a very strong contribution. At this time there were no Gospels, and the writings of Paul in Greek were the chief available Christian documents. Various churches had his epistles, which could be more widely circulated and studied. In due course the *Corpus Paulinum*, the collected letters of Paul, became the first assembly of Christian literature to be received as Scripture in the same sense as the Old Testament.[24] In the process Peter, martyred at Rome, had to be magnified and made to stand as the principal representative of the authority of all the original Apostles, as he appears in the Gospels and the Acts, so that by enlisting his testimony in support of Paulinism it could be conveyed and certified that this expression of Christianity was the consistent and genuine apostolic teaching.[25]

In the state of Christianity in the late first and early second century the Roman take-over bid was highly successful. Non-Jewish believers, many of them belonging to churches Paul had founded, were responsive and in their ignorance readily swallowed what was communicated to them with such apparent authenticity, and all the more because the Simeonite government of the Church seems not to have been in a position by reason of the political circumstances to register an effective protest when it was most needed. The consequences were so significant for the future of Christianity that fuller clarification is required to elucidate what took place.

NOTES AND REFERENCES

1. The details are furnished by Tacitus, *Hist.* IV. lxxxi, and Suetonius, *Vespasian*, VII.

2. Rev. xiii. 1–8. The Revelation reflects the Christian view in Asia Minor near the end of the reign of Domitian when there was great persecution.

3. See the article on Jochanan ben Zakkai in the *Jewish Encyclopaedia* (Funk and Wagnalls).

4. Eusebius, *Eccl. Hist.* III. xi.

5. See *Jewish Encyclopaedia* under article Sanhedrin. The Nazorean organisation had also points of resemblance to that of the Essenes, another body which regarded itself as representing loyal Israel.

6. *Epistle of Clement to James*, prefacing the *Clementine Homilies.*

7. Epiphanius, *Panarion*, lxxviii. He chiefly depends on Eusebius, Clement of Alexandria and Hegesippus. See Eisler, *The Messiah Jesus*, p. 540 ff.

8. Schweitzer, *Mysticism of St. Paul*, p. 156. Cp. Rom. xv. 25; Gal. ii. 10; II. Cor. viii–ix.

9. *Sibylline Oracles*, Bk. IV. 130–9.

10. On the state of the Jews, see Hardy, *Studies in Roman History* (First Series), p. 53. 'The Jews were still exempted from the regulations against *collegia*; their members were no more than before compelled to conform to the imperial cult; their scruples as to the Sabbath were respected; and they were excused from military service. But these privileges were no longer free to all who called themselves Jews, whether by birth or conversion. Only those were recognised as Jews by the State, who were members of one of the synagogues, and who formally entered their names (*profiteri*) as such, and received a licence from the proper official. The two drachmae which all Jews had paid hitherto to the Temple at Jerusalem were now to be paid to the temple of Jupiter Capitolinus. . . . Under this arrangement Jews by birth were

not bound to pay the tax, but only if they attended the synagogues and were therefore Jews by religion. On the other hand, proselytes, whether Roman citizens or others, who had obtained the licence, were entitled to all the religious privileges of the Jews, though apparently both classes might in private, and as long as they were not members of a synagogue, practice Jewish manners (*vita Judaica*) without, by registration, making themselves liable to the tax.' In Roman eyes the position of the Jews was no longer that of a political entity but of an authorised religion.

11. Euseb., *Eccl. Hist.* III. xii.

12. Euseb., *Eccl. Hist.* III. xxxii.

13. By the edict of the Emperor Diocletian (A.D. 303), among other instructions, the destruction of Christian sacred books was ordered. When Christianity became the official religion of the Empire the Christian emperors Theodosius and Valentinian similarly ordered the burning of all writings hostile to Christianity, which included all books deemed heretical.

14. Euseb., *Eccl. Hist.* III. xxxv; Epiphanius, *On Weights and Measures*, xv.

15. A. Lukyn Williams, *The Hebrew-Christian Messiah.*

16. Schonfield, *An Old Hebrew Text of St. Matthew's Gospel*, p. 21 ff.

17. See Euseb., *Eccl. Hist.* V. xxviii.

18. See the *Clementine Homilies* and *Recognitions* and below Chapter 10. The epistles of Paul were expressly rejected, and he was called an apostate from the Law. See also Irenaeus, *Against Heresies*, I. xxvi. 2; Eusebius, *Eccl. Hist.* III. xxvii.

19. Irenaeus, *Against Heresies*, III. lii. 1–2.

20. *Clementine Homilies*, xvii. 13–14; *Recognitions*, IV. xxxiv–xxxv. See below Chapter 10.

21. See Col. iv. 10–11 and Phil. i. 16.

22. II. Tim. iv. 14–16.

23. Rom. xiii.

24. See Milligan, *The New Testament Documents*, p. 215 ff. Grant, *The Formation of the New Testament*, p. 25 ff. The Scillitan martyrs, executed at Carthage in A.D. 180, asked about books in their possession, declared that they had 'ancient books of divine laws (the Old Testament) and epistles of Paul a just man' (Robinson, *Texts and Studies*, Vol. 1, No. 2).

25. See Mt. xvi. 17–19 and II. Pet. iii. 15–16.

9

Robbing Peter to Pay Paul

By reason of paucity of material, the uncertainties of dating and authorship of many of the New Testament documents, and quite early endeavours to make out a case for the consistency and authenticity of what became orthodox Christian belief, the factual investigation of early Christianity is beset with grave difficulties. Valuable and painstaking work continues to be carried out by Christian scholars and divines with great insight and a remarkable degree of impartiality and objectivity. All honour to them. But being Christians, even the least conservative, a certain stop in the mind was bound to exist, making it hard to acknowledge that the Founding Fathers of Christianity could have acted with as much duplicity as it is agreed many of their ecclesiastical successors did. Consequently, and despite much that is in the New Testament itself, there has been a natural reluctance to intimate that those whose names have been prefixed with the elevated designation of saints could be guilty of quite outrageous behaviour. Could this possibly be true of the authors of writings held to be Divinely inspired? Could piety and the expression of high moral sentiments be associated with power-seeking and wilful fraud? To reply in the affirmative would seem to deny the validity of a clear distinction between the spiritual and the secular, between what is holy and what is profane. The reality of revelation could be called in question.

The author of the epistle of James puts the problem clearly.

'The tongue,' he says, 'no one can tame: it is an ungovernable evil, saturated with deadly poison. With it we bless the Lord our Father, and equally with it we curse men made in the image of God. This should not be, my brothers. Does a fountain gush fresh and brackish water from the same vent? . . . If you have bitter jealousy and rivalry in your minds, do not boast and lie where truth is concerned. That wisdom never came from Above: it is earthly, materialistic and diabolical. For where bitter jealousy and rivalry exist, there will be found anarchy and every ugly business.'[1]

Studying early Christianity we have to face up to the fact that there was no moment in time at which haloes came off and horns began to sprout. The orthodox were not the goodies and the heterodox the baddies. The distinguishing of certain writings as sacred entitles them to no difference of treatment from other writings. Inspiration is not to be regarded as electric current which God has switched on for some books and switched off for others. Within the covers of the Bible we can meet with forgeries, manipulations and deliberate inventions just as much as outside it. Scholarship is well aware of this; but when a biblical work, especially in the New Testament, is evidently not by the person claiming to be the author everything is done to avoid using the word forgery. The same is true of sayings attributed to Jesus and known not to be genuine. We speak of such books as by someone of the Pauline or Petrine school of thought, of changed or invented sayings as 'secondary'. If we did not employ evasions it would appear that the Holy Spirit was an accessory to fraud.

It is on record, however, that down to the final determination of the canon of Scripture some of the books which are in the Bible were disputed. It was argued by quite orthodox Christians of the early centuries that certain books were not genuine productions of the apostolic authors by whom they purported to have been written. Occasionally the forger's name was suggested. Paul mentions that in his own lifetime false letters in his name were in circulation. What had to be suited was what was deemed to be the interests of the Church. Considerations having nothing to do with truthfulness were at work in the slant given to compositions and in the sentiments contrary to their own attitudes which various persons of note were made to express. All this kind of thing was a commonplace of the propaganda of antiquity, and what we have to appreciate is that it was a commonplace for the early Christians as well. This was the way the game of promotion and indoctrination was played. For those without scruples, who believe that ends justify means, it is so still.

While the Christian virtues and the characteristics of the new man in Christ were eloquently extolled by their spokesmen, many of these same individuals without conscious hypocrisy were busy violating them by falsification, slander and intrigue. No one need doubt that there were Christians who remarkably lived up to their ideals; but the image of the Church as a model society is entirely contradicted by the evidence. This demands that we remove rose-tinted glasses which betray our vision, and then we can become more acutely aware of much that has partially been obscured. There was uglier business going on than has previously been entertained. The Christians responsible could well have believed they were doing the right thing, to obtain greater freedom for the propagation of the Gospel, to prevent the Christian communities disintegrating through defection, immorality, and the proliferation of diverse doctrines, and to compensate for the loss of the cohesive power of an effectively functioning Christian authority.

The initiative, as we have asserted, was taken by the church at Rome, which we find increasingly occupying a position of leadership. This church not only had the distinction of being at the centre of the Empire in which most of the Christian communities were located, and thus could enjoy the prestige attaching to the seat of the acknowledged world government, it was also associated with the names of two deceased apostolic figures who were both widely known and representative of the opposing camps in the conflict which had raged in the Church a generation previously. To obtain the required results it was necessary to build up these figures in importance, as those who spoke authoritatively for Jesus Christ, Peter as being mandated by him while on earth and Paul as the recipient of his revelation from heaven. Then—and this was vital—these two had to be brought at the end into complete harmony. And since Paulinism was now favoured by the post-war church at Rome this meant that Peter had to be shown to have subscribed to the tenets of Paul.

The advancement of this design involved a considerable and developing literary activity, the clever construction of some documents and the editing of others, and the writing up of the story of Christian beginnings in the desired sense. The design was far-reaching and so successful that it coloured a large part of what became the New Testament. What we read in the Gospels, Acts and certain late Epistles is to an appreciable extent Western Christianity's presentation and interpretation of the Christian message and Christian beginnings. The story, which makes skilful use of genuine oral and written tradition, is slanted, and reinforced with specially composed documents. It is not the whole story, or the true story. It omits almost everything which would suggest that the original character of Christianity was not in accord with what the Church was now teaching. This is not to say that there was an instruction to falsify; but that writers were persuaded that they had to set things down in a way that endorsed what on apparently high authority was being put forward as the truth. Forgery assisted the formation of real convictions.

The practice of forgery in the early Church is well attested. Not only does Paul mention it, and the author of the Revelation puts a curse on anyone who adds to or subtracts from what was in his book, but much later in the latter part of the second century we have Dionysius bishop of Corinth declaring, 'As the brethren desired me to write epistles, I did so, and these the apostles of the devil have filled with tares, exchanging some things and adding others, for whom there is a woe reserved. It is not, therefore, matter of wonder, if some have also attempted to adulterate the sacred writings of the Lord, since they have attempted the same in other works that are not to be compared with these.'[2] A case in point is the epistles of Ignatius in the second century which survive in two versions, one greatly expanded.

The passage we have just quoted comes from a letter sent to Soter bishop of Rome in reply to one received from him, which Dionysius says was read to the community at the Sunday meeting in the same way as had been customary with the epistle of Clement of Rome to the Corinthians, dating it is held from near the end of the first century. Dionysius confirms what we have already learnt from Irenaeus that the church at Rome had assumed a position of leadership and had held this for a considerable time. This church was the repository of the teaching of Peter and Paul, and therefore every other church and all the faithful everywhere ought to agree with it. 'The practice has prevailed with you from the very beginning,' writes the bishop of Corinth, 'to do good to all the brethren in every way, and to send contributions to many churches in every city. Thus refreshing the needy in their want, and furnishing what was necessary to the brethren condemned to the mines, by these contributions which you have been accustomed to send from the beginning, you preserve—as Romans—the practices of your ancestors the Romans. This was not only observed by your bishop Soter, but also increased, as he not only furnished great supplies to the saints, but also encouraged the brethren that came from abroad, as a loving father his children, with consolatory words.'

For the development of this Roman hegemony we have to look to the period roughly between A.D. 70 and 110. During the reign of Vespasian (d. A.D. 79) the Christians, as Eusebius informs us,[3] were not interfered with officially. The emperor was only concerned to round-up those who claimed descent from David to check Messianic outbreaks. The peace of the

Church probably continued for about another decade. This suggests that the Christians in general were not making themselves particularly obnoxious to the authorities, and in the West were following the advice given by Paul the Roman citizen in his letter to the Roman believers. This comes out in the admonition credited to Peter (I. Peter): 'Give your obedience for the Master's sake to every human institution, whether it is to the emperor as paramount, or to governors as sent by him for the punishment of evil-doers and the commendation of well-doers; for so is the will of God, that you should silence the ignorant assertions of foolish men by well-doing. Give your obedience as freemen, or rather as slaves of God, not using your freedom as an excuse for depravity. Honour all, love the brotherhood, revere God, honour the emperor.'[4]

What makes this letter significant is that it is a directive emanating from the church at Rome ('your elect sister-community in Babylon sends you regards'[5]) addressed to the Gentile converts in Asia Minor. There are indications that the circumstances which produced the letter were the attacks on the Christians towards the end of the reign of Domitian, arising from the emperor's new policies, which particularly affected the churches of Asia Minor.[6] It must therefore be dated about A.D. 90–5.

The document is strongly evidential. It purports, falsely, to have been written by the apostle Peter, martyred in A.D. 64, and partly his name has been used as having an appeal to Asian believers with whom Paul was out of favour as we find in the pseudo-Pauline letter to Timothy (II. Timothy), 'You are well aware that all the Asiatic believers have turned from me.'[7] But when the contents of I. Peter are carefully studied we realise that 'Peter'—not only in the passage on obedience to the authorities—has been brought over to the camp of Paul, and liberally makes use of the letters of Paul, especially that which was written to the Romans.[8]

When we come to that still later forgery II. Peter the process of Petrine endorsement of Paul has fully matured. After explaining to those now in grave doubt about the return of Christ that the delay was due to God's compassion, and that the cataclysmic Day of the Lord would yet come suddenly and unexpectedly, the author proceeds in the name of Peter: 'Consequently, dear friends, because we expect these things let us be anxious to be found by him in peace, spotless and unblemished, and regard the forbearance of our Master as our salvation. Our dear brother Paul, according to the wisdom given him, has also written you to the same effect, as indeed is true of all his letters where he speaks of these matters, letters in which there are certain things by no means easy to understand, which the unskilled and unstable twist to their own ruination as they do the rest of the Scriptures.'[9]

The particular Pauline reference in the text is to the letter to the Asian Christians (Ephesians).[10] Communicating again with this region 'Peter' has still to respect to an extent objections to Pauline doctrine in the East. But by this time the apostle to the Jews has been brought wholly into line with the apostle to the Gentiles. He claims to be fully familiar with the letters of Paul and accepts them as Scripture, which could not be true of the real Peter. Readers of this epistle are meant to believe that the former opponents are now buddies.

A strong suspicion is raised that the church at Rome, asserting its establishment by Peter and Paul, 'the two most glorious apostles', was responsible for this phenomenon. No other church was so interested in such a conjunction. The Asian Christians could perhaps be more readily imposed upon since the time and circumstances of the deaths of Peter and Paul were probably not known to them. No early testimony is extant which speaks of these events.

We must now probe deeper, and note two things, the early Christian books having association with Rome, and the emergence of John Mark as a key figure linking Peter and Paul.

In addition to the epistles to churches which are attributed to Paul and written from Rome, namely Philippians, Ephesians and Colossians (and treating Philemon as an appendage of Colossians), we have the Pauline pastoral epistles to Titus and I. and II. Timothy. Then there are the two epistles of Peter, the epistle to the Hebrews, the Gospel of Mark, and of quasi-canonicity the epistle of Clement to the Corinthians and *The Shepherd* by the Roman Christian Hermas.

This is an important array of documents, and no other church than the Roman can compare with it in point of the number of Christian writings which came to be received as inspired either emanating from it or appearing to do so.

There is some difficulty about the origin of Hebrews. The unnamed author was a Hellenistic Jew familiar with the works of Philo of Alexandria, which would be well known at Rome. Philo himself had visited Rome. The Roman Church did not credit the epistle to Paul, though this attribution was made later by the Alexandrian Church. It could, however, have been written from Rome, since Clement of Rome makes considerable use of its contents in his letter to the Corinthians. Much depends on whether the conclusion of the epistle is part of the original or an addition, for here we have the statement: 'Let me add the news that brother Timothy has been released. If he comes soon I will see you with him. Give my regards to all your leaders and all the saints. The Italians send you their regards.'[11]

Passing over for the present the Gospel of Mark, we come to Clement. There is little doubt that the author of this epistle to the Corinthians was the Roman bishop of that name who held office at the close of the first century. We are not concerned here with the character and purpose of the epistle; but the work is important for our inquiry in that it witnesses to the position of leadership being taken by the Roman Church, and illustrates that Rome was holding before other churches the special example of the apostles Peter and Paul, especially the latter.

Clement writes: 'Through jealousy and envy the greatest and most righteous pillars of the Church were persecuted and contended unto death. Let us set before our eyes the good apostles:

Peter, who because of unrighteous jealousy suffered not one or two but many trials, and having thus given his testimony went to the glorious place which was his due. Through jealousy and strife Paul showed the way to the prize of endurance . . . he was a herald both in the East and in the West, he gained the noble fame of his faith, he taught righteousness to all the world, and when he had reached the limits of the West he gave his testimony before the rulers, and thus passed from the world and was taken up into the Holy Place—the greatest example of endurance.'[12]

While Clement elsewhere refers to the apostles of Christ in general in no case does he mention any others by name. The good apostles are Peter and Paul, and of these Paul is the superior.

The Shepherd is a fascinating work of visions and parables of great interest for the study of Christian thought. The hand of more than one author has been detected, the primary one being Hermas, a Christian slave writing during the second quarter of the second century. We are only required to take note of the book here because of its Roman origin and the great esteem in which it came to be held.

We turn now to the figure of John Mark and to the Gospel attributed to him. He appears in the Acts as the nephew of Barnabas, a leading personality in the Christian community at Jerusalem. This community suffered persecution by Paul, and consequently was afraid of him when he returned to the city after his conversion. But Barnabas befriended him, and was later responsible for inducing Paul to come and work at Antioch where a mixed community of Jews and non-Jews had been established as a result of the proclamation of the Gospel. When Paul with Barnabas set out from Antioch on a missionary journey they took Mark, whom they had brought from Jerusalem, with them. They went first to Cyprus, Barnabas' country of origin, but shortly after leaving the island Mark refused to go further and returned to Jerusalem. The reason for his decision is not specified. The result was that when Paul wanted Barnabas to accompany him on his second journey, and Barnabas wished to take Mark with them, Paul would not have this. They broke up with considerable display of feeling, Barnabas with Mark sailing for Cyprus, and Paul with Silas setting out for Phrygia and Galatia. No more is heard of Mark in the Acts. Tradition speaks of him evangelising Egypt, and finally becoming the interpreter of Peter, travelling with him on his visits to the Christian communities abroad. In this connection it may be assumed that he came to Rome.

Here then we have a man who had been associated with both Paul and Peter, and if the two apostles were to be shown to be in accord Mark was the obvious intermediary, and his reconciliation with Paul had to be established. The Pauline letters from Rome wish us to believe that at the end Mark served Paul and must therefore have been won over to Paulinism. In Colossians we read, 'My fellow-prisoner Aristarchus sends you his regards, as does Barnabas' relative Mark—about whom you have been advised: welcome him should he visit you—and so does Jesus known as Justus. They belong to the Circumcision, and they alone have been my co-workers for the Kingdom of God: they have been a great comfort to me.'[13] Mark is included among Paul's fellow-workers in the letter to Philemon, and in II. Timothy we find: 'Pick up Mark and bring him with you, for he is valuable to me in administrative work.' But Mark has also not abandoned Peter, for in the pro-Pauline I. Peter, written from Rome, 'Peter' sends to Asia not only the regards of the Roman Church, but also those of 'my son Mark'.

Thus when, as part of the propaganda of the Roman Church designed to promote the unification of the churches under Roman leadership in the chaos caused by the war, the first biographical account of Jesus came to be composed, the name of Mark was most appropriate to be identified with it, one who had been associated with Peter and Paul but was in an outside position, not himself being one of the twelve Apostles of Jesus. The Gospel was not directly credited to Peter. Later it came to be accepted that Mark reflected what Peter had taught, having accompanied him as interpreter and taken notes of his addresses. The chief authorities are Papias (c. 135) and Irenaeus (c. 175). According to Irenaeus, after the death of Peter and Paul at Rome Mark set down the teachings of Peter, while Luke, the companion of Paul, set down the teachings of Paul.[14]

We are so familiar with the Gospels that we may not have appreciated what a remarkable event was the publication of the first specimen. Mark's Gospel broke new ground in Christian literature, wedding recollections of what had been given out about Jesus and his teaching to a non-Jewish literary art form. It represented a design to provide for the first time a pen-portrait of Jesus which would both offer Christians a kind of standard delineation which would assist a unified expression of their convictions and clarify for non-Christians what it was desired should be their understanding of the character and mission of one who was regarded as the founder of a pernicious Jewish superstition.

Mark's Gospel is a masterly performance. While Peter comes into prominence among the Apostles he is not yet accorded a position of unique privilege. Neither does he express any outstandingly Pauline sentiments. This would argue that the Gospel was written not many years after A.D. 70. There are a number of grounds for accepting this dating discussed by Dr. Brandon in his valuable work *The Fall of Jerusalem and the Christian Church*.[15] We may here summarise the matters to which he draws attention in the course of his analysis.

The Gospel is strongly apologetic, clearly endeavouring to dissociate Christianity from Judaism in the relationship between Jesus and his opponents the Scribes and Pharisees. Jesus shows himself not to be bound by Jewish teaching and observances: he condemns his opponents and rouses them to condemn him. Mark is also anxious to establish that the Christians repudiate Jewish political Messianism. There is no Davidic genealogy at the head of the Gospel. Jesus is asked a compromising question about the payment of tribute to

Caesar, which he evades by an ambiguity. 'The significance of the question . . . amounts to nothing less than a request to the Christians' Lord to define his views about the right of the Jews to rebel against their Roman masters. . . . In xii. 35–7 Jesus is represented as commenting, during his public teaching in the Temple, on the scribal doctrine of the Davidic descent of the Messiah and exposing it to condemnation on the score of illogicality by a quotation from Psalm 110.' Further, Mark, who usually translates Aramaic terms, in the description of the apostle Simon as 'the Cananaean', neglects to explain that the term meant 'the Zealot', presumably because this would link Jesus with the Jewish revolutionaries. In the trial of Jesus the Jews are blamed and the Roman governor does not endorse that Jesus is a criminal. At the cross the centurion testifies that the victim is Son of God.

Dr. Brandon proceeds to describe Mark's treatment of the family of Jesus and of the twelve Apostles. The kindred of Jesus are against him, and he virtually repudiates them; the Apostles are weak and vacillating, and finally abandon him. 'Accordingly it must be concluded that the author of the Markan Gospel was writing at a time when he found it expedient to belittle the status and reputation of those who had recently been leaders of the Jerusalem Church: at a time, in other words, when such disparagement would not be deemed a dangerous disloyalty to a strong and accepted authority, and before the memories of the persons concerned had become invested with an unassailable halo of sanctity.'

The evidence of Mark points to the beginning of the rehabilitation of Paul's teaching and theology, concludes Dr. Brandon, where the Messiahship of Jesus is set aside in its political context and the doctrine of the Son of God is developed. 'In the Gospel of Mark we thus have embodied the first reactions of a Gentile Church, probably that of Rome, to the destruction of Jerusalem.' These views are wholly in line with what we have urged, though it is not observed that the phenomena indicate a movement by the Roman Church to assume leadership of the Christians on a Paulinist basis in replacement of the authority of the family of Jesus and the surviving Apostles.

When Matthew and Luke came to be written later the Roman Christian objectives had reached an advanced stage. Though these Gospels were composed elsewhere than in Italy, in all likelihood in Egypt and Greece respectively, Mark has to be incorporated as a major source. It is evident from these Gospels that the Roman version of Christianity had prevailed. Yet in the areas of their composition the churches were not prepared to cast away the Jewish Christian tradition which had been preserved. The coherence of Christianity could best be assured by a compromise combination of the basically incompatible testimonies of West and East. The Nazorean heritage was not left out, but worked over, so as to become subordinated to the doctrine favoured by Rome which appealed strongly to a Gentile Church. Jesus is more emphatically revealed as Son of God than in Mark, but sayings of his remain, particularly in Matthew, which strikingly contradict the Western viewpoint, such as those which emphasise the restricted mission of Jesus and his Apostles to Israel and stress obedience to the Mosaic Law, and those which endorse the Davidic Messiahship.

An important feature of this development, agreeable to the process of harmonising Peter and Paul, is that the stature of Peter is exalted as pre-eminent among the Apostles and he subscribes to Paulinism. Thus in Matthew we have Peter announcing that Jesus is not only Messiah, but also the Son of the Living God. And Jesus tells him, 'To you I will give the keys of the Kingdom of Heaven. Whatever you prohibit on earth shall be prohibited in heaven, and whatever you permit on earth shall be permitted in heaven.'[16] In Luke, after the Last Supper, we have the unique words of Jesus to Peter, 'Simon, Simon, Satan has begged to have you that he may prize you loose like husks from the grain. But I have prayed that your loyalty may not fail, and on your restoration you must confirm your brothers.'[17] Is this a suggestion by Luke that Peter is to be converted to the teaching of Paul? The Neo-Paulinist Gospel of John, later still than Matthew and Luke, introduces final charges to Peter by Jesus after his resurrection. Peter is asked repeatedly whether he loves him better than the other Apostles do, and he is told to tend the Christian lambs and sheep. He is even advised of his Roman martyrdom.[18] Thus it is progressively conveyed that Peter is the chief of the apostolic band, entitled to speak for them or in their stead. His is a voice which all Christians everywhere must heed, and no Christians would dare to challenge his supremacy, a supremacy now become vested in the Roman Church. But Peter only occupies this position so far as the advocates of the new Christianity are concerned because he speaks as the mouthpiece of Paul at a time when in the East the name of Paul was not so honoured. Only by requisitioning the person of Peter could the East be won for Paulinism.

With the Acts of the Apostles a much clearer picture is presented of the plan in operation. It is not for nothing that Irenaeus associates Luke with the teaching of Paul. Luke's second treatise, probably published in the first decade of the second century, dealswith the theme of the proclamation of the Gospel to the Gentiles. Some particulars are given of the Church at Jerusalem, but related in such a manner as to set the stage for and punctuate the progress of Christianity from a Jewish to a Gentile environment. It is foreign-born Jews and converts to Judaism, notably Stephen and Philip, who pioneer the break away.[19] Later, James the head of the Church is made to endorse the call of the Gentiles by an adaptation of Amos ix. 11–12.[20]

But the chief personalities in the Acts are Peter and Paul, and the role of Peter is to be the forerunner of Paul. From the beginning Peter is the principal apostolic spokesman. In his public utterances, while the Jews are to have the first opportunity of accepting Christ, he conveys that the Gospel is also directed to the Gentiles.[21] He receives the vision which calls upon him to eat unclean food, as the prelude to becoming the instrument of the conversion of the Roman centurion Cornelius. The Acts omits all reference to the presence of Peter at Antioch at the time of the dispute there as to whether Gentile believers should be required to observe the Mosaic Law, when even according to the biassed Paul Peter had ranged himself finally with Paul's opponents.[22] Instead, the Acts brings in Peter as a pro-Pauline witness at the ensuing assembly of the Nazorean Council.[23]

The hero of the Acts is Paul himself, the apostle of the Gentiles. In recounting his history the author displays strongly an intention to promote a good relationship between the Christians and the Roman Government, having already made reference to the conversion of Cornelius. The Christian missionaries are persecuted by the Jews and have no connection with the Zealot revolutionaries. Stress is laid on the Roman citizenship of Paul and Silas.[24] Paul is saved from the Jews by the Roman proconsul Gallio, brother of Seneca, at Corinth, by the Roman garrison commander Claudius Lysias at Jerusalem, and at Caesarea he is exonerated by the anti-Jewish governor Festus and the pro-Roman king Agrippa II. On Paul's journey as a prisoner to Rome he is protected by the centurion Julius, and at Melita (Malta) he is favoured by the governor Publius whom he has cured of dysentery. Finally he reaches Rome almost in triumph, and not a word is said of his subsequent condemnation and execution.

The character and aims of the Roman Christian propaganda could not be better expressed, or its policies more persuasively endorsed. Yet in the light of what we can otherwise learn about the situation the picture we are offered, however drawing upon historical material, is essentially bogus. To an appreciable extent this has already been illustrated in the course of our investigation. There is no convincing proof that Peter ever departed from the position and teaching of the Nazoreans, the testimony of the Apostles, Elders and relatives of Jesus, who held that Jesus was the Messiah, a wholly human Messiah, and remained loyal to their Jewish faith. In undisputed Pauline sources, the epistles to the Corinthians, there is no suggestion that Peter had defected to Paul. Quite the contrary. This Christian community was divided as a result of Nazorean intervention, and Peter had a following in opposition to Paul.[25] In another passage Paul contrasts what the Corinthians would deny to himself and Barnabas with what they allowed to the other apostles, to the brothers of Jesus, and to Peter,[26] all members of the Nazorean Council at Jerusalem.

The schemes of the Roman Church which were to have such far-reaching consequences for the future of Christianity would seem to be indefensible. They falsified the truth about Jesus, and actually in this connection misinterpreted Paul.[27] Yet something should be said in mitigation of the offence.

The Christians, as we have seen, were in a precarious position after the Roman victory over the Jews. They needed to dissociate themselves from political Messianism and rectify as far as they could the opinion of the authorities that they were subversives. This was felt particularly by the church at the heart of the Roman Empire. To gain freedom to assemble and to proselytise the Christians had to combat the view that they were enemies of the human race, and create the image of a community that was peaceful, moral and law-abiding. The policy of placating the Romans could not effectively be pursued without anti-Judaic protestations, and the rejection of Jewish Christianity in favour of Paulinism, which in any case to Gentiles was so much more appealing in its doctrine.

The circumstances demanded a strong leadership which the plight of the Nazorean leaders prevented them supplying at this time, and which the church at Rome was in the most advantageous position to offer. Information was coming increasingly to hand that the Christian converts in many areas, confused and bewildered by events, were apostasising or giving ear to eccentric teachers. Towards the end of the first century conditions were ripe for the introduction of cults which could offer solace, even if wrapped up in Judaeo-Hellenic mumbo-jumbo. The Christian communities for the most part were made up of people who were not particularly intelligent and who were easy victims of these who now began to prey upon their credulity.

The epistles to which we have called attention are full of warnings, admonitions and exhortations, following the Pauline line in Colossians. A few passages may be quoted in illustration.

'There are many disorderly vaporisers and bamboozlers, particularly those from the Circumcision, people who must be muzzled, the kind who subvert whole households, teaching things they have no business to do from mercenary motives. . . . Rebuke them sharply, that they may be sound in the Faith, paying no heed to Jewish myths and enactments of men who have turned away from the truth. To the pure everything is pure, but to the polluted and unbelieving nothing is pure, because both their minds and consciences are warped. They profess to know God, but by their actions they disown him, being disgusting and mutinous, hopeless for any useful service.'[28]

'In the Last Days hard times are in store; for men will be selfish, money-grubbing, brazen, arrogant, slanderous, defiant to parents, ungrateful, irreligious, lacking in affection, implacable, spiteful, uncontrolled, savage, disliking good, treacherous, headstrong, conceited, preferring pleasure to piety, maintaining a semblance of devoutness but denying its efficacy. Turn away from all such people; for from them come those who gain an entrance into households and captivate immature females, piled high with peccadilloes, swayed by whims and fancies, always learning, but never really able to grasp the truth.'[29]

Everyone comes in for attention in these letters, the old and the young, widows, slaves, officials of communities. The author of Hebrews urges constancy and self-control. 'Submit to discipline, since God treats you as sons; for where is the son whom his father does not discipline? But if you are without the discipline of which all have their share, then you are bastards and not sons.'[30] Jesus Christ is continually held up as a model of rectitude, obedience and endurance. Misbehaving Christians are even threatened with forfeiture of their expectation of salvation if they do not mend their ways. It is impossible for those who have been enlightened, and then have fallen away, to make a fresh start with repentance.[31]

Evidently it was felt that only a stable and energetic authority able to pronounce firmly on matters of faith and doctrine could cope successfully with the crisis situation. The church at Rome considered that it had been raised up at this time to discharge these responsibilities, and deemed itself justified in going to almost any lengths and employing every available weapon to secure effective control. In pursuit of its aims the use of fraud and forgery was apparently not regarded as immoral or unethical. But thereby, to the deception of future generations, Christianity was converted from a Jewish movement centred on Jesus as Messiah into a new religion worshipping him as the Divine Son of God. Henceforth Christians would be entitled to believe on the evidence of the falsified and concocted records that the Faith they espoused was indeed that which once and for all had been delivered to the saints.

NOTES AND REFERENCES

1. Jas. iii. 8–18.
2. Eusebius, *Eccl. Hist.* IV. xxiii.
3. Euseb., *Eccl. Hist.* III. xvii.
4. I. Pet. ii. 13–17.
5. I. Pet. v. 13. Babylon is an apocalyptic synonym for Rome. See Rev. xvii–xviii.
6. Euseb., *Eccl. Hist.* III. xvii–xviii and Revelation, 'Letters to the Seven Churches' in Asia. See below Ch. xi.
7. II. Tim. i. 15.
8. I. Pet. ii. and elsewhere.
9. II. Pet. iii. 14–16.
10. Eph. v. 27.

11. Heb. xiii. 23–4.

12. I. Clem. v. 1–7 (tr. Kirsopp Lake, *The Apostolic Fathers*, Loeb Classical Library).

13. Col. iv. 10–11.

14. Irenaeus, *Against Heresies*, III. i. 1. See Schonfield, *The Passover Plot*, p. 238 ff.

15. S. G. F. Brandon, op. cit., Ch. x, 'The Markan Reaction to A.D. 70'.

16. Mt. xvi, 16–19.

17. Lk. xxii. 31–2.

18. Jn. xxi. 15–19.

19. Acts vi–viii, xi. 19–21.

20. Acts xv. 13–18.

21. Acts ii. 39, iii. 26.

22. Gal. ii. 11–14.

23. Acts xv. 6–11.

24. Acts xvi. 37, xx. 25–8.

25. I. Cor. i. 12, iii. 22.

26. I. Cor. ix. 1–6.

27. See *The Christology of Paul* at the end of this volume.

28. Tit. i. 10–16.

29. II. Tim. iii. 1–7.

30. Heb. xii. 7–8.

31. Heb. vi. 4–8, xii. 25.

10

Counterblast

THE propaganda of Roman Christianity, employing the great names of Peter and Paul, was extremely persuasive. The churches which were reached were in many instances unable to tell that the material purporting to come from such eminent personages and containing such greatly needed and helpful counsel was not genuine. There was deep thankfulness in these communities in their difficult situation following the destruction of Jerusalem that a new seat of Christian authority had come into being established by outstanding apostles. In the mercy of God guidance had not been withdrawn.

The question of guidance was of great importance. The authority of the Nazorean Council derived from personal knowledge and experience of what Jesus had said and done in his public life: its chief members had received his direct mandate and could pass this on to their successors. The creators of the new authority had to establish a valid title to secure adhesion on the part of the churches. This is why it was so vital to them to use the name and fame of Peter. But it was also essential to assert a claim to the possession of a higher mandate, that of the continuing voice of Jesus speaking not from earth but from heaven. Hence the importance of Paul, who had been the first to set up an independent authority on the grounds that by revelations he was the recipient of the guidance of the Christ in heaven through the Holy Spirit.

The church at Rome built on the Pauline foundation, and

so was able to make guidance by the Holy Spirit the chief source of Christian authority for the future. In due course any doctrine which the Church found it desirable to proclaim as Catholic Truth could be attributed to this guidance, even when there was no warrant for it in the New Testament itself.

Initially, however, despite great successes the church at Rome did not have everything its own way in formulating the new Christianity. In the East and in Egypt the Christian communities were still considerably under the influence of the original Jewish Christian teaching, and a number of them had a substantial proportion of Jews and converts to Judaism among their members. The epistles from Rome bear witness to this in their attacks on the advocates of Judaic doctrines. In these communities no justification was seen for overturning the instruction of the Apostles which had emanated from Jerusalem before the war. This was indeed a time of grave uncertainty and circumstances called for an agonising reappraisal; but it was not evident that the situation required a wholesale abandonment of former positions.

Some, certainly, would bitterly resent and oppose the contentions of the Petro-Pauline propagandists. But even those who were greatly impressed by the seeming authenticity of the epistles now put forth, and were especially attracted by the Gospel of Mark, would to an extent resist the implication that the original apostolic body had been superseded. There were yet living members of the family of Jesus and numerous persons who had known and heard his Apostles. The prevailing tendency would be towards compromise. And this is what we find in the Gospels of Matthew and Luke, which combine Eastern and Western sources of information, the former particularly incorporating sayings and ideas which cannot be reconciled with the terms of the new Christianity, to the discomfort of subsequent exegetes.

We must not neglect the intimations that the more straightforward road towards adjustment was not by any means the only one. There were all the consequences of Dualistic thinking manifested long before the Jewish War in eschatological mysticism. The conditions after the war and the frustration of Second Advent hopes helped to encourage excursions into spiritual philosophy and cosmology, which brought Gnosticism into conjunction with both Judaism and Christianity, and engendered a crop of fringe cults.[1] These were to prove extremely troublesome in the second century and later, but their roots go back to at least the first century, and their ultimate origins are much earlier. Egypt offered a fertile soil for these developments. While their eccentricities are not here our concern, it has to be acknowledged that the doctrines of these movements, inspired by highly intelligent teachers in their chief manifestations, greatly complicated Christian issues, and as a reaction to them brought about the definition of Christianity in a Trinitarian formula.

Gnosticism, however, entered very little at the beginning into the opposition of primitive Christianity to Western thinking. The real struggle was between the apostolic doctrine that Jesus was the Messiah of God descended from David and the new teaching based on interpretation of Pauline Christology that he was the Divine Son of God sent for human salvation and was not a political figure. Paul himself accepted that Jesus was born of the line of David, though demonstrated to be Son of God by the resurrection,[2] but the Church of the West was anxious not to stress the Messianic aspect in its endeavour to procure the toleration of the Roman Government. In the East, where there was much hostility to Roman hegemony and considerable loyalty to the authority of the Nazorean Council, there was no such inhibition. The ruling family, the Heirs of Jesus, gloried in their Davidic descent and called attention to it from their genealogical records.

Thus the authors of the Gospels of Matthew and Luke would not and could not, if their books were to find acceptance, omit the cardinal testimony of a substantial part of the Church. The Gospel of Mark had had a powerful effect, and was therefore employed by the other Evangelists, but the fact that the end of Mark is lacking has suggested to scholars a scarcity of copies of the work and a loss of popularity once Matthew and Luke were in existence. These neither neglected nor played down the Messianism of primitive Christianity, while responsive to the Paulinist teaching of the West. This comes out particularly in the Nativity narratives.

While Jesus is born of a virgin through the agency of the Holy Spirit he is none the less in Matthew the predestined king of the Jews, and through Joseph his legal father is descended from David. Luke makes the angel Gabriel announce to Mary, 'You will conceive in your womb and have a son, whom you are to call Jesus. He will be a great man, and be termed "Son of the Most High", and the Lord God will give him the throne of his ancestor David: he will reign over the house of Jacob for ever, and his sovereignty shall be without end.'[3] The angel of the Lord also announces to certain Jewish shepherds at Bethlehem, 'I bring you news of a great joy which will be shared by all the people, that today in David's town a deliverer has been born to you, none other than the Lord Messiah.'[4] No Roman official would have had any joy from reading these words.

So long as there were Jews at the head of Christian affairs in the East, that is to say down to A.D. 132,[5] there was some check to the relinquishment in this region of features of the Church's original teaching, though its waning effectiveness was further weakened by the persecuting policy of Domitian.

One of the products of that persecution, the book of Revelation published in Asia Minor, in spite of subsequent revision retains reference to Jesus as 'the Lion of the tribe of Judah, the Root of David'. This apocalypse, emphatically anti-Roman, continues to proclaim, 'The dominion of the world has become the dominion of our Lord and his Messiah, and he shall reign for ever and ever'.[6] The statement is of great importance since 'our Lord' here is not Jesus but God himself, and Jesus is distinguished from God as his Messiah. The basic position of the Revelation is that of Psalm ii, a favourite with the early Christians.

Another work, *The Teaching of the Twelve Apostles* (*Didache*), which also underwent some later changes, nevertheless preserves the same tenet in the eucharistic prayer over the cup of wine: 'We give thanks to thee, our Father, for the holy vine of David thy servant, which thou didst make known to us through Jesus thy servant; to thee be glory for ever.'[7] The relationship of Jesus to God is the same as that of David to God, to whom alone prayer is to be addressed. The prayer, like others in the *Didache*, reflects Hebrew liturgical forms. The production in the East of documents in the name of the Twelve Apostles was one way of hitting back at Western Petro-Paulinism.

It is by no means easy to speak of early reactions to what was being put out from the West because of lack of records. But one effect of the prominence given to Peter through the Roman initiative may possibly be seen in the outcrop of Petrine literature in the second century, such as *The Preaching of Peter*, the *Gospel of Peter*, the *Teaching of Peter*, and the *Revelation of Peter*. An uncanonical quotation which brings in Peter as leader occurs in the Homily known as the *Second Epistle of Clement to the Corinthians*.

On the other hand, of uncertain derivation, are the canonical epistles in the names of James and Jude, brothers of Jesus, which attack Paulinist doctrine. II. Peter is a kind of reply to Jude, borrowing from it and at the same time endorsing the authority of Paul.

After the middle of the second century in the *Memoirs* of Hegesippus we have the records, fragmentary unfortunately, of a man who endeavoured to promote a truly catholic Christianity by collecting traditions of East and West and thus furnishing material of consequence for a general ecclesiastical history. We also observe in the remains of the *Exposition of the Dominical Oracles* by Papias of Hierapolis (c. A.D. 135) the concern of another Eastern Christian to assemble as much as possible of what the Apostles and Elders had taught of the things said and done by Christ as recalled by those who had heard him.

A telling counterblast to the new Christianity of the West, however, could only come from the Nazoreans, the direct heirs of the apostolic doctrine. Ever since the destruction of Jerusalem they had undergone great vicissitudes which made it extremely difficult for them to have adequate contact with other bodies of Christians and thus to be sufficiently informed of what was going on. They were in danger from the Romans, especially their leaders of the family of Jesus who proclaimed their Davidic descent, as actual or potential rebels. They were regarded as a menace by rabbinical Judaism, now concerned to put a damper on apocalyptic and Messianic enthusiasm in order that the Jews should be able to settle down quietly under the new conditions and avoid the risk of Roman reprisals and restrictions of their religious liberties. Consequently, the rabbinists from about A.D. 90 sought to ban them, the Essenes, and all Last Day fanatics from the synagogues.[8] They were looked at askance by many Christians on account of their Jewish nationalism and maintenance of Jewish observances, and churches which favoured the new teaching about Jesus increasingly despised them for their refusal to acknowledge his deity.[9]

Oppressed and afflicted, forced to live for the most part in outlying areas in Galilee, Auranitis and Gaulanitis, the Nazoreans nevertheless continued active and made numerous Jewish converts. In certain places they could openly have synagogues and communities. They suffered especially in the persecution initiated by Domitian, and later in the Jewish revolt under Bar-Cochba when they refused to recognise this leader's Messianic claims.[10] Having their own problems they could devote little attention to developments in the Church at large, and probably before the first quarter of the second century they were not too familiar with what had been happening. By the time they could make a rejoinder there had been changes of emphasis in their own outlook, and some groups had acquired various eccentricities as a result of new teaching and relationships with remnants of Baptist, Essene, Samaritan and other sects of 'Saints' of the pre-war period.

Our information about the Nazoreans is still slender, and outside the New Testament no documents are earlier than A.D. 150. Many of the authorities who can be quoted are not well-informed or are hostile. We therefore have to run ahead somewhat to glean what we can of Nazorean reactions to the Petro-Pauline propaganda. While what we can learn derives from sources extending from the second century to the tenth, and allowing for the fact that much of it is second-hand knowledge, there is a remarkable amount of consistency in the traditions which argues both for their antiquity and general reliability.

Antagonism to Paulinism was not, of course, a Nazorean novelty of the second century. We have already considered its original causes. Feeling must indeed have been strong to leave behind such a legacy of enmity, so that for centuries in their teaching the Nazoreans harked back to the initial conflict, embroidering the account with additional hostile details. But rankling memories of what after all had taken place a long while ago would not sufficiently account for the intensity of the animosity betrayed subsequently. Remote generations could not have kept these memories alive so acutely unless much had transpired later to fan the flames.

We see the justification for the persistent and virulent attacks on Paul in the realisation by the Nazoreans that an idolatrous religion had been founded on his thinking, a religion which blasphemously identified Jesus with God. The crime was aggravated by an assertion that the new Faith was the true apostolic Faith; by having invented and perverted many things about Jesus; by having been plotted in Rome, enemy of God's people; and by the audacious falsehood that the venerated Peter had apostasised and given his blessing to Paulinism. As most of the Church progressively went over to the new religion, and dared to call the Church of the Apostles heretical, and when this religion finally became that of the Roman Empire and mercilessly persecuted the inheritors of the Truth and drove them away, the seed sown by Paul had indeed become a tree bearing bitter fruit. No wonder that by the Nazoreans he was vilified and execrated continually! He was the whipping boy, made to pay posthumously for the follies of his successors.

The first admission of the existence of two opposing Christianities comes from Justin Martyr in his *Dialogue with the Jew Trypho*. Justin was born in Samaria at Flavia Neapolis, the modern Nablus. He studied philosophy and later became a Christian. His travels as an evangelist finally brought him to Rome, where he suffered martyrdom about A.D. 165. While Justin subscribed in the main to Western Christianity, he still adhered to some of the tenets of the East, including that of the restoration of Jerusalem and the millennial reign of Christ on earth. He did not agree with Nazorean Christianity, but tolerantly refused to condemn it as the Neo-Pauline Christians were doing. In the *Dialogue* Justin allows that the Jewish followers of Jesus were entitled, if they chose, to observe the Mosaic Law, though he does not approve of their requiring Gentile believers to do so. He cannot go along with those Paulinists who would have no intercourse with the Jewish Christians or give them hospitality, and denied that they would be saved. He himself was prepared to associate with them in all things as kinsmen and brethren.

We can see from Justin's statements that by the middle of the second century Western Christianity had achieved dominance and the old Faith of the Apostolic Church was now being treated as sectarian. The fundamental difference between the two Christianities was that the new proclaimed that Christ *was* God, while the old declared that Christ was *of* God. Justin sides with the Christodeists, holding that Christ existed as God before the ages and submitted to be born as man while remaining God even as man. But he will not denounce those who hold the contrary conviction, that Jesus was solely man, anointed by election and thus becoming the Christ. The vital thing, whether Jesus was God or not God, is that he should be acknowledged as Christ.[11]

This, however, is not the position of Irenaeus a few years later, who though he too came from the East and was a millennarian is more decisively in the Roman camp as a result of his close relations with the Roman Church when bishop of Lyons. He emphatically affirms the dogma of the West that as Son of God Jesus Christ *is* God, and expresses its creed in terms that anticipate the Nicene formula of the fourth century.[12] But he did not depend wholly on Western thought, being also influenced, as Justin may have been, by the Fourth Gospel, whose author was the protagonist in the East of the deity of Christ as the incarnate Word of God.

Irenaeus attacks the Nazoreans as heretics under the name of Ebionites. The name is from the Hebrew for 'the Poor', a designation employed both by the Essenes and the early Christians to signify their humble following of the way of God. Later Christian writers would have it either that Ebion was the name of the man who founded the sect, or that at any rate the name was rightly bestowed on those who had a poor opinion of the dignity of Christ. Whether one branch of the Nazoreans particularly adopted this name is not known for certain; but it must be allowed that Ebionism came to represent those Jewish Christians who deviated in some respects from the main body, being strict vegetarians and therefore opposed to animal sacrifices. It would, however, be going too far on the available evidence to regard the Ebionites as a denomination wholly distinct from the Nazoreans.

According to Irenaeus, those of this persuasion believe that Jesus was born in the normal manner as the son of Joseph and Mary and declared to be the Christ at his baptism. 'They use the Gospel of Matthew only,' he says, 'and reject the Apostle Paul, maintaining that he was an apostate from the Law. As to the prophetical writings, they endeavour to expound them in a somewhat singular manner: they practice circumcision, persevere in the observance of those customs which are enjoined by the Law, and are so Judaic in their way of life, that they even adore Jerusalem as if it were the House of God.'[13]

The passage is important in many respects. The reference to the use of the prophetical writings indicates that the Jewish Christians employed similar methods to those of the Essenes in interpreting the Old Testament in the manner found in the commentaries among the Dead Sea Scrolls. Of course in relation to Jesus as Messiah this had been done in testimonies in the Gospels and elsewhere; but what Irenaeus states is confirmed by remains of the Nazorean *Commentary on Isaiah* quoted by Jerome.[14] Evidently, too, the Nazoreans turned towards Jerusalem in prayer like other Jews.[15] But we are particularly interested that it is here for the first time stated that the Nazoreans acknowledged only one Gospel, that of Matthew, and that they would have nothing to do with the Pauline epistles, denouncing Paul as an apostate from the Law.

Regarding the Nazorean Gospel, Irenaeus elsewhere says that Matthew had written his Gospel in Hebrew, and he probably deduced this from what Papias of Hierapolis in Asia Minor had set down some fifty years previously that 'Matthew compiled the Oracles in Hebrew, and each one interpreted them as he was able'. Papias was almost certainly referring to a primitive collection of Biblical passages which proved that Jesus was the Messiah, which Matthew may well have prepared and a copy of which was in the possession of the Nazoreans.[16] But it is established from many Patristic sources that they also had a Hebrew or Aramaic Gospel comparable to those in the New Testament, reputed to be by Matthew, but commonly known to the churches as the *Gospel according to the Hebrews*, and of which extracts have been preserved. A discussion of the subject would take us too far afield,[17] but we may briefly say, because this is relevant, that the composition of a Gospel of the type of the canonical books would be unlikely as the natural literary expression of a Jewish body. The cause of its production would more probably be deliberately to counter the New

Testament Gospels and undermine their effect on Jewish Christians by furnishing a document that was consistent with Nazorean teaching and tradition. The passages available for examination tend to support this view, and it would appear that in due course more than one form was in circulation, such as that significantly entitled *The Gospel of the Twelve* or *According to the Apostles*. The remains we have exhibit knowledge of canonical Matthew and Luke. It is possible that John was also known. The only effective way to reply was by composing a corrective Gospel.

We have abundant evidence that many groups from eccentric Christians to outright Gnostics were producing Gospels from the second century onward to get their ideas across under apostolic names, and their literature also included Acts, Epistles and Revelations. We learn from Epiphanius bishop of Salamis in the fourth century that the Jewish Christians had created an anti-Pauline Acts of the Apostles. Of the Ebionites he writes: 'They have other Acts, which they call those of the Apostles, in which are many things filled with their impiety, whence they have incidentally furnished themselves with arms against the truth. For they set forth certain Ascents and Instructions in the *Ascents of James*, representing him as holding forth against both temple and sacrifices and against the fire on the altar, and many other things filled with empty talk; so that they are not ashamed in them to denounce Paul in certain invented utterances of the malignant and deceitful work of their false Apostles.'[18]

Epiphanius is an important if erratic witness. He was himself of Jewish origin and became a violent champion of Christian orthodoxy. He became acquainted with another Jewish convert to Nicene Christianity called Joseph who had been a student in the household of the Jewish Patriarch Hillel II. This Joseph reported that in Jewish possession were Hebrew copies of Matthew, John and the Acts of the Apostles,[19] and it is to be inferred that these were books obtained from the Nazoreans rather than translations of the canonical Gospels made either by the Church or by the Jews themselves. When a Jewish Gospel parody was produced in the *Toldoth Jeshu* this was based on the Nazorean-Ebionite Gospel and not on the canonical texts.[20]

We have some confirmation, therefore, that the Jewish Christians felt obliged to combat the onslaughts of the Church Fathers and reveal the errors of the New Testament writings. We should not conclude that the Nazoreans were entirely inventing: they must have had a certain amount of genuine traditions which they had preserved and which gave a different picture of Christian beginnings. But polemics forced them to go much further when Christianity became the official religion of the Roman Empire and they became the victims of Christian persecution. Their attacks on Paul as the root cause of what had happened became more virulent, and they were now saying that his parents had been Greeks, that he came to Jerusalem because he desired to marry the high priest's daughter and therefore became a proselyte to Judaism. When his suit was rejected, angry at the slight, he wrote against circumcision, the Sabbath and the Law.[21]

Lately further light has been thrown on the Jewish Christians and their attitude to the dominant Christian Faith by an Arabic manuscript in Istanbul dating from the end of the tenth century.[22] This document reflects to a considerable extent developments between the fifth and tenth century and much relates to the Islamic challenge to Christianity. But the author, a Muslim controversialist, appears to have had access to Jewish Christian literature or sources of information which furnished him with ammunition, and what he adduces reveals much more of the Nazorean arguments and traditions and rabid anti-Paulinism.

We have yet to deal with another vital consequence of the bid for leadership of the church at Rome initiated in the latter part of the first century, which involved a denigration of the original Christian authority vested in the Apostles of Jesus and members of his family, and conveyed that Peter was the supreme spokesman for the Twelve, and that he had been converted to Paulinism. This enterprise, when it had fully matured and brought into being the new Christian religion, could only give rise to a counter-attack by the Nazoreans in which it was demonstrated that the true teaching of and about Jesus was held by the Apostles mandated by him while on earth, that the rightful chief representative of Jesus had been his brother James, and that Peter had never defected to Paulinism.

The only substantial presentation of the Nazorean response is contained in the pseudo-Clementines, the *Homilies* and *Recognitions*. These works unfortunately are only available to us in Latin translations from the Greek, to an extent abridged and edited, made towards the end of the fourth century by Rufinus of Aquileia. The original compositions probably belong to the early third century. As they stand the ideas expressed are not exclusively Ebionite, and there is a mingling of the doctrines of various Syrian bodies. But incorporated in the text are elements from second-century works, and these are often Jewish Christian.

The Clementines have two main ingredients, which are interwoven. The first is a romance telling how a Roman family was broken up by misfortune and its members scattered abroad undergoing many sufferings. But there is a happy ending, since all are finally reunited, having become or becoming Christians. This tale previously existed as a distinct book of which we have a Syriac exemplar.[23] The second ingredient is a narrative of Peter's pursuit of the anti-Christian Simon Magus from city to city to combat his teaching and influence. This too probably goes back to an independent work entitled *The Travels of Peter*. In the Clementines the hero of the romance part of the story is Clement of Rome, converted by Barnabas, who journeys to Palestine to become Peter's disciple, and it is in the course of Peter's travels that Clement becomes reunited with his father, mother and two brothers. Among other distinct works drawn upon are *The Preaching of Peter* and the *Ascents of James* referred to by Epiphanius.

Preserved by the Clementines is a clear aim to counter Western propaganda. It is not Peter who has joined the Paulinists but the esteemed Clement of Rome who comes to Palestine and joins Peter and the true Apostolic Church, which is headed by James. Paul is alluded to as 'the enemy' and the arch-heretic Simon Magus is also used as a medium through whom Paul and Pauline teaching are attacked. The obvious intention was to reach Christians who had gone over to the opposing camp. Prefacing the *Homilies* is a forged letter from Peter to James, of which we may quote a part. Here we have a retort in kind.

'Peter to James, the lord and bishop of the holy Church under the Father of all, through Jesus Christ wishes peace always.

'Knowing, my brother, your eager desire for that which is for the advantage of us all, I beg and beseech you not to communicate to any one of the Gentiles the books of my preachings which I sent to you, nor to anyone of our own race before trial; but if anyone has been proved and found worthy, then to commit them to him, after the manner in which Moses delivered his to the Seventy who succeeded to his chair. Wherefore also the fruit of that caution appears even till now. . . . In order, therefore, that the like may also happen to those among us as to those Seventy, give the books of my preachings to our brethren, with the like mystery of initiation, that they may indoctrinate those who wish to take part in teaching; for if it is not so done our word of truth will be rent into many opinions. And this I know, not as being a prophet, but as already seeing the beginning of this very evil. For some among the Gentiles have rejected my legal preaching, attaching themselves to certain lawless and trifling preaching of the man who is my enemy. And these things some have attempted while I am still alive, to transform my words by certain various interpretations, in order to the dissolution of the Law; as though I also myself were of such a mind, but did not freely proclaim it, which God forbid! For such a thing were to act in opposition to the Law of God which was spoken by Moses, and was borne witness to by our Lord in respect of its eternal continuance. . . . But these men, professing I know not how, to know my mind, undertake to explain my words, which they have heard of me, more intelligently than I who spoke them, telling their catechumens that this is my meaning, which indeed I never thought of. But if, while I am still alive, they dare thus to misrepresent me, how much more will those who shall come after me dare to do so!'[24]

In the *Recognitions* 'Peter' warns believers against accepting any other authority and teaching than that of the Nazorean Council and attacks the new Christianity of the West.

'Our Lord, confirming the worship of the One God, answered him (i.e. Satan): "It is written, Thou shalt worship the Lord thy God, and him only shalt thou serve." And he, terrified by this answer, and fearing lest the true religion of the One and True God should be restored, hastened straightway to send forth into this world false prophets, and false apostles, and false teachers, who should speak indeed in the name of Christ, but should accomplish the will of the demon. Wherefore observe the greatest caution, that you believe no teacher, unless he brings from Jerusalem the testimonial of James the Lord's brother, or of whosoever may come after him. For no one, unless he has gone up thither, and there has been approved as a fit and faithful teacher for preaching the word of Christ . . . is by any means to be received. But let neither prophet nor apostle be looked for by you at this time, besides us. For there is one true Prophet, whose words we twelve Apostles preach; for he is "the acceptable year of God", having us Apostles as his twelve months.'[25]

Paul had contended that his gospel was the true one because he had received it by direct revelation from the Christ in heaven, unlike the twelve Apostles who depended on the teaching of Christ while on earth. The new Christianity, which gave rise to the Catholic Church, continued to hold that in the formulation of its doctrine it was progressively guided by revelation through the Holy Spirit. Peter in the Clementines combats this claim in his controversy with Simon Magus (alias Paul). Simon argues:

'You (Peter) professed that you had well understood the doctrines and deeds of your teacher, because you saw them before you with your own eyes and heard them with your own ears, and that it is not possible for any other to have anything similar by vision or apparition. But I shall show that this is false. He who hears anything with his own ears is not altogether fully assured of the truth of what is said; for his mind has to consider whether he is wrong or not, inasmuch as he (i.e. Christ) is a man as far as appearance goes. But apparition not merely presents an object to view, but inspires him who sees it with confidence, for it comes from God. Now first reply to this.'

Peter has a ready answer. 'The Prophet, because he is a prophet, having first given certain information with regard to what is said objectively by him, is believed with confidence; and being known beforehand to be a true prophet, and being examined and questioned as the disciple wishes, he replies. But he who trusts to apparition or vision and dream is insecure. For it is possible either that he (i.e. the one who reveals himself) may be an evil demon or a deceiving spirit, pretending in his speeches to be what he is not. But if anyone should wish to inquire of him who he is who has appeared, he can say of himself what he will. And thus, gleaming forth like a wicked one, and remaining as long as he cares to do, he is at length extinguished, not remaining with the questioner as long as he wished him to for the purpose of examination.'[26]

We can summarise the sense of the extract to make it clearer. The Pauline is saying, 'He who relies on what a man says cannot be sure he has received the truth, since the man may be right or wrong. But he who obtains his revelation by a vision knows that he is getting information from a superhuman source, from God himself, and therefore the truth of what he is told is guaranteed.' The Petrine answers, that there is a difference when the man is known to be a true prophet, and has given evidence that he is. 'The man does not appear and disappear. He remains with the disciple to explain his words, and can be questioned indefinitely. But an apparition provides only a brief encounter. Before it can be questioned at length it has gone. Moreover, the apparition can falsely claim to be someone whom it is not, and the disciple has no opportunity to test whether it may not be a demon in disguise deliberately deceiving him.'

We may bring our treatment of the rival positions to an end here, though the evidences have by no means been exhausted. Our concern has been sufficiently to establish and illustrate that Christianity as we know it must not be imagined to be identical with what Jesus taught about himself and what his immediate Apostles proclaimed. Catholic Christianity is based on a radical deviation, which progressively by dubious ways and means was converted into an orthodoxy. Historical conditions, which we have depicted, favoured the supremacy of a Church and its doctrines predominantly Gentile in outlook and composition. But the direct heirs of original Christianity did resist strenuously to the limited measure of their capacity. The victory was not won without a prolonged struggle, and a running battle sustained for centuries. Just as the insignificant Jews dared once and again to match themselves against the might of the Roman Empire, so did the Jewish believers in Jesus as the Messiah manfully contend with the overwhelming forces the Roman Church was able to unleash against them.

NOTES AND REFERENCES

1. As an introduction to the subject the author commends *Gnosticism and Early Christianity* by R. M. Grant.

2. Rom. iv. 3.

3. Lk. i. 31–3.

4. Lk. ii. 10–11.

5. 'Down to the invasion of the Jews under Hadrian there were fifteen successions of bishops (of Jerusalem), all of whom, they say, were Hebrews

from the first and received the knowledge of Christ pure and unadulterated. . . . For at that time the whole Church under them consisted of faithful Hebrews, who continued from the time of the apostles until the siege (of Jesusalem) which then took place' (Euseb. *Eccl. Hist.* IV. v.). Their names are given as James, Simeon, Justus, Zaccheus, Tobias, Benjamin, John, Matthew, Philip, Seneca, Justus II, Levi, Ephraim, Joseph and Judas.

6. Rev. xi. 15.

7. *Didache*, ix. 2.

8. The rabbinists attempted to suppress the reading of apocalyptic writings, which many Jews regarded as inspired, and denounced those who calculated the Time of the End. Under Gamaliel II a prayer against sectaries was composed by Samuel the Little to be used in public worship in the synagogues. This may be the prayer inserted in the Eighteen Benedictions, originally commencing, 'And for sectaries let there be no hope' (i.e. of a share in the world to come). The rabbinical reference is Talmud Babli, *Berachoth*, fol. 28b–29a. One ruling seems directed against the Essenes: 'If a man said, "I will not go before the Ark (i.e. the sacred chest containing scrolls of the Torah) in coloured raiment," he may not even go before it in white raiment' (Mishnah, *Megillah*, iv. 8–9).

9. The Church Fathers in their natural opposition to Jewish Christianity ignored all evidence that it represented an unbroken tradition from the time of the Apostles.

10. 'In the Jewish war which lately raged, Bar-Cochba, the leader of the revolt of the Jews (A.D. 132–5), gave orders that Christians alone should be led to cruel punishments, unless they would deny Jesus Christ and utter blasphemy' (Justin, *I. Apol.* xxxi. The majority of those affected in Palestine must have been Jewish Christians at this time.

11. Justin, *Dial. with Trypho*, xlvii–xlix.

12. Irenaeus, *Against Heresies*, I. x. 1, II. i. 5.

13. Irenaeus, *Against Heresies*, I. xxvi. 1–2.

14. Jerome, *Commentary on Isaiah*, quoted by Schonfield, *Saints Against Caesar*, p. 180 f.

15. Jews in the West turn to the East during the recitation of the Eighteen Benedictions. The Nazoreans when they fled to Mesopotamia had to turn towards the West in order to face Jerusalem.

16. See Schonfield, *The Passover Plot*, pp. 234–8.

17. See the discussion in Bacon, *Studies in Matthew*, especially his Appended Note IV, 'Matthew and the Jewish-Christian Gospels'. See also Schonfield, *According to the Hebrews*.

18. Epiphanius, *Panarion* (*Refutation of All Heresies*), xxx. 16 and 23.

19. Epiphanius, *Panarion*, xxx. See Schonfield, *According to the Hebrews*, p. 217 f.

20. See Schonfield, *According to the Hebrews*.

21. Epiphanius, *Panarion*, xxx.

22. The manuscript is No. 1575 in the Shehid 'Ali Pasha collection in Istanbul, and entitled *The Establishment of Proofs for the Prophethood of Our Master Mohammed*, by 'Abd al-Jabbar al-Hamadani chief Qadi of Rayy (d. 1024/5). This important text has been edited and translated by Prof. Shlomo Pines as regards the anti-Christian section and proved to contain much Jewish Christian material. See Pines, 'The Jewish Christians of the Early Centuries of Christianity According to a New Source' (*Proceedings of the Israel Academy of Sciences and Humanities*, Vol. II, No. 13, Jerusalem, 1966).

23. See Mingana, 'A New Life of Clement of Rome' in *Some Early Judaeo-Christian Documents in the John Rylands Library*, Manchester: The University Press, 1917.

24. *Epistle of Peter to James*, i–ii.

25. *Recognitions*, IV. xxxiv–xxxv. There is no room for Paul as a thirteenth apostle.

26. *Homilies*, XVII. xiii–xiv. There can be no doubt that the author is hitting at Paul, because he makes Peter say to Simon Magus, 'You alleged that you knew more satisfactorily the doctrines of Jesus than I do, because you heard his words through an apparition.'

11

Trials and Tribulations

'LET him who has the wit to do so compute the numerical value of the Beast. . . . His number is 616.' So writes the seer of the Revelation.[1] 'A devouring tyrant marked by the letter four,' proclaims the Jewish Sibyl.[2] Both references allude to the Emperor Domitian. It was under this son of Vespasian that the theocratic conflict was resumed. The ensuing half century was marked by renewed apocalyptic fervour, strife and terror, war and persecution.

The Messianic struggle between Jew and Roman had not been exhausted by the war of A.D. 66–73. The flames had been subdued in blood, but they had not been wholly quenched. The fires smouldered underground and found fresh fuel in the faith of the vanquished that retribution must overtake the heathen conqueror. It simply could not be that Almighty God would fail to put forth his power in wrath and judgment. 'How long will it be, holy and true Sovereign Lord, before thou dost judge and avenge our blood on those who dwell on earth?'[3] It only wanted a man at the head of Roman affairs to take alarm, a man half-crazed with morbid fears and fancies, for the outbreak to be revived and develop with mounting fury.

In many ways Domitian was like the emperor who had had to meet the earlier menace of Messianism by drastic means. For Christians he became 'the bald Nero'. He too in the earlier part of his reign gave evidence of an intention to govern well; but the vicious side of his character all too soon predominated, and led him into the commission of great crimes. He was highly superstitious and from his youth had been wont to consult Chaldean soothsayers. His sense of insecurity led him eventually both to magnify himself and to seek to destroy all who might conceivably conspire against him. In a corner of his warped mind he began to entertain a dread of the Jews, that mysterious and obstinate people whom his brother Titus and his father Vespasian had never really conquered. These Jews, as he knew, had strange gifts of prophecy, and still believed that one of their royal line would bear rule over the earth. They had a weapon to which he was peculiarly vulnerable, and which they were again employing with telling effect in the dissemination of dire predictions of Rome's imminent doom.

Suetonius reports how susceptible was Domitian to the influence of dreams and auguries, and towards the end of his life the omens seemed to presage nothing but disaster.

'During eight months on end there was so much lightning at Rome, and such accounts of the phenomenon were brought from other areas, that at last he cried out, "Let him now strike whom he will." The Capitol was struck by lightning, as well as the temple of the Flavian family, with the Palatine-house and his own bedchamber. The tablet also, inscribed upon the base of his triumphal statue, was carried away by the violence of the storm, and fell upon a neighbouring monument. The tree which just before the advancement of Vespasian had been prostrated, and rose again, suddenly fell to the ground. The goddess Fortune of Praenaste, to whom it was his custom on new year's day to commend the Empire for the ensuing year, and who had always given him a favourable reply, at last returned him a melancholy answer, not without mention of blood. He dreamed that Minerva, whom he worshipped even to a superstitious excess, was withdrawing from her sanctuary, declaring that she could protect him no longer, because she was disarmed by Jupiter.'[4]

It is therefore by no means improbable that the tightening up of regulations affecting the Jews, Domitian's edict to seek out and destroy descendants of the House of David, and his hostility to the Christians in the East, had a connection with forebodings to which the Jewish and Christian oracles contributed.

There can be no doubt of the resurgence in the latter part of the first century of apocalyptic literature, and now it was more violently anti-Roman than in the past. Several specimens have survived, notable among them the Fifth Book of the *Sibylline Oracles*, the *Apocalypse of Ezra*, the *Apocalypse of Baruch*, and the Revelation in the New Testament. The first and last mentioned have many points of resemblance, and a statement in *Baruch* about the fecundity of the Messianic Age was reported by Papias as a saying of Jesus.[5] To quote at length from these documents would occupy many pages; but for those to whom they are unfamiliar a few extracts are indispensable, since without them the situation to be envisaged cannot be made clear.

From the *Sibylline Oracles* we take the following passages.

'From heaven a great star shall fall on the dread ocean and burn up the deep sea, with Babylon (i.e. Rome) itself and the land of Italy, by reason of which many of the Hebrews perished, holy and faithful, and the people of truth. . . . Woe to thee, thou city of the Latin Land, all unclean, thou maenad circled with vipers, thou shalt sit a widow on thy hills, and the river Tiber shall bewail thee, his consort, with thy murderous heart and ungodly mind. Knowest thou not the power and design of God? But thou saidst: "I am alone, and none shall despoil me." Yet now shall God who lives for ever destroy both thee and thine, and no sign of thee shall be left any more in that land, nor of the old time when the great God brought thee to honour. Abide thou alone, thou lawless city: wrapt in burning fire, inhabit thou in Hades the gloomy house of the lawless.'[6]

'One day shall the voice of God be heard from above throughout the broad heaven as a peal of thunder. The rays of the very sun shall fail, the moon shall not give her bright light, when God shall rule. There shall be thick darkness over all the earth. . . . In the time of the end, and the last days of the moon, there shall be a mad world-wide war, treacherous and guileful. . . . For fire shall rain down from the floor of heaven upon men, and fire, water, thunderbolts, gloom and murk in the sky, with wasting of war and a mist of slaughter to destroy all kings together and all men of might. Then shall the piteous ruin of war thus have an end: none shall any more make war with sword and steel and spear: this shall be unlawful henceforth. And the people of wisdom, which was forsaken, shall have peace, having made trial of calamity, that thereafter they might have joy.'[7]

'From the billowy clouds of heaven there came a blessed one, a man bearing a sceptre in his hand (i.e. the Messiah), which God had delivered to him, and he triumphed nobly over all, and gave back to all the good that wealth which aforetime men had taken from them. He took and utterly burnt with fire the cities of them who before had done evil, and the city which God loved (i.e. Jerusalem) he made more bright than the sun, moon and stars: her he adorned, and he made a holy house in visible shape, pure and beautiful. . . . It is the last time of the saints, when God who thunders from on high, founder of the great temple, brings these things to pass.'[8]

'And one chief man shall come again from the sky, who stretched forth his hands upon the fruitful tree, the best of the Hebrews, who once shall stay the sun in its course, calling upon it with fair speech and holy lips.'[9]

In the last of these quotations we have a purely Christian oracle relating to the return of Jesus Christ. He is the second Moses, who also stretched forth his hands (Ex. xiv. 27, xvii. 12), and his name is given by allusion to Jesus (Joshua) son of Nun (Josh. x. 12–13). There are many evidences that the Christians made use of the earlier and later Jewish pseudepigraphic and apocalyptic writings, some of which they interpolated in order to introduce references to Jesus.[10]

The doom of Rome at the hands of the Messiah is predicted in the *Apocalypse of Ezra* in the vision of the Lion and the

Eagle, and in the *Apocalypse of Baruch* in the vision of the Vine and the Cedar. In the first of these visions the Eagle is the Roman Empire, and the Lion (of the tribe of Judah) is the Messiah, 'whom the Most High hath kept for the consummation of the days, who shall spring from the seed of David'. He will bring the ungodly before him in judgment and then destroy them; but the survivors of God's people will be delivered and made joyful.[11] In the second vision the proud Cedar is again Rome and the Vine is the Messiah. When the consummation approaches the principate of the Messiah will be revealed:

'The last leader of that time will be left alive, when the multitude of his hosts will be put to the sword, and he will be bound, and they will take him up to Mount Zion, and there my Messiah will convict him of all his impieties, and will gather and set before him all the works of his hosts. And afterwards he will put him to death, and protect the rest of my people which shall be found in the place which I have chosen (i.e. Jerusalem). And his principate will stand for ever, until the world of corruption is at an end, and until the times aforesaid are fulfilled.'[12]

It is to be noted in the doom literature of Jews and Christians after the time of Jesus, and especially after the fall of Jerusalem, that the Messiah has become a much more militant figure. It is a Christian error, often repeated, that the Jews of the time of Jesus were expecting a warrior Messiah and that therefore his understanding of the Messianic office was in complete contrast to contemporary thinking. This is demonstrably untrue.[13] It was only when Jewish suffering at the hands of the Romans was intensified that the Messiah was seen as overcoming the enemy in battle. Yet even so he is depicted as holy and just. The Eastern Christian view underwent a similar development in relation to Jesus, especially his Second Advent, as shown in Luke's Gospel and in the Revelation.[14]

The Emperor Domitian manifested himself as the very personification of heathen Roman arrogance and hostility to the people of God. His crimes are certified by the Roman historians, and his great extravagances led him to plunder his subjects and annexe private estates. His egotism insisted that when his officials communicated with him they should address him as 'Our Lord and our God'. His first measure against the Jews was to make sure that neither they nor proselytes to Judaism evaded payment of the Jewish Tax. Suetonius recalls that in his youth he had seen an old man forced to expose his genitals in a crowded courtroom in order that it should be confirmed whether or not he was circumcised.[15]

Domitian came to entertain a superstitious fear of the Jews which was associated with his forebodings about the security of himself and the Empire. He was concerned, therefore, not only to halt the flow of proselytes to Judaism but to make it much more difficult for people who were attracted to the Jewish way of life. The Jews were the only community enjoying immunity from participation in the imperial cult, and those joining them could be held to be motivated by disloyalty or even treasonable intentions. To the warped mind of Domitian there was a Jewish Peril which menaced him, so that those he suspected of plotting against him were regarded as involved in Jewish indoctrination. In his last year he arrested and executed his kinsman Flavius Clemens, banished the wife of Clemens to the island of Pontia, and destroyed the eminent Acilius Glabrio and others. The charge against them was Atheism and following Jewish practices.[16] According to the Christian historians Clemens and his wife Domitilla were crypto-Christians.[17]

There is little evidence, however, of persecution of the Christians in the West. At this time they were following the policy of placating the authorities and dissociating themselves from Jewish Messianism. It was otherwise in the East where the anti-Roman apocalyptic literature was produced. Domitian was particularly concerned to ensure that a new Messianic claimant should not arise from the proscribed descendants of the House of David. Hegesippus tells a story of the grandsons of Jude the brother of Jesus being apprehended and brought before the emperor. They admitted being of the line of David; but when asked about their means they explained that their sole possession was a farm worth a comparatively trivial sum which they cultivated by their own labour. Interrogated about the Messiah and his kingdom, they said it would be revealed from heaven at the end of the age, when the Messiah would come in glory to judge the living and the dead. Domitian decided that they were ignorant peasants from whom no danger was to be feared, and released them.[18]

None the less action against the Christians was deemed to be required, and instructions may have been issued to the eastern governors and officials to tighten up on the maintenance of religious disciplines and customs, especially the worship of the emperor which had originated in Asia Minor. It was known that the Christians refused this worship, and consequently the populace could be encouraged to denounce them. The situation is depicted in an extreme form in the *Revelation*, published in this area at the end of the reign of Domitian. We read here not only that those who refused to worship the image of the Beast, the imperial regime personified by Domitian, were to be slain, but further that everyone without exception had to receive a stamp on their right hand or forehead, so that none should be able to buy or sell who did not bear this stamp.[19] One way in which timid Christians could avoid the risk of denunciation was by becoming full proselytes to Judaism, when they were automatically released from Gentile religious duties. This course was frowned upon but not prohibited. It may be such weaker brethren who are attacked in the Letters to the Seven Churches in the Revelation, as claiming to be Jews, when they are not, and who are of the synagogue of Satan.[20] Of the seven churches addressed no less than six of the cities in which they were located are known to have had temples of the imperial cult.

As the Book of Revelation now stands it purports to be by one John, who had written it on the island of Patmos off the coast of Asia Minor. According to tradition the author had been deported to the island, but returned to Ephesus after the death of the emperor, assassinated in A.D. 96. The John concerned was held to be the Beloved Disciple of the Fourth Gospel, but early doubts were expressed as to whether he could be the same since the language and style of the Revelation is vastly different to that of the Gospel. The Greek is poor and contains many hebraisms. One modern view is that the book is a Christian overworking of a purely Jewish apocalypse. Of course the author of the Fourth Gospel and the Beloved Disciple need not have been the same person.[21] An early theory ascribes the authorship of the Revelation to Cerinthus, possibly a Jewish Christian, who came to Asia Minor from Egypt. What is known of his views has a likeness to what is in the book, and it is of interest that much of the Fifth Book of the *Sibylline Oracles*, which also has a kinship with Revelation, originated in Egypt. The ascription to Cerinthus was not a bad guess, but guesses are not enough, though they can be useful. A late Jewish source attributes the Revelation to Simeon son of Cleophas, then an old man, who was executed as a descendant of David and a Christian in the reign of Trajan.

While nothing conclusive can be said about the origin of the book, it is so strongly anti-Roman that it could only have been put out in the East at a time of great trial for the followers of Jesus which intensively revived expectation that his return was at hand. The 'patience and faith of the saints' is speedily to be rewarded.

One of the worst features of the imperial regime was the encouragement of informers. And now it was open to anyone from reasons of jealousy or spite to denounce persons as Christians, or for personal gain to blackmail them by threatening to lay information. The situation cannot have been very different to what it was some fifteen years later when the younger Pliny as governor of Bithynia in Asia Minor wrote his well-known letter to the Emperor Trajan requesting guidance.

'Having never been present at any trials of the Christians,

I am unacquainted as to the method and limits to be observed in examining and punishing them. Whether, therefore, any difference is to be made with respect to age, or no distinction is to be observed between the young and the adult; whether repentance admits to a pardon; or, if a man has been a Christian once, it avails him nothing to recant: whether the mere profession of Christianity, albeit without any criminal act, or only the crimes associated therewith are punishable; in all these points I am greatly doubtful.

'In the meanwhile the method I have observed towards those who have been denounced to me as Christians is this: I interrogated them whether they were Christians; if they confessed I repeated the question twice again, adding a threat of capital punishment; if they still persevered, I ordered them to be executed. . . . There were others also brought before me possessed with the same infatuation; but being citizens of Rome, I directed them to be carried thither.

'These accusations, from the mere fact that the matter was being investigated, began to spread, and several forms of the mischief came to light. A placard was posted up without signature, accusing a number of people by name. Those who denied that they were Christians, or had ever been so, who repeated after me an invocation to the gods, and offered religious rites with wine and frankincense to your statue (which I ordered to be brought for the purpose, together with those of the gods), and finally cursed the name of Christ (none of which, it is said, those who are really Christians can be forced into performing), I thought proper to discharge. Others who were named by the informer at first confessed themselves Christians, and then denied it; true, they had been of that persuasion formerly, but had now quitted it (some three years, others many years, and a few as much as twenty-five years ago). They all worshipped your statue, and the images of the gods, and cursed the name of Christ.'[22]

We have given here only an extract which relates specifically to the kind of trial Christians would receive at the hands of a conscientious and fairly humane official. Trajan's reply is also extant. The Christians are not to be searched for; but when they are denounced they are to be punished (i.e. by execution) if found guilty. They are to be pardoned, however, if they repent and give proof by invoking the gods. Denunciations are to be disallowed if they are anonymous.

The very nature of the tests points to the conviction that the Christians were hostile to the Empire, and this could only have arisen emphatically as a result of the revival of Second Adventist fervour with its production of a fresh crop of anti-Roman and Judgment Day literature.

The Christians, again notably in the eastern Provinces, had acquired the reputation of being a doom folk, invoking evil upon the human race out of their inveterate hatred of mankind and despising of the gods. The uneducated populace was in the highest degree superstitious and readily alarmed. They regarded the very presence of Christians in their midst as calculated to bring upon them plagues, famines and every kind of calamity. Commonly the denunciation of Christians was due to such unreasoning fears, and for many decades as the Acts of the martyrs establish it was the ordinary people who were chiefly concerned to cry out against the Christians and insist on their destruction. The authorities held that the opinions of the Christians were treasonable and subversive, and therefore it was proper to punish them when they had been denounced and refused the test of loyalty. But not until the latter part of the second century were they considered dangerous enough to warrant direct police action against them.

The general pagan attitude towards the Christians affected the Jews, who in many cities of the Empire had long been subject to attack as anti-social and atheistic and were a prey to periodic demonstrations and antisemitic outbreaks. For these peaceful Jews the development of Christianity as a distinct religion constituted a fresh menace to their security, since a clear distinction between the two Faiths had not been established in the public mind before the end of the first century, and there were many Jewish Christians in the synagogues and Gentile proselytes to Judaism who were Christians. The decrees of Domitian were already making it much more difficult for non-Jews to practice the Jewish way of life; but now it was seen by the Jewish authorities that action was required to impress upon officials and the public that Judaism repudiated the new religion. The action could be taken with even more justification since the new Christianity of the West was both repugnant to Jews in its deification of Jesus, and had already begun in its propaganda to seek to procure Roman toleration by its anti-Judaic teaching. That at this period Western Christians suffered very little from persecution, and that no Roman edicts specifically prohibited Christianity so that governors were obliged to proceed actively against its professors, may in no small measure have been due to the influence of the Roman Church's literature.[23]

We have already had occasion to observe that towards the end of the reign of Domitian there was a move by rabbinical Judaism to make it impossible for Jewish Christians to worship in the Jewish synagogues. But the Fourth Gospel, early second century, is the first Christian source to speak of a Jewish policy to expel believers in Jesus from the Synagogue. This is the only Gospel to employ the term *aposynagogos*, 'banning from the synagogue'.[24]

It is an anachronism on the part of the author of the Gospel to make such expulsion date from the time of Jesus himself, and in any case wrong to speak of a formal act of exclusion. Jewish sectaries were made to exclude themselves, since they would not be able to recite the prayer against them inserted in the synagogue services in Palestine about A.D. 90. Some time must have elapsed before the inclusion of the prayer became at all general. Justin Martyr, near the middle of the second century, had heard that the Christians were cursed in the synagogues,[25] though in fact the curse did not single out Christians in particular. He had also heard that the Jews had sent out special envoys to announce that a godless and lawless heresy had sprung up, that of the Christians, derived from one Jesus, a Galilean deceiver 'whom we crucified, but his disciples stole him by night from the tomb, where he was laid when unfastened from the cross, and now deceive men by asserting that he has risen from the dead and ascended into heaven'.[26]

Justin, like the author of the Fourth Gospel, is anachronistic, since he will have it that the emissaries were sent from Jerusalem shortly after the death of Jesus. What he had picked up and garbled related to action taken by the rabbinical authorities in Palestine in the nineties in connection with the additional prayer against heretics. It was the practice of the new Sanhedrin to continue what had been done in the past, to appoint apostles to convey decisions affecting all Jews to the synagogues of the Diaspora. The institution of the anti-sectarian prayer would have been a case in point, calling for both an oral and written explanation of why the measure had been taken. It was the circumstances of the development of Christianity into a distinct and anti-Jewish Faith, which did not come about until the reign of Domitian, which was the cause of the contemporary Jewish official action. It was only then that such action became imperative.

It is most improbable that Justin could have known the wording of the Jewish communication, except by hearsay. The details he furnishes could not have appeared in it in the phrasing he employs, but he may well have got the gist of the message right. He would have known that Paul before his conversion had received letters from the high priest at Jerusalem addressed to synagogues, as this was in the Acts of the Apostles. No doubt he had also read the statement in Matthew about the Jewish explanation of the resurrection, that the disciples had come by night and stolen the body of Jesus, 'and this saying is commonly reported among the Jews until this day'.[27] 'This day' would have been around A.D. 90 when Matthew's Gospel was composed, and it is quite possible that the Jewish version of the resurrection story originated about this time and that the epistle to the synagogues made reference to it. So, although Justin mixed up dates and cannot be relied upon for his text, we have both Jewish and Christian evidence of steps taken by both sides to repudiate identification. Everything points to the last decade of the century, when conditions brought this about, as the historic moment of separation.

Justin has one other important reference in his *Dialogue with Trypho*. He makes the Jew Trypho speak of a rule laid down by the rabbis that Jews should avoid contact with Christians and all discussion with them of matters at issue between the two Faiths.[28] On the other side, speaking for the Christians, we have the epistles of Ignatius bishop of Antioch early in the second century in the reign of Trajan.

Writing to the Magnesians Ignatius says, 'If we are living until now according to Judaism, we confess that we have not received grace. . . . Christianity did not base its faith on Judaism, but Judaism on Christianity, and every tongue believing on God was brought together in it.'[29] He tells the Philadelphians, 'If anyone interpret Judaism to you do not listen to him; for it is better to hear Christianity from the circumcised than Judaism from the uncircumcised. But both of them, unless they speak of Jesus Christ, are to me tombstones and sepulchres of the dead, on whom only the names of men are written.'[30]

So far as the Christians were concerned the Jews had been abandoned by God. The two Faiths henceforth were in inflexible opposition, and both were anxious to destroy the one bridge between them represented by Jewish Christianity. For Church and Synagogue the Nazoreans were now heretics, and both could agree with the dictum of Jerome, 'that while they will be both Jews and Christians, they are neither Jews nor Christians'. It has had to wait until the twentieth century for a move to set aside this antique verdict, without which there can be no advance towards reconciliation, and the real character and mission of Jesus will continue to be rejected by Christian and Jew alike.

It is of no avail to cite the courage and steadfastness of

martyrs as evidence of the truth of their beliefs. All Faiths have furnished those who sealed their testimony with their blood, and it establishes nothing to inquire whether this was a Christian or a Jew, or of any other persuasion, who died. What counts is the bringing of people and information together as comprehensively as possible in circumstances that compel no one to occupy a position of rigidity. So long as those who stand for the good wage war on those who also stand for the good the war with evil is always lost; for the good cannot fight the good without becoming evil and using the weapons of evil.

Of this spectacle our history affords an eloquent illustration. Jews, Christians and Jewish Christians were locked in conflict at a time when tribulation was their common lot. It was fully in keeping with such folly that the East at this juncture should produce an outstanding personality in the Christian camp, who spoke much of truth and goodness and love, and belied them all with his aggressiveness, egotism and bigotry. 'Love one another' was this man's continual theme, and yet he could write, 'If anyone comes to you and does not bring this teaching, do not receive him into your homes, do not even bid him welcome; for he who bids him welcome shares in his evil deeds.'[31] This man, whom we know as John, was next to Paul the chief architect of Christian ideology.

NOTES AND REFERENCES

1. Rev. xiii. 18. Some MSS. read 666. The figure 616 has allusion to the imperial stamp or seal inscribed in Greek with the year of the emperor's reign. Tradition dates the Revelation at the end of the reign of Domitian (died A.D. 96). The imperial stamp for the year 95–6 would bear the legend ID KAISAROS, 14th year of Caesar's reign, which consists of ten heads or letters and numerically adds up to 616 (10+4+20+1+10+200+1+100+70+200). The solution of this ancient puzzle is the author's based on examples of the stamp which have been recovered.

2. D equals 4, standing for Domitian. *Sibyl Or.* V. 39–40.

3. Rev. vi. 10.

4. Suetonius, *Domit.* XV.

5. *Apoc. Baruch.* xxix. 5–6. See Papias, quoted by Irenaeus, *Against Heresies*, V. xxxiii. 3–4.

6. *Sibyl. Or.* V. 156–79. Cp. Rev. xviii. 7–8, etc.

7. *Sibyl. Or.* V. 344–85.

8. *Sibyl. Or.* V. 415–33.

9. *Sibyl. Or.* V. 256–9.

10. The books of *Enoch* and the *Assumption of Moses* are quoted in the New Testament. Christian interpolations are found in the *Testaments of the XII Patriarchs*, the *Apocalypse of Abraham* and the *Ascension of Isaiah.*

11. *Apoc. Ezra*, Vision V, x. 60–xii. 51.

12. *Apoc. Baruch*, xl.

13. See Schonfield, *The Passover Plot*, p. 34 ff.

14. See Lk. i. 69–71, xix. 27, and Rev. xix. 11–21.

15. Suetonius, *Domit.* XII.

16. Dio Cassius, *Hist.* lxvii. 14; Suetonius, *Domit.*, X and XV.

17. Eusebius, *Eccl. Hist.* III. xviii.

18. Quoted by Eusebius, *Eccl. Hist.* III. xx.

19. Rev. xiii. 15–17.

20. Rev. ii. 9, iii. 9.

21. See ch. xii below, and *The Passover Plot*, pp. 25–48.

22. *Letter of Pliny to Trajan* (tr. by W. Melmoth, revised by W. M. L. Hutchinson, *Loeb Classical Library*).

23. It is worthy of remark how much liberty the Christians enjoyed for a considerable time, and how much freedom to propagate their beliefs. Pliny mentions in the letter quoted that Christianity was not confined to the cities, but had spread through the villages and countryside.

24. Jn. ix. 22, xii. 42, xvi. 2.

25. Justin, *Dial.*, xcvi. For a full discussion of the early relations between Jews and Christians see James Parkes, *The Conflict of the Church and the Synagogue.*

26. Justin, *Dial.* xvii; cviii.

27. Mt. xxviii. 11–15.

28. Justin, *Dial.* xxxviii.

29. Ignat., *Magnesians*, viii. 1 and x. 3.

30. Ignat., *Philadelphians*, vi. 1.

31. II. Jn. 10–11.

12

The Man Called John

NEXT to Paul's epistles the Johannine documents (Gospel, three epistles, and the Revelation) are the largest collection in the New Testament attributed to any one author. Since Paul's death some thirty years previously no comparable figure had emerged among the Christians capable of exerting such a powerful effect on Christian doctrine by the range of his intellect, his command of language, and his dynamic personality. Now there arose the man called John, so outstanding that he was able to provide Eastern Christianity with a counterpoise to the Petro-Pauline combination of the West. The paucity of reliable knowledge about him may partly be accounted for by the strong inducement which existed to claim him as a direct rather than an indirect link with the person of Jesus himself and with the original apostolic band. His name could even cause him to be identified later with John the son of Zebedee, the hot-headed and impetuous Galilean fisherman, who with his brother James and Peter constituted the trio of apostles whom Jesus had chosen as his intimates. This extraordinary error, perpetuated down to the present day by leaning over backwards to make the evidence fit, reveals how much the Church has delighted in the Jesus of the Fourth Gospel and wished it to be believed that this portrayal of him was first-hand and authentic.

There was every incentive, especially among Eastern Christians piqued and at the same time greatly attracted by the doctrine of the West, to infer that the son of Zebedee and the Beloved Disciple of the Fourth Gospel were identical, though there was no clear proof of it. Indeed, if this disciple had been the son of Zebedee there was no occasion for anonymity after the other Gospels had been written. This would hold good whether the disciple or someone else had written the Fourth Gospel. The association with Jesus of Peter, James and John was already recorded and widely known. If of these three John had survived to the end of the first century the fact would have been familiar to many, a circumstance to be much publicised, not least by John himself if he was the last of the original Apostles.

Such a disclosure would have contributed most helpfully to the encouragement of Christians when they most needed it. Shyness and self-effacement were certainly not characteristics of the 'Sons of Thunder'. Evidently the Fourth Gospel is not altogether tongue-tied about the sons of Zebedee, because it mentions them in company with Peter, Thomas and Nathaniel, and two other disciples, in a story which goes on to state that one of the party was the Beloved Disciple.[1] Here would certainly be the place to make clear that the disciple in question was one of the sons of Zebedee. But this is not done. The natural conclusion is that this disciple was one of the two who are not named, and the author would expect to be understood in this sense. There is a somewhat analogous situation at the beginning of the Gospel, where two disciples are with John the Baptist and hear him speak about Jesus who is passing by. Here one of the two is disclosed to be Andrew the brother of Simon Peter,[2] and there would have been even more reason to disclose the fact if the other had been John the brother of James the son of Zebedee.

Whoever the Beloved Disciple may have been the author of the Gospel did not wish it to be supposed that he was John the son of Zebedee, and everything he says of the unnamed disciple depicts a quite different individual.[3]

The available external evidences point to the same conclusion. These have been fully set out by Robert Eisler in his important book *The Enigma of the Fourth Gospel.* We have testimony that both the sons of Zebedee, John as well as James, had been executed in Palestine in the early days of Christianity, and the words of Jesus quoted by Mark confirm that both had suffered by the time that Gospel was written.[4] When Paul wrote to the Galatians there were three eminent leaders in Jerusalem, James, Peter and John. But the James of Paul was not the son of Zebedee, but the brother of Jesus, and we cannot therefore assume that John in this case was the son of Zebedee. The John who is associated with Peter in the Acts could have been the son of Zebedee; but by the time of the Council of Jerusalem he has ceased to be mentioned. The Beloved Disciple of the Fourth Gospel was also associated with Peter, and his name appears to have been John. But this disciple has a house at Jerusalem and was known to the high priest. On the cross Jesus entrusted his mother to his care. It is brought out that he lived to a great age, so that it came to be believed that he would not die before Jesus returned from heaven to inaugurate his kingdom.[5] Of this John it was reported that he had been a Jewish priest, and even that he had worn the high priest's golden frontlet. In his later years he resided in Asia Minor and was buried at Ephesus. The information comes from a reasonably reliable source, a letter from Polycrates bishop of Ephesus at the end of the second century addressed to Victor bishop of Rome.[6]

The real issue is only obscured by dragging in John the son of Zebedee. What we need to know is whether the dynamic personality who flourished in Asia Minor at the beginning of the century was the venerable Jewish priest who had been the Beloved Disciple of Jesus or some other man, a third John.

That there was a third John playing a very active part in Christian affairs at this time is no speculation. He was known as John the Elder (presbyter) and is mentioned in a well-known passage found in the *Exposition of the Dominical Oracles* by Papias of Hierapolis, another Asian Christian, published about A.D. 140. Papias was concerned to collect the oral traditions of the teaching of Jesus and recorded what anyone who had followed one of the Apostles could tell him, as these apostles themselves, including the sons of Zebedee, had long been dead. From the same sources he also wanted to know what two other authoritative persons, Aristion and John the Elder, were still saying, implying that they still survived.[7] Papias knew that these two had access to traditions about Jesus, but he does not identify John the Elder with the Beloved Disciple of Jesus, who was not one of the Twelve Apostles and who must have been dead before Papias began to gather his material, even if he did live to a ripe old age.

Eusebius, who gives the quotation from Papias, goes on to surmise that John the Apostle may have written the Gospel while John the Elder could have written the Revelation, and he refers to those who have drawn attention to the fact that there were two tombs at Ephesus, both of them called John's. Eusebius then claims that Papias had himself been a hearer of Aristion and John the Elder, which actually Papias does not say. It even got about that Papias had taken down the Fourth Gospel at John's dictation.[8] What we may accept is that in the names of the Elders Papias recorded certain teachings, and either through Papias or Polycarp such teachings were known to Irenaeus, who used some of them in his work *Against Heresies* in the last quarter of the second century.

The authorship of the Johannine literature was a puzzle from a very early date. From the time of Irenaeus onward there were the gravest doubts that the Gospel and the Revelation were by the same hand. While it was agreed that John's Gospel and the first epistle of John were by the same author, there was uncertainty whether he had been responsible for the second and third epistles. It is quite surprising that so much ignorance and confusion could have existed so quickly, unless there were circumstances which had fostered such confusion. The problem of which John was which was one of these circumstances, the different quality of the Greek of the Gospel and the

Revelation was another, and there was a third in the mixed character and disturbed state of the text of both works.

The Revelation is in some textual disorder both at the beginning and end. It is doubtful whether the Letters to the Seven Churches formed part of the original book, and there is a strong suspicion that christological changes have been introduced to bring the text into closer harmony with the Gospel. The disfavour with which the Revelation came to be regarded by those who had abandoned belief in an earthly reign of Christ is understandable. The work also denounced Rome with all the vehemence of Jewish apocalyptic. One of the first to challenge its authenticity was the Roman ecclesiastic Gaius. By contrast, the Fourth Gospel had its detractors in the East, though there too there were some who opposed both books, whom Epiphanius calls Alogi because of their opposition to the Logos doctrine, and also apparently they opposed the notion of the Paraclete. On the whole, however, the East backed the Fourth Gospel, especially against the Romans in the famous Quartodeciman controversy.

It was of great consequence to Eastern Christianity to be able to call as a witness an actual disciple of Jesus, and to believe him to be the author of the Gospel. But if he was indeed a Jewish priest then much in the Gospel is quite inconsistent with his having written it as it stands. There is a mystery here heightened by the ample evidence that the text is in much greater disarray than the Revelation. Passages are in the wrong order, breaking continuity of time and thought. Large chunks of discourse and theological exposition have been superimposed on the narrative, and these elements are often anti-Judaic and of an advanced christological character, in which Christ is the Divine Son, altogether out of keeping with what could be the convictions of a Jewish priest. Whoever was responsible for this material was no Jew. Apart from his expository passages he has prepared long discourses of Jesus to the Jews and to the Apostles. The addresses to Jews are broken up by narrative information, while the address to the Apostles, delivered after the Last Supper, is interpolated as a continuous discourse which interrupts the story. In each instance the audience interjects occasional questions or comments, a familiar Greek literary device designed to permit the argument of the speaker to develop. All this material is highly artificial and in striking contrast to other elements in the Gospel which reveal accurate knowledge of the topography of Palestine and Jerusalem in the time of Christ, of Jewish manners and customs, and of the ritual of the Temple prior to its destruction.

To any impartial judgment it must be evident that two different individuals are represented, one who has furnished reminiscences from his own information and personal experiences, and another who has taken over these records and utilised them for his own purposes.

The characteristics of the first individual would well fit the one we know as the Beloved Disciple, a Jewish priest of Jerusalem who had been a follower of John the Baptist and may be presumed to have had Essene connections. The final chapter of the Gospel implies that he lived to a great age. According to Irenaeus he survived until the reign of Trajan (A.D. 98–117), and Epiphanius, who is not very reliable, dates his death in the emperor's last year. By this time he would certainly have been a centenarian. There are stories of him in his old age, and Polycarp who was martyred in A.D. 167 at the age of eighty-six claimed that as a young man he had seen and heard him.[9] Tradition has it that the Beloved Disciple was not minded to write a Gospel, but was finally persuaded to set down or dictate his recollections. The Fourth Gospel certainly appears to include such memories, but exhibits few if any indications of extreme age. It is impossible to ascribe to the aged Jewish priest the vigorous polemicism of the work and its hostility to the Jews, or to imagine him recalling the long discourses attributed to Jesus.

The peculiar features of the Fourth Gospel must be attributed to a much younger man with very strong views and convictions and a Greek background, and who was still alive a good many years after the latest date for the death of the Beloved Disciple. We should therefore identify him with John the Elder, who also wrote the three epistles of John.

The question inevitably arises of what was the relationship between the two men? The author of the Gospel and of the first epistle of John seems anxious to convey that the association was so close that he was entitled to speak as the Beloved Disciple's mouthpiece, so much so that he can refer to Jesus as the one 'whom *we* have heard, whom *we* have seen with our own eyes . . . and whom our hands have touched'.[10]

There are two curious statements in the Gospel itself. The first is a note which follows the account of the piercing of the side of Jesus on the cross, when there came blood and water from the wound. It reads: 'He who saw it has stated this, and his statement is completely trustworthy, and he knows he is telling the truth, that you too may believe.'[11] The story of the soldier's lance was not in any of the other Gospels, and such an important novelty was felt to require certification. What the note conveys is that the person penning the Gospel is reporting what he heard from one who was an eye-witness and was still living but had not the capacity to write himself. Another note is furnished in connection with the saying of the risen Jesus to Peter about the Beloved Disciple, 'Supposing I wish him to remain until I come, what concern is that of yours? You follow me.' The great age of the Beloved Disciple had fostered the belief that he would survive until the Second Advent. The note tries to correct this impression by pointing out that what Jesus had said did not actually imply this, and proceeds: 'He is the disciple who testified to these matters, and recorded them, and we know that his testimony is trustworthy.'[12] Here again we have the person giving out the Gospel confirming the authority and reliability of his informant. It is the same man writing who in one of his letters uses the same kind of endorsement to include himself: 'You know that our testimony is trustworthy.'[13]

The attestations tend to confirm the tradition that the

Beloved Disciple in extreme age had dictated some of his recollections, and they suggest that the amanuensis was John the Elder, who proceeded to edit, expand, and publish them to present his own opinions and teaching in a manner which gave them the weight of apparent genuineness. There was nothing to distinguish between the authentic contributions of the Beloved Disciple and what was supplied by the Elder. Henceforth in the Gospel the two voices were so blended by the Elder's art that though study of the text reveals by its nature how substantial have been his changes and additions it can never be determined exactly what remains of what the Beloved Disciple had told his scribe.

What could have induced the Elder to perpetrate such a deception? A strong possibility is that his action was governed by the belief that the doctrines to which he subscribed were vital truths which it was imperative to express to combat contemporary errors. This is conveyed not only by the Gospel, but by the three epistles, the first especially. Possession of the material supplied by the last living link with Jesus enabled him, as he may have held providentially, to give out his doctrines in a way and with an authority that would lend them maximum and indeed unique weight. The opportunity was irresistible. The disarray of the text of the Gospel remains a problem. Did the book as we have it have to be sent out hastily in detached sheets which were clumsily edited and published? Certainly a better job can now be done to straighten out the order, which suggests that the confusion was not intentional.[14] This could argue that the Elder was anxious to prevent the aged Jewish priest knowing what had been done and repudiating and denouncing the Gospel.

This, of course, is conjecture; but there has been preserved what could be an intimation that the Beloved Disciple was opposed to the opinions of John the Elder.

The hint, if it is one, is found in what is known as the Anti-Marcionite Prologue to the Fourth Gospel, though it dates from the fourth century. There we find stated: 'The Gospel of

John was revealed and given to the churches by John while yet in the body, as one Papias of Hierapolis, a dear disciple of John, has reported in his exoteric, that is, his last five books. Indeed he took down the Gospel in writing while John dictated. Marcion the heretic, however, who had been disapproved by him (i.e. John) because of his contrary opinions, was cast out by John. Indeed he (i.e. Marcion) had brought to him writings (or letters) from the brethren who dwelt in Pontus.'[15]

This is a careless Latin translation from a lost Greek original, and can partly be corrected. We should read, 'as one Papias . . . has reported in the last of his five books of Exegetics'. That Papias acted as John's secretary is of course a comment by the writer of the Prologue. But why bring in that the heretic Marcion had been rejected by John because of his contrary opinions? We are surely meant to understand that Marcion had wished to act as John's scribe; but that John refused to permit this in case heretical ideas should be introduced without his knowledge, and instead entrusted the task to Papias. Marcion had initially gained the old man's confidence on account of letters of commendation he had brought to Ephesus from the brethren in the Pontic region.

The author of the Prologue has got his facts wrong, as we know that it was not to Ephesus but to Rome that Marcion went about A.D. 140 with his letters of introduction. He was only born about A.D. 100 and would have been a child at the time he is supposed to have visited John at Ephesus. The Elder had written against those who did not accept that Jesus Christ had come in the flesh (Docetists), and Marcion later subscribed to this view. We also have a story that the venerable Polycarp, who had been a hearer of the Beloved Disciple, encountered Marcion at Rome. 'You know me,' said Marcion to Polycarp. To which the saint rudely replied, 'Yes, I know you, the firstborn of Satan.' We can account in one way or another for all the elements in the Anti-Marcionite Prologue; but there does remain the whisper of some tale that the Beloved Disciple had wished to change his amanuensis, whom at first he had trusted, on discovering that he held heretical opinions.

There remains appositely to say something more about the Revelation. The evidence is at least clear here that John the Elder taught in terms derived from this book. The Revelation could conceivably have been written by the Jewish priest who was the Beloved Disciple of Jesus, though not in its entirety. The Greek is poor and the product of one who thinks in Hebrew or Aramaic, and there are many references to the Temple and its ministries. The author's favourite Biblical books are the Song of Moses in Deuteronomy, and the prophets Zechariah and Ezekiel, all of the tribe of Levi. As a man of distinguished family, and probably a Roman citizen, John the priest might have been banished to the island of Patmos by the Emperor Domitian. We cannot be sure that he did write the book, but it is likely enough that he had it in his possession with other apocalyptic works and Essene writings at his home at Ephesus. He had been a disciple of John the Baptist in his youth, and the Fourth Gospel has been discovered to have a number of points of comparison with the Dead Sea Scrolls.

What is important for us is that such a book should have been interpolated and amplified both to bring it into line with the special teaching of the Fourth Gospel and to employ it as a means of influencing the Asian churches. Regarding the first, we may note in the Revelation the presentation of the Christ as the Lamb of God, and when he comes for judgment he is called the Word of God. He is also referred to as 'the reliable and trustworthy witness'[16] in the fashion of John the Elder. Concerning the second, the whole work is framed as an epistle, and the visions are preceded by the seven admonitory letters, where the writer speaks in tones strongly reminiscent of the anti-Jewish elements in the Gospel and of the attacks on Christian sectaries in the epistles of John the Elder.

But scholars have noted other points of comparison. The John of the Revelation insists that he has the message of the

Spirit which is being communicated to the churches. The Fourth Gospel similarly emphasises the work of the Spirit. In the Revelation the special number of the redeemed are virgin males: 'These are they who have not been defiled with women: they are celibate.'[17] So the John of the Gospel speaks of those privileged to become sons of God as not being born of the will of the flesh or of the will of man,[18] and in the first epistle tells us, 'Whoever is born of God does not sin, because his seed remains in him; and he cannot sin, for he is begotten of God.'[19]

After so much of indispensable preliminaries due to the confused traditions and inadequacy of the records John the Elder here begins more particularly to make himself known to us. No Jewish priest, no Jew, could have expressed these sentiments, and though there were Jewish sects and individuals who refrained from marriage, their virginity was not regarded as a spiritual grace. But John is called by Epiphanius 'the holy virgin', one who rejected sexual intercourse as sinful. In the *Acts of John*, attributed to his disciple Leucius, John is made to say:

'Little children, while yet your flesh is pure and ye have your body untouched and not destroyed, and are not defiled by Satan, the great enemy and shameless foe of chastity; know more fully the mystery of the nuptial union: it is the experiment of the serpent, the ignorance of teaching, injury of the seed, the gift of death . . . the impediment which separateth from the Lord, the beginning of disobedience, the end of life, and death. Hearing this, little children, join yourselves together in an inseparable marriage, holy and true, waiting for the one true incomparable bridegroom from heaven, even Christ, the everlasting bridegroom.'[20]

We know nothing of John the Elder's early life and upbringing or how he became a Christian. He was an educated Greek, and like other Greeks he may have set out in quest of truth, attaching himself to various teachers, and finally to the Beloved Disciple—the name he coined for the old Jewish Priest—as the last person living who had been in direct touch with Jesus. Possibly he had had contact with Gnostics and antinomians, and having learnt that only Jesus had perfectly revealed God[21] he wished to hear about him at first hand, and as an ascetic to devote himself wholly to him. We may suggest that through his association with John the priest he came to reject that Jesus had not really become man and suffered, as Docetists were alleging, and in the Gospel he retains for Jesus all the evidences of his humanity. Yet, while he makes no distinction between the God of the Hebrews and the Father God in whose name Jesus spoke, he does take the view that the Jews had failed to know God and therefore rejected Jesus who was the embodiment of his will. Thus there are elements in the Gospel which do have a Gnostic flavour.

Wherever we look in the Johannine literature we meet with a man who has reached clear and intense convictions. His quest has brought him to his goal. He is a Gnostic in the sense that he *knows* the truth. But he knows it uniquely as by a personal revelation, and he regards himself as singularly called and equipped to communicate it to others. He is obsessed with the profundity of his discoveries, so that he is entitled to dogmatise and uncompromisingly to denounce all who differ from him and will not bow to his authority. In a time of stress and great uncertainty, of corruption and apostasy, he has been raised up, as he believes, to be the saviour of the Church, to strengthen and unite the Christians. He is the deliverer of Christ's last word in the Last Times, the prophet charged with proclaiming the Son of God's full and final self-revelation to his followers.

John the Elder comes before us in his writings as the Paul of the East; but what he had to accomplish doctrinally was much more difficult. Paul had turned away from the Jesus who spoke on earth, and proclaimed a gospel he had received by revelations which he attributed to the Christ in heaven. But if the truth as John saw it was to have weight with Christians it could only do so through an unchallengeable authority, the voice of the historical Jesus speaking as the incarnate Word of God.

Circumstances made this possible, since all the original Apostles of Jesus were dead. But there was one man, a very old man, still alive, who had known Jesus personally. He was both the only one who could contradict John's interpretation of Jesus, and the only one who could invest it with convincing verisimilitude. If the aged disciple could be induced to dictate what he remembered of Jesus, and if John could obtain possession of this precious material and use it as the groundwork for his projected Gospel without the old man knowing what was being done, then everything was set for what were startling novelties to be received as genuine on the indisputable testimony of one who had been a hearer of Jesus and an eyewitness. This is why the trustworthiness of the witness is emphasised. The new Gospel was successfully given out, and the Revelation, as we have seen, was suitably edited to bring it into line as far as was practicable.

Thus in the Fourth Gospel, as in the letters to the Seven Churches, it is not the real Jesus speaking, but John the Elder who is speaking in his name. The fraud can be detected, however, not only because the Christ of the Fourth Gospel expresses himself in a manner which so often is unJewish, but far more because the evidence of the first epistle of John reveals that Jesus speaks in the way the creator of his supposed utterances writes. We have to be very thankful for the existence of that epistle. There is no call for us to be horrified at the idea that a gifted and even spiritually-minded Christian, whose work has a place in a collection of what many hold to be inspired documents, could be guilty of such gross deception. It should be clear to us by now that there are several bogus books in the New Testament, and others which are purposefully misleading. Our own moral judgments must not be applied to the literary productions of antiquity, where it was not considered at all improper to forge, interpolate and slant documents in a good cause. John would certainly have believed that his design was righteous and God-guided. He would not doubt for a moment that he had been specially raised up by God for the task to be performed, that he was being led by the Spirit. The remarkable way in which everything was working with him at every stage confirmed it.

The consideration of John's christology is the subject of a short study at the end of this volume, and we need say little about it here. It is the man himself with whom we must be occupied; for it is profitless to discuss the Christ of John until we have understood how much this Christ is a reflection not only of John's spiritual and intellectual powers, but of his character and moods. The visualisation of Jesus is to an appreciable extent an unconscious self-portrait of the artist.

John is a commanding personality, a man born to rule, harsh when he is severe, arrogant and egotistical, but also capable of sweetness, generosity and humility where his friends are concerned. He is an ardent ascetic and deeply introspective, one who has undergone a prolonged struggle in his search for certainty. Triumphant in the conclusions he has reached he sees himself as born of the Spirit[22] to become the pure and undefiled mouthpiece of the Truth, invested with the responsibility of making it known by all means and at all costs. He is incapable of perceiving any contradiction in the methods he employs to promote it. His self-deception here is absolute. For him Truth is writ large with a capital T. It had come into the world with the incarnation of the Divine Word, and the Gospel and epistles stress how Jesus has revealed the Truth from the True God his Father and communicated it to his disciples who now are followers of the Truth.[23] The mission of Jesus is thus what John believes is his own mission. If we study the language of the Johannine writings carefully and perceptively we can apprehend that John regards himself as the repository of the Truth, and no one else has it except those who fully subscribe to his teaching. All who are otherwise-minded do not belong to the virgin elect ones, but to the world from which Christ distinguished and redeemed his own.

'Do not love the world,' John writes to his flock, 'nor what is in the world. If anyone loves the world, there is no love of the Father in him. For everything that is in the world, desire of the flesh, desire of the eyes, and the hollow sham of life in general, belongs not to the Father, but to the world. And the world with its desire is passing away. Children, it is the Last Hour. And as you have heard, "Antichrist will come", well, there are plenty of antichrists in existence now, by which fact we know it is the Last Hour. They went out from us, but they did not belong to us. You, however, are consecrated by the Holy One. You do *know*, all of you. I have not written to you because you do not know the Truth, but because you do know it, and because no lie has any connection with the Truth.'[24]

Gnostics like Valentinus with his *Gospel of Truth*, the text of which has been recovered and was published in 1957, and the author of the quasi-Gnostic *Odes of Solomon*, which personifies Truth, were simply building on the Johannine foundation.[25] The Truth is for those who have received the grace of *knowing*. John can write to one of his own communities as 'the Elect Lady and her children, whom I truly love for the Truth's sake, and not only I but all indeed who have known the Truth, which continues in us and will be with us forever.'[26] So Papias, following John's teaching, proclaimed that he took no pleasure 'in those who relate foreign commandments, but in those who relate such as were given by the Lord to the Faith, and are derived from the Truth itself'.[27] Both in the name of Jesus and in his own name John speaks much of believers loving one another; but this chaste love is for the Elect according to John and not for anyone else, even if they go by the name of Christians.

The Christ of John is so very like himself, loving his own but condemning others. God may have loved the world, but only those who believe in the Son and have the Son obtain eternal life. No one can get to the Father except through the Son. All who fail to acknowledge the Son are condemned. John has the same attitude towards those who accept or reject his own teaching. The treatment of the Jews is significant. The whole history of this people was associated with God's revelation of himself to them and of his communication with them. But John's Jesus is a rabid antisemite. He declares that the Jews because they do not accept him do not know the Father and that they are of their father the Devil. They are liars, and he dissociates himself from the Jewish story of Divine guidance by stating that he was before Abraham and by speaking of '*your* Law'. He announces that all who came prior to himself were thieves and robbers.[28]

The most singular aspect of Johannism is the promise Jesus makes to his disciples to send the Paraclete, or Adviser. When the Fourth Gospel appeared with such a substantial amount of new teaching given by Jesus which was not in the other Gospels and often inconsistent with what was in them, the obvious question would be asked by many, If this teaching is genuine why was it not known before, why was it held back for so long? The Paraclete doctrine seems designed to anticipate this criticism.

There are four passages on the subject in the Fourth Gospel which we may bring together in the natural order.

'If you care for me, carry out my instructions; and I will beg the Father to give you another Adviser to be with you permanently, namely the Spirit of Truth, which the world cannot receive, because it neither perceives it nor knows it. But you will know it, because it will dwell with you and be with you. I will not leave you forsaken: I will come to you. When the Adviser comes, which I will send to you from the Father, the Spirit of Truth that emanates from the Father, it will testify of me, and you too shall testify because you have been with me from the first. I have a great deal more to tell you, but you cannot receive it now. When it comes, however, the Spirit of Truth, it will initiate you into the full truth. It will not speak of its own accord, but say exactly what it hears, and convey to you what comes. It will glorify me, because it will receive what is mine and convey it to you. I have spoken to you thus while I am with you. But the Adviser [*gloss*, the Holy Spirit] which the Father will send in my name, will give you full instructions, and remind you of everything I have told you.'[29]

Throughout we may use the masculine gender instead of the neuter in relation to the Spirit of Truth; but this Spirit, though an editor has wanted to suggest it, is not the Holy Spirit, which the author states was breathed upon the disciples immediately after his resurrection.[30] The Spirit of Truth is to be sent much later, after Jesus has returned to the Father and has interceded with him to send it. It will reveal the fuller truth about Jesus which he could not communicate while on earth. And what it reveals will be received mediumistically. The Spirit will be in contact with Christ, listening to him, and conveying what comes.

In this promise of Jesus, then, the Christians are informed that they are to expect someone, who will be the instrument of conveying to them more advanced doctrine, the fuller revelation of Jesus, since the spirit-guide of that person will be the Spirit of Truth manifesting itself in him as the Adviser, Advocate, Comforter—the Greek word Paraclete having all these significations. The whole point of this promise in the Fourth Gospel is to endorse the claim of the author to be the ultimate Christian prophet and seer. He has introduced himself in this light at the beginning and end of the Revelation, where the Angel of Jesus may be equated with the Spirit of Truth of the Gospel. Through this angel John has seen and heard everything, and is told, 'These things are trustworthy and true, and the Lord God of the spirits of the prophets has sent his angel to show to his servants what must shortly transpire.' The angel is the angel of Jesus, whom John has seen as a glorified figure, and the Father has indeed sent him in the name of Jesus as promised: 'I, Jesus, have sent my angel to testify these things to you for the churches.'

This is a very exceptional man with whom we are dealing, a religious fanatic both highly gifted and wholly assured that he is the divinely appointed agent of Christ to declare the Truth, rally the divided and distracted Church, unmask the false teachers and strengthen the Elect of the Last Times. He is the

John the Baptist of the Second Advent. It is little wonder that the influence of his dogmatic assertions, his mystical eloquence and command of language, should have captivated and controlled Christian thought down to the present day. So much so, that readers of his writings have taken in their stride all those passages in which an ascetic bigotry and intolerant animosity find expression, because the same man so freely speaks of love. By the sentiments John has attributed to Jesus on earth he has magnified him in quite a different way to what was done by Paul, but only to betray him more grievously than Judas.

Yet we can pay tribute to the effectiveness of John's zeal and persuasive imagination. He created a clear-cut christology which allowed of no deviation. Christians were challenged to stand up and be counted in terms of the new and overriding revelation. When they were hard-pressed from without and within in the region where he taught he provided what they sorely needed, a deep joy in believing, a zestfulness at the inflowing of eternal life, a fresh confidence as the recipients of the most assured verities, and the capacity to rise superior to persecution and adversity in the certainty of a glorious vindication. 'I am Resurrection and Life. Whoever believes in me will live even if he has died, and everyone who lives and believes in me will never die at all.'[31]

The John who is so convinced he possesses the Truth is no less enamoured of Life. Here is no venerable and infirm disciple of Jesus, who could never have preserved in his memory such torrential outpourings of Dominical doctrine, but one who can zestfully do battle with all the alertness and vigour of a man in his prime. The survival of the disciple gave him opportunity, which he seized with both hands, to give out his own teaching as the singular repository of the recollections of the last living contact with Jesus. Confronted with the electrifying and stimulating potency of the Paraclete personality many were only too ready to yield to a confusion of identities arising from a common name and bask in the glory of a figure of apostolic stature who so providentially had arisen in the East to match the pretensions of the West.

Johannism was not adopted without misgivings and even resistance, and tradition has left traces of the suspicion aroused by the radical change in the image of Jesus and the curious circumstances in which it had been made known. But everything at the time militated against obtaining concrete evidence, and exuberant support for the new teaching stilled opposing voices. The Johannine puzzle remains, but what has been adduced may throw some light on what possibilities exist for arriving at a solution. There is always hope that more decisive documentation may turn up.

NOTES AND REFERENCES

1. Jn. xxi. 2–7.

2. Jn. i. 35–40.

3. See Rogert Eisler, *The Enigma of the Fourth Gospel.*

4. See Eisler, op. cit., ch. xv. Papias had written in the second book of his *Expositions* that both John and James had been killed by the Jews. This could only have been before A.D. 70 when for brief periods Jewish authorities in Palestine were able to carry out a death sentence. James of course was executed by the Jewish king Agrippa I.

5. Jn. xxi. 20–3.

6. Quoted by Eusebius, *Eccl. Hist.* V. xxix.

7. Quoted by Eusebius, *Eccl. Hist.* III. xxxix.

8. So Fortunatian's preface to the Fourth Gospel, c. A.D. 313, and others subsequently. The Texts may be found in Eisler, *The Enigma of the Fourth Gospel.*

9. Eusebius, quoting a lost letter of Irenaeus to Florinus (*Eccl. Hist.*, V. xx.), gives us a passage in which Irenaeus spoke of his early association with Polycarp, who had been a hearer of John, and whose reports of what John had said he remembered clearly.

10. I. Jn. i. 1.

11. Jn. xix. 33–5.

12. Jn. xxi. 23–4.

13. III. Jn. 12.

14. See the rearrangement in Schonfield, *The Authentic New Testament.*

15. See Benjamin W. Bacon, *Studies in Matthew*, Appended Note III, *The Anti-Marcionite Prologues*; also Eisler, op. cit., chs. iii–v.

16. Rev. iii. 14.

17. Rev. xiv. 14.

18. Jn. i. 13.

19. I. Jn. iii. 9.

20. *Acts of John* (tr. by M. R. James, *The Apocryphal New Testament*, ref. p. 266).

21. Jn. i. 14–18 and I. Jn. i. 2.

22. Jn. iii. 6, vi. 63.

23. Jn. i. 14, 17; iii. 34; vi. 32–3; viii. 13–19, 32, 40, 44; xiv. 6; xviii. 37; I. Jn. ii. 2; iv. 6; II. Jn. 1–2; III. Jn. 3–4, 12.

24. I. Jn. ii. 15–21 and cp. Jn. xvii. 11–12.

25. See R. M. Grant, *Gnosticism and Early Christianity*, pp. 128–34.

26. II. Jn. 1. John says much of loving one another (Jn. xv. 17; I. Jn. ii. 5, iv. 20).

27. Papias, quoted by Eusebius, *Eccl. Hist.* III. xxxix.

28. Jn. vii. 28; viii. 19, 58; viii. 17 and x. 34; viii. 44, 55; x. 8.

29. The Gospel order as we now read the text is xiv. 16–18, 25–6; xv. 26–7; xv. 17–19. The first passage is out of place and should be last as in our quotation. See Schonfield, *The Authentic New Testament*, translation of John's Gospel.

30. Jn. xx. 22–3.

31. Jn. xi. 25.

13

The Time of Transition

IN THE first half of the second century A.D. Christianity moved decisively away from Judaism, from the hope of the Kingdom of God on earth, from any real identification with the Jesus of history, and became as a result very much the religion with which we are familiar. We have traced some of the contributory factors and attitudes, and must now look more closely at particular aspects of the situation.

The Messianic revival, which had been assisted especially in the East by the policies of the Emperor Domitian, petered out very quickly so far as the Christians were concerned after his assassination in A.D. 96. Christianity had not the same incentives as the Jews to sustain it politically. But both communities were spiritually affected and distressed at the unaccountable deferment of their expectations. Not only faith, but frustration and questioning, characterises the apocalyptic literature of the period. Of what avail was it to announce cataclysms and judgments, when it appeared that Rome would continue to rule in her pride and the wicked flourish?

Despite pleas for constancy, loyalty and endurance, many more Christians were disillusioned and either left the Church or followed those teachers who offered less earth-bound interpretations of the nature of Christianity. To combat disbelief in the Second Advent the Gospels of Matthew and Luke provided parables to illustrate that Jesus had anticipated that his return might not be for a considerable time. Nevertheless Christians must be always ready since the event would come suddenly and without prior warning. Jesus was made to say that he himself had no knowledge of the date, which was a secret the Father had not revealed even to him. Similarly predictions were circulated which showed that it had been foretold what was now taking place of Christians becoming lukewarm and apostasising, being led astray by false teachers and falling into evil ways.

From the beginning of the proclamation of the Gospel to the Gentiles without the discipline of commitment to the prescriptions of the Jewish way of life the risk was there that the types of people who largely availed themselves of the free offer of the new salvation would bring into the Church the turpitudes of pagan society. The shocked Paul had fought against these intrusions, and to an appreciable extent they could be curbed so long as the Christians were in expectation of the imminent return of Christ in judgment. But now the way was open for a more emphatic breakdown of morality in the churches, not only because nothing had happened to carry conviction that the Second Advent was at hand, but because Christianity was to a much greater extent divorced from Judaism. Even the connecting link of Jewish Christianity had substantially been broken.

New Testament epistles which reflect the state of affairs present an image of anything but an ideal Christian society. Conditions were at their worst on the eastern fringe of the Roman Empire where as non-Christian sources make abundantly clear standards of conduct were much more permissive than in the West. We can convince ourselves of what things were really like in the churches from the following extracts.

'I would remind you,' says the author writing in the name of Jude the brother of James, 'though you once knew all this, how the Lord having saved the people from the land of Egypt afterwards destroyed those who did not believe. The angels too, who did not keep to their own province, but forsook their native habitat, he has kept in close confinement in subterranean gloom for the Judgment of the Great Day, even as Sodom and Gomorrah and the towns in their vicinity, having after the same manner as these taken to obscene ways and indulgence in unnatural vice, are presented as an example, suffering the penalty of perpetual burning.

'Notwithstanding this, these dreamers similarly defile the flesh, defy disciplines, and speak slightingly of dignities. . . . Woe to them! They have travelled the road of Cain, and plunged greedily for gain into the vice of Balaam, and perished in the mutiny of Korah. These are the hidden snags sharing the entertainment of your love-feasts, feeding themselves fearlessly, empty clouds carried away by winds, trees that are autumn-blasted and barren, dead twice over, torn up by the roots, raging breakers of the sea foaming with their own shame, wandering stars for whom is reserved the blackness of darkness for ever. . . .

'You however, dear friends, recall the words spoken in advance by the envoys of our Lord Jesus Christ, when they told you, "In the Last Times deceivers will come, followers of their ungodly impulses." These are the separatists, unspiritual materialists. You however, dear friends, develop yourselves in your most sacred faith, praying by the Holy Spirit, retaining God's regard, awaiting the mercy of our Lord Jesus Christ for Eternal Life. Take pity on some, of course, and save them with eager resolution, snatching them from the blaze. Take pity on others too, but save them with repugnance, loathing even the tunic soiled by the flesh.'[1]

The author of II. Peter writes in similar vein, borrowing some of the imagery of Jude. He fulminates against false teachers.

'Many will follow them in their immoral courses, with the result that the True Way will be maligned. Yes, in their rapacity these false teachers will cheat you with their fabricated messages. But not for long will their judgment dawdle, or their destruction drowse. . . . These men . . . will surely perish in their corruption, suffering injury as the reward of inflicting injury.

'These are the people who deem wantonness in the daytime a special pleasure: blots and disgraces, luxuriating in their seductive wiles, even when feasting with you, with eyes full of adultery that never rest for a moment from sin, enticing unstable souls, and with a mind fully trained in gaining their ends. . . . With their high-flown nonsensical talk they entice with their base physical passions those who have only just escaped from those who live in error. They promise them liberty, while they themselves are the slaves of corruption; for a man is enslaved by whatever he gives way to. For if, escaping from the world's pollutions by knowledge of the Lord and Saviour Jesus Christ, they are vanquished by being again enmeshed by them, their last state is worse than their first. Far better for them never to have known the way of righteousness, than knowing to have gone back on the sacred injunction delivered to them. They only confirm what the true proverb says, "The dog has returned to his vomit, and the washed sow to her wallowing in the mire."

'The letter I am writing you now, dear friends, is my second, and my intention with these letters is to stimulate your clear thinking by reminder. . . . In the first place you must realise this, that in the Last Days there will surely come scoffers, following their own desires and saying, "What has become of the promise of his advent, for since the fathers fell asleep everything goes on exactly as it has done since the beginning of Creation?" They choose to ignore the fact that the sky and earth, formed by the word of God out of water and by water, has been a long time in existence, yet the world of those days perished, inundated by water by these agencies. By the very same word the present sky and earth have been stocked with fire, kept for the Day of Judgment and the destruction of ungodly mortals. There is this too that must not escape your notice, dear friends, that a single day with the Lord is as a thousand years, and a thousand years as a single day. The Lord is not dilatory in fulfilling his promise as some reckon dilatoriness: he is forbearing to you, not wanting any to perish, but all to come to repentance.'[2]

No doubt, as with many pulpit utterances, such words never reached those for whom they were chiefly intended: they fell on the ears of the residue of the faithful, who squirmed deliciously and drank in avidly the tale of terrible sins which they were too modest, too conforming, or too virtuous to commit, and of retributions appropriate to the crimes. Yet the admonitions must have had some of the intended effect. The convictions of many believers would be reinforced and strayed lambs would be brought back penitently into the fold.

The conditions are no less reflected in the letters to the seven churches of Asia in the Revelation. There are Christians who have forsaken their former love, who have among them adherents of the teaching of Balaam, who instructed Balak to lay a trap for the children of Israel, to make them eat food dedicated to idols, and to indulge in sexual vice. There are those who have a name for being alive, but are really dead. Others are neither frigid nor fervent, but merely tepid.[3] We have the external testimony of Pliny that there was a considerable falling away among the Christians. Many of them were prepared to carry out the sacred rites to the emperor and to curse the name of Christ.

The accusation was widespread that the Christians performed shameful deeds at their love-feasts. Justin refers to what was alleged, 'the upsetting of the lamp, promiscuous intercourse, and eating human flesh'.[4] Athenagoras similarly speaks of the heathen charges of 'atheism, Thyestean feasts, and Oedipodean intercourse'.[5] These Christian philosophers were at pains to repudiate such allegations, and indeed by the middle of the second century this could be done with far more justification. But fully allowing for hostile invention and exaggeration, there is evidence enough in what we have quoted from the New Testament records that earlier on orgiastic practices were not unknown at gatherings ostensibly Christian.

To check the rot that had set in more than strong language was necessary. The sheep had to be separated from the goats. One means of doing this was to foster a cult of virginity, one of the activities of the Johannine group as we have seen. Indications of this trend appear already in Matthew's Gospel in the discussion on divorce. When the disciples say, 'If that is how a man stands with his wife it is not advisable to marry', Jesus replies, 'It is not everyone who can go as far as that, only those to whom it is given. For there are eunuchs who have been so from birth, and there are eunuchs who have been made so by human agency, and there are eunuchs who have made themselves so for the sake of the Kingdom of Heaven. Whoever can go so far let him do so.'[6] A popular piece of fiction in the second century was the *Acts of Paul and Thecla*. Thecla is a virgin engaged to be married, but is influenced to keep her virginity after listening to Paul preach. The apostle is credited with expanding the Beatitudes to include a number of new ones to exalt virginity and abstention from all sexual intercourse.[7] One example is, 'Blessed are the continent, for unto them shall God speak.' But quite apart from fiction we have Justin seeking to prove that promiscuous intercourse was not part of the Christian mysteries. He cites the case of a Christian youth at Alexandria who requested the governor to permit the surgeons to make him a eunuch, as they refused to do so without official authorisation.[8]

The Clean-up-the-Church movement seems to have been pretty extensive and pretty drastic. The lauding of total chastity was a natural reaction to the outbreak of indulgence. The purity campaign among the Christians at this time had some community with Essenism among the Jews at an earlier period and with contemporary Gnostic disgust with the flesh. Some forms of Gnosticism were influenced by Essene teaching and Christianity was considerably affected. The Essene emphasis on the Two Ways, of Life and Death, and the Two Spirits, of Good and Evil, Truth and Error, found fresh expression in the Johannine literature, in the *Teaching of the Twelve Apostles* and in the *Odes of Solomon*.

There was revived in the Church the view that within the People of God there was a much smaller body of the truly Elect, the faithful and moral remnant, those who had indeed become as innocent as little children and were therefore fit to enter the Kingdom of God, as in the *Gospel of Thomas* recovered from Egypt. In reponse to a question by the disciples as to when they will see Jesus, he tells them, 'When you undress yourselves and are not ashamed, and take your clothing and lay them under your feet like little children and tread on them; then you will become sons of the Living One and you will have no fear.' The Age of Innocence is to return. The garment of shame assumed by Adam and Eve when they sinned can be cast off. The little children of the Kingdom will cease to think in terms of male and female, so that 'the man is not the man and the woman is not the woman'; for Man was originally created androgynous.[9]

Egypt was evidently the region in which these ideas flourished and developed. Before the middle of the first century A.D. we already find much that was to affect their growth in the works of Philo the Jewish philosopher of Alexandria, who also contributed materially to the enunciation of the Logos doctrine. The intellectual atmosphere of Alexandria was highly conducive to the promotion of Gnostic thought, which was greatly assisted in its expression by both Jewish and Christian teaching, and the state of Christianity in the second century made the Church in the East responsive to a great deal that was being promulgated in Gnostic circles. Transplantation from Egypt to Asia Minor was readily accomplished. Waning confidence in the Second Advent created a condition in the Church highly receptive to the notion that all matter was evil and corrupt, and therefore the Kingdom of God could not be realised in any earthly and physical sense.

Gnosticism emphasised the escape of the self from the sinfulness of flesh and its reunion with the pure realm of Light.

Its essence was the revelation to the individual of his true self, whence he had come and whither he must return. The systems explained that the Fall had not taken place with Adam: it had taken place in the Heavenly Sphere at the very beginning of Creation. Man himself was the product of that higher spiritual Fall, since he was generated as the result of the creation of lower spiritual beings, angels and powers. Thus the Wisdom of God became imprisoned by the created world and could not get back to its Source without a rescue operation. In the end God had to come himself in the Son, descending to earth through all the spheres without contamination to effect the redemption.

The systems were various, but had a broad likeness which resided in the attempt to produce a philosophical explanation of the universe and of the phenomena of being. They originated in a quest for the true significance of the ancient pagan mythologies and cosmogonies, and became related to Jewish and Christian ideas through the relative simplicity of Biblical teaching. Christianity especially, with its doctrine of the Incarnation and its purpose, offered in many respects a ready made vehicle for the expression of the Gnostic message.

The whole Church was seriously exercised by the arguments and erudition of teachers like Basilides, Valentinus and Marcion, who flourished in the first half of the second century, and compelled to define its creed much more precisely. In the process Trinitarianism emerged and Christianity was driven forward towards the formulation of a universal orthodoxy.

It is most essential to understand to what extent the doctrines of Christianity were now being shaped by the Gnostic challenge and the rejection of the physical as inherently evil. Matthew's Gospel, which may have been composed in Egypt around A.D. 90, already witnesses to the beginnings of detachment from sex, not only in the eunuch passage we have quoted, but also in the doctrine of the Virgin Birth which first appears in this Gospel. Evidently it was not considered fitting that Jesus should be conceived as a result of sexual intercourse.

But the developments that followed went much further, well beyond the position of John's Gospel which omits the nativity story. The conflict was no longer between those who followed the original teaching of the Church that Jesus was wholly human and those who asserted that he was also the Divine Son of God. Now it was between those who upheld the Incarnation and those who contended that Jesus Christ had not come in the flesh at all, but only seemed to be a man. The docetic doctrine was the inevitable outcome of the conviction that the flesh was itself sinful and sex was of the Devil.

If Jesus Christ was God then he could never have assumed humanity, for if he had done so he would not be sinless. It was repugnant that he should have had the normal bodily functions, that he should be capable of digestion and excretion, not to mention the emission of sperm. It was argued that he only appeared to be a man and that the food of which he seemed to partake was automatically burnt up. Equally he could have had no earthly mother as well as father, and all that might be allowed was that he had passed through Mary like smoke.

Docetism necessarily affected the question of the crucifixion, since obviously Christ could not suffer if he was God. Docetic tendencies are found in the *Gospel of Peter* where on the cross Jesus feels no pain. The *Acts of John* is more extreme. To the multitude at Jerusalem Jesus is being crucified, but at the very same time he appears to and speaks with John on the Mount of Olives. John tells of Jesus, 'Sometimes when I would lay hold on him, I met with a material and solid body, and at other times again when I felt him the substance was immaterial and as if it existed not at all. . . . And oftentimes when I walked with him, I desired to see the print of his foot, whether it appeared on the earth; for I saw him as it were lifting himself up from the earth: and I never saw it.'[10]

The Church repudiated docetism; but it left its mark in the doctrines of the Immaculate Conception, which declared that by a special dispensation the mother of Jesus had been born without the taint of original sin, and the Perpetual Virginity of

Mary. In her sinlessness she had borne only the Son of God and never had sexual intercourse with her husband. The brothers and sisters of Jesus were explained as being the children of Joseph by a previous marriage.[11]

But there was something else to be accounted for. If Jesus was truly God as well as man, why had he performed no miracles before he was baptised by John the Baptist? To meet this criticism the more familiar *Gospel of Thomas*, not the Gnostic work, was composed, which related a number of miracles by Jesus as a boy. Unfortunately they do not redound to his credit for the most part and make him appear as something of a problem child.[12]

The accentuation of the deity of Christ at a time when there was a turning away from the material world and all its ways made it extremely difficult henceforth to think of Jesus in any genuine sense as a man. A true union of Godhead and manhood might be a theological formula acceptable in the abstract, but concretely the combination could not be made to work out convincingly. Those who acknowledged the deity were forced to impose limitations on the characteristics of humanity.

Under the impact of Gnosticism Jesus Christ was converted from Son of God to God the Son. It was either this or yielding to a dualistic concept of Deity; for Gnostic thinkers were contending that the Supreme God was not the creator of the universe. This was the work of a lower Power, since the Supreme God was wholly good and therefore could not have created matter which was evil. The Creator God, the Demiurge, was equated with the God of the Old Testament, the God of the Jews. Jesus Christ had come to reveal the Unknown Father and redeem believers from the power of the Lord of this world. The Devil of the Christians thus appeared as the Lord of Hosts of the Jews. But Christians accepted the Old Testament and held the universe to have been created through Christ as the Word of God. The only way to combat the Gnostic view without abandoning the deity of Christ was to assert the Unity of God in Trinity. The Unity by itself, as held by the Jews, would have excluded Christ's deity to which the Church was now fully committed. The question of the relationship of the Holy Spirit to the other two Persons in the Godhead was never finally resolved to the satisfaction of all Christians, and Arianism preserved the doubt inherent in Paulinism which suggested that in some sense the Father had preceded the Son. But had it not been for Gnosticism the Trinitarian formula might never have been devised.

Thus in little more than a century after the death of Jesus Christianity for all its relics of a Jewish origin, including that of being a chosen people, patently presented itself in the guise of a religion of the Gentile world, competing in future with that world's other religions, especially with those having some affinity like Mithraism. On the one hand its engagements were with apologetics, to enable it to compete on more equal terms as a permitted Faith, and on the other hand with combating various 'heresies' which weakened its power. To dominate demanded consistency, and therefore both an onslaught on every kind of deviation and acceptance by men of intelligence who could expound Christianity in a manner which would commend it to the sophisticated. The Faith had to be shown to be morally and intellectually superior to other Faiths. The measure of the Church's success is certified by its ability to secure converts of the calibre of Aristides and Athenagoras, Quadratus and Melito, Clement of Alexandria and Origen. The philosopher's robe ceased to be an alien garb for a Christian, and it is of interest that the earliest encounter with a Christian authority recorded in the Talmud describes the Christian as a 'philosoph'.[13]

The Christian protagonists had no difficulty in demonstrating the worth of monotheism as compared with polytheism. Judaism had always been able to do that. But they were still far from convincing when it came to explaining the Christian mysteries. Even more now these seemed to liberal and acute minds both foolish and incomprehensible. It was a weakness in the Christian position that with all its elaborate theologising the majority of the converts continued to be drawn from the uneducated masses. Athenagoras tries to make a virtue of the circumstance. After castigating those who make the art of words rather than the demonstration of deeds their occupation and profession, he continues: 'But among us you will find uneducated persons, and artisans, and old woman, who, if they are unable to prove the benefit of our doctrine, yet by their deeds exhibit the benefit arising from their persuasion of its truth: they do not rehearse speeches, but exhibit good works.'[14] The situation had not materially changed from what it had been when Paul wrote to the Corinthians that the world had failed to know God by wisdom. 'There are not many sages among you in the world's sense. . . . Instead God has selected what is foolish in the world to shame the wise.'[15]

What had improved by the reign of Hadrian, which marks the effective beginning of the era of Christian *apologia*, was Christian morality in general. The Church had made widely available a code of behaviour based on the Ten Commandments and the Sermon on the Mount,[16] and this was being strictly enforced. The Apologists, therefore, were able to point in all sincerity to the conduct of Christians both as a recommendation for just treatment and in refutation of those reports of what went on at the love-feasts, which as we have seen on Christian testimony had not been wholly the baseless inventions of opponents.

But it was still true, what was chiefly urged against the Christians, that the majority of them were ignorant, simple-minded and gullible. It was this fact which made them an easy prey to the wiles of teachers of novel doctrines and charlatans. They never could have been so carried away by almost every kind of persuasion if they had been more discerning and better educated. And indeed Christianity might never have departed so radically from its original Jewish expression had this been the case.

One of those who pointed these things out was the philosopher Celsus, who made a considerable study of Christianity and set down his findings in a work entitled *A True Discourse*. Origen's reply to this work long after its author's death is more spirited than brilliant. Celsus makes fun of Christian stock phrases which put a premium on ignorance, such as 'Do not examine, but believe!' and 'Your faith will save you!' He deliberately exaggerates a little in claiming that Christians say, 'The wisdom of this life is bad, but foolishness is a good thing!'[17] Elsewhere he declares that at first when the Christians were few in number they maintained common convictions, but when they multiplied they were split into many sects which only had in common the name of Christians. This was an indication of how little their opinions were based on reason. What held them together was a rebellious nature and fear of external foes, and in all other respects they were at loggerheads and had no consistency of doctrine.[18]

We have another picture of how Christians appeared to outsiders in the writings of Lucian of Samosata, described by Lord Macaulay as 'the last great master of Attic eloquence and Attic wit'. Lucian holds up the Christians to ridicule in the *Death of Peregrine*. He relates the history of Peregrine, an unscrupulous rogue and charlatan, who wished to be known as Proteus. After early criminal behaviour Peregrine in his wanderings encounters the Christians and embraces their creed.

'I can tell you,' Lucian writes to Cronius, 'he pretty soon convinced them of his superiority; prophet, elder, ruler of the synagogue—he was everything at once; expounded their books, commented on them, wrote books himself. They took him for a god, accepted his laws, and declared himself their president. The Christians, you know, worship a man to this day—the distinguished personage who introduced their novel rites, and was crucified on that account. Well, the end of it was that Proteus was arrested and thrown into prison. This was the very thing to lend an air to his favourite arts of clap-trap and wonder-working; he was now a made man. The Christians took it all very seriously: he was no sooner in prison than they began trying every means to get him out again—but without success. Everything else that could be done for him they most devoutly did. They thought of nothing else. Orphans and ancient widows might be seen hanging about the prison from break of day. Their officials bribed the gaolers to let them in to sleep inside with him. Elegant dinners were conveyed in; their sacred writings were read; and our old friend Peregrine (as he was still called in those days) became for them "the modern Socrates". In some of the Asiatic cities, too, the Christian communities put themselves to the expense of sending deputations, with offers of sympathy, assistance and legal advice. The activity of these people, in dealing with any matter that affects their community, is something extraordinary; they spare no trouble, no expense. Peregrine, all this time, was making quite an income on the strength of his bondage; money came pouring in. You see, these misguided creatures start with the general conviction that they are immortal for all time, which explains the contempt of death and voluntary self-devotion which are so common among them; and then it was impressed upon them by their original lawgiver that they are all brothers, from the moment they are converted, and deny the gods of Greece, and worship the crucified sage, and live after his laws. All this they take quite on trust, with the result that they despise all worldly goods alike, regarding them merely as common property. Now an adroit, unscrupulous fellow, who has seen the world, has only to get among these simple souls, and his fortune is pretty soon made; he plays with them.'[19]

There is nothing malicious in Lucian's treatment of the Christians, and he gives them full marks for their self-sacrificing care for one another. But like Celsus he finds them extremely naive and easily imposed upon.

This defect in a movement largely composed of the ignorant and credulous, however good and worthy as individuals, was patent to the Christian leaders. For external representation they put a good face on the matter and stressed the blessing of simple faith and innocence, but internally they were disturbed and concerned. The *Teaching of the Twelve Apostles*, which could profitably have had a place in the New Testament, is very frank with advice.

'Let every apostle who comes to you be received as the Lord, but let him not stay more than one day, or if need be a second day as well; but if he stay three days he is a false prophet. And when an apostle goes forth let him accept nothing but bread till he reach his night's lodging; but if he asks for money he is a false prophet.... And no prophet who orders a meal in a spirit (i.e. while under spirit control) shall eat of it: otherwise he is a false prophet. And every prophet who teaches the truth, if he do not what he teaches, is a false prophet.... Let everyone who "comes in the name of the Lord" be received; but when you have tested him you shall know him, for you will have understanding of true and false. If he who comes is a traveller, help him as much as you can, but he shall not remain with you more than two days, or, if need be, three. And if he wishes to settle among you and has a craft, let him work for his bread. But if he will not do so, he is making a traffic of Christ; beware of such.'[20]

For the first time here, and clearly with good cause, we meet with the word *Christemporos*, a Christmonger, one who trades on the name of Christian for personal gain or advantage.

Better organisation and closer agreement on points of doctrine progressively built up a better image of the Church, but could never remove the stigma that the chief appeal of Christianity was to those who could take its tenets on trust and not ask awkward questions.

Judaism in the second century did not have to contend so much with such problems, since its theology was simpler and less systematic and its people were better educated. But it did have to emphasise discipline and require adherence to the code formulated in the Mishnah as a statement of the Oral Law. There were some scandals arising from Gnostic dualism and sectarian activities. But the Synagogue unlike the Church did not stress the other-worldly, and looked forward in faith to the day of redemption and restoration. Its chief difficulty at this period lay with those whose impatience led them again to contemplate violent action for the deliverance of Israel. Two Jewish revolts were staged, initially with considerable success. The first, in the reign of Trajan, in A.D. 115–16, was mainly outside Palestine, in Mesopotamia, Cyprus, Cyrene and Egypt. This was quelled by the Roman generals Lusius Quietus and Q. Marcius Turbo. The second attempt in A.D. 132–5, in the reign of Hadrian, was almost entirely confined to Palestine. This had far greater religious justification and was also more protracted, as in Simon Bar-Cochba the Jews had a Messianic leader of great courage and skill, and fought with fanatical zeal. Hadrian had to bring his ablest general C. Julius Severus from Britain before the Romans finally got the upper hand, and their casualties were exceptionally heavy. Jewish suffering was equal to if not greater than in the war of A.D. 66–70. A new pagan city Aelia Capitolina was established by Hadrian on the site of Jerusalem, and for some time to come Jews were forbidden entrance except once a year. But a Christian church found a lodging in the city under a Gentile bishop Marcus.

These events in Jewish history undoubtedly influenced current Christian thinking in two respects. They reinforced anti-Judaic feeling among Christians, who now found themselves further confirmed in the conviction that the Jews had been repudiated by God for their rejection of Christ, and they encouraged those who favoured a heavenly rather than an earthly kingdom as the reward for believers. Well before the end of the second century the Christian Church had passed beyond its recall to the aims and faith of Jesus and his original Jewish followers. Henceforth the Jesus of Christianity would be alien to his brethren, and indeed their enemy and persecutor through the teaching and example of the Church, and Jesus as purely Jew and human Messiah would be alien to Christians for whom he had become the incarnation of the Second Person of the Trinity.

The dichotomising of Jesus effectively dichotomised the

People of God. In their circumscribed relationships with one another neither Jews nor Christians could any longer see straight or think straight. The chief sufferer was mankind, with whose peace and wellbeing both professed to be concerned. For the duration of the great schism, however long it might continue, the power-drunkenness of imperialism in various guises, associated with the name of Rome at the crucial period of our story, would continue to dominate the human scene. The Messianic Hope of a Kingdom of God among men based on mutual service would remain unfulfilled.

NOTES AND REFERENCES

1. Jude 5–23.
2. II. Peter ii–iii. 9.
3. Rev. ii–iii.
4. Justin, *First Apology*, xxvi.
5. Athenagoras, *A Plea for the Christians*, iii.
6. Mt. xix. 10–12.
7. Translated by M. R. James, *The Apocryphal New Testament*, p. 272 ff.
8. Justin, *First Apology*, xxix.
9. *The Gospel of Thomas*, sayings 38 and 23. See *The Secret Sayings o, Jesus* by Robert M. Grant and David Noel Freedman (*Fontana Books*), which provides a valuable commentary on each saying as well as an excellent study of the background and associations of the work.
10. Translated by M. R. James, *The Apocryphal New Testament*. See p. 252 ff.
11. See the *Book of James*, or *Protevangelium* (tr. by M. R. James, *The Apocryphal New Testament*, p. 38 ff.).
12. *The Gospel of Thomas* (tr. by M. R. James, *The Apocryphal New Testament*, p. 49 ff.).
13. Babylonian Talmud, *Shabbath*, 116a–b. The incident can be dated in the first quarter of the second century. See Travers Herford, *Christianity in Talmud and Midrash*, p. 146 ff.
14. Athenagoras, *A Plea for the Christians*, xi.
15. I. Cor. i. 26–7.
16. *The Teaching of the Twelve Apostles* (*Didache*) contains such a code. We have several examples of a compendium of the ethical sayings of Jesus, one of which is given in Justin's *First Apology*, xv–xvi.
17. Origen, *Against Celsus*, I. ix.

18. Origen, *Against Celsus*, III. x–xv.

19. Lucian, *The Death of Peregrine*, 11–13 (tr. by H. W. and F. G. Fowler); *The Works of Lucian of Samosata*, vol. iv, p. 82 f.

20. *The Teaching of the Twelve Apostles*, xi. 3–xii. 5 (tr. by Kirsopp Lake); *The Apostolic Fathers*, vol. i, p. 327 ff.

14

The Christian Problem

SO FAR as the theme of this book is concerned there is no call to pursue further the history of the Church either externally or internally. Within one hundred and fifty years of the death of Jesus the Christian Faith in its principal features had in substance assumed the form in which it would be perpetuated. There would be changes and challenges in respect of particular doctrines, and when after another hundred and fifty years Christianity became the official religion of the Roman Empire there would be additional accommodations to paganism. But what are still regarded as Christian fundamentals had been sufficiently defined to make it possible to speak in terms of broad convictions. Once this stage had been reached the Church could begin to make much greater conquests in converting to its teaching whole tribes and peoples: it could move from the defensive to the offensive.

From the beginning of the third century Christianity was subjected to intense persecution at the hands of the Romans under various emperors, and this helped to promote a large measure of unity. The persecution was itself one of the symptoms of the manner in which the Empire was deteriorating, and finally Christianity came to be seen as a powerful force for promoting and restoring integration. Its services were enlisted in support of its former adversary.

In the course of our survey we have considered some of the more important circumstances and individual contributions which affected the evolution of Christianity. The resultant religion was a remarkable achievement in spiritual architecture and creative engineering incorporating both old ideas and novel features. It was clearly marked out for a successful future. Here, indeed, was a great religion which stood in the tradition of the great religions of the past civilisations of the Near East, of Egypt and Babylon, infused with the purer spirit of Hebrew monotheism, morality and prophetic universalism, and the exalted philosophical concepts of the Greeks. Here the venerable Nature and Saviour cults were given new life in a Faith which could therefore satisfy the emotional requirements of the common man, and at the same time invest him with dignity as a person, both cared for by God and assured of eternal happiness with God. Here in fact was a religion which lifted Gentilism on to a higher plane, sublimating its grossness and removing its neuroses, while satisfying its intellectual demand for a comprehensive theology.

Under the name of Jesus Christ the God-man doctrine was brought to a peak of cosmic dramatic expression linking heaven and earth, the world of spirit and the everyday life of human experience, capable of meeting the need of every kind of worshipper and devotee that such a concept could attract. In the Church there was also laid under tribute the Jewish vision of a People of God, which produced the sense of a new collectivity guided and inspired by God, purposeful in its corporate programme and assured in respect of its ultimate destiny. In what Christianity supplied over a long period of social development, especially in the West, and in the ways in which its ethics and doctrines assisted that development, it was of great value, even if at times it impeded rather than aided progress by reason of its spokemen's inflexibility. It was needed and it appeared.

But nothing of all this has any relevance to the question of whether what Christianity has taught is true. That any religion works does not mean that it is right. It is in the nature of all religions that they should work for those who are persuaded that they represent the determined vehicle of communication between the Seen and the Unseen. From primitive times the divinities have manifested themselves to those who had faith in them, have guided, protected, punished, and answered petitions. A thousand years and more before Christianity prayer was being addressed to 'Our Lord' and to 'Our Lady' as well. The history of religion, as of society for which it caters, is one of intellectual progress, but fundamentally religion because of its function, and because the human animal as a whole has changed so little, continues to reflect the instinctive responses of man to the mysteries with which he is surrounded both near and far. This is predominantly at a low level.

In its development Christianity assumed the form of another religion, and gradually furnished itself with all the apparatus of a religion in the antique sense, ritual, liturgy, priesthood, holy places and persons. By so doing it exhibited a preference, to be linked more closely with the heritage of the religious past than with the forces beginning to move away from a cultic expression of a spiritual ideology.

Looking back in all honesty, which has been the object of this volume, it is possible to speak of a retrograde movement in Christianity and of a lost opportunity. At first the circumstances seemed to favour a very considerable break-through. Philosophically, the old mythologies were being discredited and allegorised. There was a disposition to synthesise and an eager spirit of speculative inquiry was abroad. Christianity was born in the pure monotheistic environment of Judaism, a Faith which had passed beyond idolatry. It was possessed of a challenging dynamic in the universalistic message of Messianism. The destruction of the Temple at Jerusalem as a ritualistic cult centre provided a chance of escape into a freer atmosphere of worship than in buildings made by hands. There was an exciting fresh enterprise to be pursued in preparing mankind for the end of war and the downfall of power-politics and the transformation of the world into the pleasant and peaceful Kingdom of God. There had been many visions of the brotherhood of man, but concrete action could now be taken to contribute to their realisation. Religion in the old sense could be left behind, so that humanity could enjoy the fuller life of the unimpeded circulation of the Spirit.

But all too quickly it appeared that the Gentiles were no more ready for the teaching of Jesus than the Hebrews had been for the teaching of Moses and the Prophets. They wanted a god after the imagination of their pagan hearts and were given him in Jesus Christ. Messianism went into cold storage, and stage by stage Christianity took on the colouring and trappings of its non-Jewish environment. It did preserve, however, the evidences of its origin by insisting that there was one God and by safeguarding the historicity of Jesus. Consequently the potentiality was there throughout the centuries for the revival in one form or another of the original impulses whenever conditions in general were conducive to their expression. In this respect Christianity as a religion has always carried within itself what eventually would be bound to bring about its destruction.

Of course the conversion of Christianity into a religion of the Gentiles may be viewed differently, as a means of loosening the ties of heathenism and in this way providing a halfway house on the road towards greater enlightenment and the elimination of superstition. It may be well here to quote a Roman Catholic authority.

'One of the elements of the religious life . . . without in any way modifying the intransigence of Christian Monotheism, attenuated, as we might say, that which its apparent severity might make difficult to accept in the case of relatively primitive minds accustomed to all the religious varieties of polytheism. The cultus of the saints, which began with that of the martyrs, provided them with a satisfaction which they instinctively sought, and carried on the idea of a populous heaven such as they loved, and an earth in which many localities were as before consecrated by the memory of holy presences. . . . Christianity, which provided an answer to the highest aspirations of souls eager to find a truly divine God, adapted itself in this way to the instinctive human desire to find a religion near to mankind, and this in two ways. First and foremost it did so by its doctrine of the Incarnate God, who really became a man among men, but it also did so by this practice of the cult of the saints which, by introducing between man and God a chain of intercessors and friends, seemed to shorten the distance and bring about the union between earth and heaven.'[1]

The same authority might have gone very much further in listing Christian accommodations to heathenism, the most notable example of which is the elevation of the Virgin Mary as Mother of God to the place occupied by the ancient Mother Goddess and Queen of Heaven. Not for nothing were Christian churches often erected on the sites of pagan temples.

It has long been the contention of Protestantism of the old school that what it was pleased to call Popery was nothing else but 'baptised Paganism', and there is ample evidence that in many connections the designation is appropriate. A good deal of it was collected in that curious but still illuminating nineteenth-century work *The Two Babylons*[2] by the Reverend Alexander Hislop, where the author sought to establish conclusively 'that Rome is in very deed the Babylon of the Apocalypse; that the essential character of her system, the grand objects of her worship, her festivals, her doctrine and discipline, her rites and ceremonies, her priesthood and their orders, have all been derived from ancient Babylon; and, finally, that the Pope himself is truly and properly the lineal representative of Belshazzar'.

The point that needs to be made about the Reformation is that it was only in the atmosphere of the radical changes taking place in Europe from the thirteenth to the sixteenth century, socially, politically, culturally and intellectually, that it could begin to become apparent to many Christians how much of heathen ways and superstitions had found their way into the Church. When men were being driven forward into a new age of enlightenment they could then discover, as by a revelation, that the Church had been the legatee of heathenism and in many respects constituted a refined by nevertheless anachronistic idolatry which had been outgrown.

What the Protestants could not readily detect was that the fundamental doctrines of the Church deriving by interpretation from the New Testament were involved just as much as the more blatant paganisms of Catholicism. The Church had not started to go wrong in the fourth century. The process had begun in the first century A.D. with the movement of Christianity into association with an alien religious environment. To an appreciable extent Protestantism was only reverting to an earlier and less contaminated phase of the process of Gentilisation. It was not capable of going behind it, or seeing any necessity to do so, since it was imagined that through the New Testament contact had been made with the original content of the Christian Faith. To advance further, towards the questioning and repudiation of second-century Christianity, was not possible before the dawn of the Age of Reason and the arrival of Unitarianism, though this did not seriously affect the continuance of Protestantism any more than the Reformation had affected the continuance of Roman Catholicism.

By being less hidebound, however, less tied to fixed positions, Protestantism took the Church forward into an area of greater flexibility of opinion where the individual conscience became a higher authority than what the Church decreed. To this extent it provided a spiritual liberation which opened up the possibility of moving with the times in a manner far beyond what was practicable for Catholicism. The Catholic has had to wait until today for a very cautious movement, hedged with reservations, in the same direction.

Even so, the modern Protestant talk of a New Reformation[3] is not really due to an initiative from within, but a response to the external pressures of a period which has witnessed more striking and far-reaching changes than those which sparked off the first Reformation. As a result both society in general has become much more critical of the Christian dogmas, and

Christian scholars much more analytical and objective in their treatment of the Gospels and the origins of Christianity. There was nothing that need be regarded as sacrosanct, taken for granted or at face value. The field of religious inquiry was fully open to all, with the specialists and theologians only having a pull in so far as they were better equipped with the requisite learning.

What has been happening for many people, both inside and outside the churches, has been a quite tremendous jump into maturity which has made everything specifically Christian, except its social and ethical implications, appear irrelevant and legendary. For most people in the West religion has meant Christianity, and consequently in rejecting the Christian God and the doctrine of his incarnation in Jesus Christ with all the attendant miracles there has been a pronounced trend towards agnosticism and atheism. This is not because of a desire for irreligion, but because the religion of the Church no longer made sense in terms both of knowledge of the universe and of the terrifying state of world affairs.

The Church has had every reason to see the red light and to be conscious that it is lagging well behind contemporary ideas of what must be done to extricate mankind from its perilous situation. There is new emphasis on the social and political responsibilities of Christianity, and divers attempts to create a new theology which will not be divorced except in expression and interpretation from the old. The disunity of the Church is regarded as a great weakening of its witness, and ecumenism is seeking to remedy this grave defect. But so far there does not appear to be any real awareness of the nature of the Christian problem, and solutions are not to be found either in modern gnostic-type theologies or in going over to a religionless Christianity such as Bonhoeffer foresaw.[4]

Obviously very serious and perceptive thinking is called for. The Church is losing out all the time that its representatives hum and haw and flap about, making their pronouncements with so much qualification that people are confused and exasperated. Ecumenism could mean not a fresh definition of the Christian message to lead mankind forward towards the Kingdom of God, which is what is needed, but a defeatist retreat from reality and relapse into sacerdotal obscurantism and an out-dated near idolatry. If this should happen Christianity has no future except for the minority of the faithful. The Gospel must always be ahead, infused with a dynamic that calls men into co-operation with a plan to change the world infinitely for the better, otherwise it is no Gospel at all. The original Gospel promised peace on earth and the overthrow of power-politics, not by reason that God had incarnated and suffered with and for men—that doctrine was the first Christian heresy—but by reason that the Messiah (the Christ) had appeared to prepare a people to govern the nations in righteousness on a basis of service, and would reappear when that people was ready for its appointed function. The suffering of the Messiah at the hands of the rulers of the existing world order witnessed that all the people of God must suffer under that order in the worthwhile cause of the redemption of mankind so as to have their love of humanity intensified and therefore to be fit to reign. The new world order would be built on all that love implies of sacrifice, devotion, forbearance, conciliation and affection.

The pages of this book have been designed to illustrate the progressive movement of Christianity away from its initial inspiration, not by going to the Gentiles but by falling into the ways of the Gentiles, which were idolatrous, deifying the Messiah and building a Gentilised religion around that deification. To clarify the process the conjunction of Jewish history with Christian history has been indispensable. It has required more than nineteen centuries for it to begin to be practicable for a pure monotheistic conception of God to be accepted by Gentiles, just as it took nearly all the time from Abraham to Jesus for the Hebrews to do so. The dilemma of the Church is that it finds itself unprepared for this change. Through its tradition, which it asserts to be the Truth, it remains enmeshed in the Gentilised faith of its devising, and cannot readily extricate itself.[5] Once that tradition was in advance of Gentile religious thinking in the West; but now it is substantially in arrears. Its concern still is to expound a doctrine of God that requires that at a certain moment of history God uniquely manifested himself corporeally in the man Jesus. Consequently the Church still looks askance at the Jews with some remains of an ancient antisemitism because Judaism from which Christianity sprang excludes such a notion. The Church cannot even bring itself to ponder meaningfully and constructively the Messiahship of Jesus in a Jewish sense. Where it assents at all to the proposition that Jesus believed himself to be the Messiah it has to propound by a falsification that Jesus rejected the contemporary Jewish interpretation of the Messianic office. It refuses to contemplate that Jesus was just the kind of Messiah that spiritually-minded Jews had anticipated. By all means the Messiahship must be subordinated to the Incarnation thesis.

Reading through reams of modern Christian theology it is hard to find any awareness that the Messianism which gave Christianity its name, Messianism in its native Jewish expression, may hold the secret which could give the Church life from the dead.[6] We must say that either Messianism was the essence of the Gospel, or that Christianity from its very inception was a fraud. Everything else can go, but here is the rock on which the Kingdom of God was to be founded. As a religion Christianity is an anachronism. As a Messianic enterprise for mankind channelled through a sentient dedicated nation it has pressing and desperately needed work to do. If help does not come from a combined Christian and Jewish effort then salvation will come from another quarter, and the Kingdom will be given to a nation bringing forth the fruits thereof. But what a revolution is involved if the Messianic impetus initiated by the Jew Jesus is to be regained! We have looked very sharply and without blinkers at *Those Incredible Christians* in hope that the ecclesiastical mind may be capable of making a positive response. If it cannot the Christian laity may be able to take over. It is at least a pointer in the right direction that the burden of Christian thought now is the Church in the World. Substitute for the Church, which today has such an institutional flavour, the People of God, politically as well as spiritually, and the Gospel could go forth again with unarmed and persuasive power, the power of example.

This book must therefore close on an invitation, which is also a prayer, for Christians to turn with new insight to the consideration of what our story has revealed, not in anger but in meditation. The old rabbis said these things: 'Be rather the object of curses than curse thyself.'[7] 'A man should always be among the persecuted rather than among the persecutors; for of birds, none are so persecuted as turtle-doves and pigeons, and yet Scripture has designated them as an offering on the altar.'[8] 'They who being reviled revile not again, who take no heed of insults, and act out of love, rejoicing in afflictions, of them Scripture says, "Them that love him are as the sun when he goeth forth in his strength".'[9] This is what being a Jew meant to Jesus, as we may see in the Sermon on the Mount. And this is why Christians must go back to the beginning and search out anew in the context of the Jewish vision, which the Church forsook, the mysteries of the Kingdom of God.

NOTES AND REFERENCES

1. See 'The Triumph of Christianity', Bk. IV of *A History of the Early Church*, by Jules Lebreton, S.J. and Jacques Zeiller, p. 356 f., Collier Catholic Readers Series.

2. See the Introduction, p. 3 of *The Two Babylons*.

3. See, for example, *The New Reformation?* by John A. T. Robinson, Bishop of Woolwich, S.C.M. Press.

4. D. Bonhoeffer *Letters and Papers from Prison*. The title is *Prisoner for God* in the American edition.

5. T. E. Lawrence (Lawrence of Arabia) rightly pointed out in *The Seven Pillars of Wisdom* that 'Christianity is a hybrid faith compounded of the Semitic as to its origin, and the non-Semitic as to its development. It therefore carries within itself a problem, which as yet it is unwilling to resolve, and of

which indeed it is not correctly aware . . . due to the extraordinary manner in which the Semitism in Christianity has been sublimated.'

6. As illustration the quotations may be consulted in the books by the Bishop of Woolwich, *Honest to God* and *The New Reformation?*

7. The Talmud, *Shabbath*, fol. 1. 55a.

8. The Talmud, *Aboda Zara*, fol. 93a.

9. The Talmud, *Baba Kama*, fol. 93a.

Supplementary Studies

1. THE CHRISTOLOGY OF PAUL

THE key to Paul's christology is to be found in the kind of man he was, in his training, and in his need to expound his religious philosophy both for the benefit of his Gentile converts and his own self-justification.

We know a great deal about Paul's personality from his writings and autobiographical statements, how intelligent he was, how sensitive and introspective. Since we have already given some account of him and his teaching in chapters 4–7 of this book it is needful only to recall here that by birth and upbringing Paul was a Pharisee, identified in the most impressionable period of his life with the doctrine and discipline of this form of Judaism. As a youth he came to Jerusalem to study the Torah, and is said to have sat at the feet of the famous Rabban Gamaliel. The information is important because it directs us where to seek for knowledge that will explain Paul's concept of Christ.

The Christian idea of Pharisaism is that it was predominantly legalistic, whereas it was also highly speculative and theologically profound. The Pharisaic faith included belief in angels and demons, the mapping of the heavenly abodes, Paradise and Gehinnom, magic and astrology, the mystery of the Archetypal Man, special creation and pre-existence, the Above and Below, the Messiah, transmigration of souls, revelation and Divine intervention, predestination, the Day of Judgment, the resurrection of the body, and the life everlasting. Pharisaism had its esoteric aspect, and those who were specially trained and qualified could follow the difficult and dangerous path that led directly to the heavenlies, and permitted access—to use the phrase employed—'behind the Curtain'. How hazardous was this undertaking may be gathered from the account given of the four rabbis who, some fifty years after Paul's death, penetrated into Paradise, of whom one died, one went out of his mind, the third became confused in his theology, and only the fourth returned in peace.[1]

We are given clues in Paul's letters which indicate that as a young man he had delved deeply into Jewish occultism. He had a disposition towards mysticism, heightened perhaps by a physical ailment, an unprepossessing appearance, and a certain morbidity and egocentricity. For the satisfaction of his inmost cravings, his desire for righteousness and holiness, it was natural that he should gravitate towards the higher ranges of his religion, those pursuits and exercises which could offer the prospect of full communion with God. He tells us that his aim was to satisfy and please God, and set himself accordingly to advance in Judaism 'far beyond many students of my own age: for none was more keenly enthusiastic than I to master the traditions of my ancestors'.[2] He makes reference to the knowledge of mysteries and secret lore,[3] and claims to have undergone the experience of being caught up into Paradise, the third heaven, and there having heard 'ineffable words which no human is permitted to utter'.[4]

The rabbis distinguished seven heavens, and seven stages or degrees of initiation. Being caught up to the third heaven, called *Pardes* (the Garden), answered to the third degree. We have an account of how one day the prophetically gifted first-century rabbi Jochanan ben Zakkai was conversing on esoteric matters with two of his colleagues. 'In my dream,' said R. Jochanan, 'I and ye were resting upon Mount Sinai, and the sound of a voice (*Bath Kol*) was sent to us from heaven, saying: "Come up hither, come up hither! Large banqueting couches are prepared and fair coverlets are spread for you, you and your disciples and their disciples, as fitted to attain to the third degree of blessedness." '[5] There were two main divisions of occult study, the one concerned the mysteries of the Creation in Genesis (*Ma'aseh Bereshith*), and the other concerned the Heavenly Chariot in Ezekiel (*Ma'aseh Merkabah*). It is laid down in the Mishnah: 'Men are not to expound . . . the Lore of Creation with two persons, nor the Lore of the Chariot with one; but if a man do so, he must be a wise man, and one who has much knowledge of his own. Everyone who meddles with the following four things it were better for him if he had not come into the world, namely, what is Above and what is Below, what is Before and what is After. And everyone who does not revere the glory of his Maker (i.e. detracts from God's Unity), it were better for him if he had not come into the world.'[6]

Much has been made by certain scholars of evidence that Paul was acquainted with the mystery cults of Asia Minor, and no doubt he does sometimes borrow their terminology. But these cults were pagan and he was a Jew: it is not therefore to these sources but to the occultism of the Pharisees that we must turn for an understanding of Paul's christology. Naturally a great deal of this teaching was not committed to writing, but there are sufficient remains to enable us to elucidate Paul's ideas and to perceive that in them he was making public much that he had learnt for the benefit of believers, giving out within limits mysteries which previously had not been made known. It was his great sorrow that his converts were still so physically minded that it was impossible to initiate them into many of the spiritual profundities.[7]

In two passages Paul makes reference to the Four Things mentioned in the Mishnah. The first is where he says, 'I am convinced that neither death nor life, neither angels nor ruling spirits, neither Present nor Future, neither Powers Above nor Powers Below, nor any other created being, will be able to sever us from the love of God which is in Christ Jesus our

Master.'[8] The second is where he prays for his converts that God 'may grant you by his Spirit to be powerfully strengthened in the inner self, that the Christ may make his abode in your minds by faith, that being deep-rooted and well-founded in love you may be able to grasp with all the saints what is the Breadth, the Length, the Depth and the Height, that you may know, what indeed surpasses knowledge, the love of Christ, that you may be filled with the immensity of God'.[9]

As we shall endeavour to make clear, Paul had specialised in the Lore of Creation rather than in that of the Chariot. This Lore dealt with the inner meaning and significance of the Creation and with the primitive nature of man in his relationship with God. No doubt it was influenced by Chaldean and platonic cosmogonical speculations, but these had been poured into a Jewish monotheistic mould. At times, it is true, the teaching became so involved that it came perilously near to detracting from the Divine Unity, as it sought to describe how the visible universe proceeded from the invisible, and had to pull up short when the borderline was reached. Some Jewish initiates failed to stop and lapsed into Dualistic heresy or mental confusion. The great questions were, What relationship to God had his self-expression (word) in Creation? and, How was man related to that self-expression?

In seeking to answer these questions the grave danger was always present that the Agency of Creation should be regarded as the Being rather than as the manifestation of the capacity of God, or that it should be thought to be God in detachment by manifestation, and thus real but lesser God. Were there in fact Two Powers in heaven? We know how later Christianity and Gnosticism dealt with these issues; but we are concerned with how Paul did and on what basis in Jewish mystical teaching.

The chief Pauline documents which treat of these matters are Ephesians, Philippians and Colossians. But there are passages in earlier writings Corinthians and Romans, and perhaps earlier still Galatians. None of the documents is peculiarly devoted to metaphysics. Usually Paul's highest mystical flights are set in conjunction with exhortations on personal conduct, on which they bear directly; and this is a distinctly Jewish trait. The Hebrew spirit will soar eagerly into the heavenly spheres, but rarely stays there: it returns to the workaday world: it insists that ideals shall be translated into action, precept into practice, the spiritual applied to the physical, the abstract to the concrete. This is why in the Jewish and Pauline teaching the heavenly and earthly processes are linked with Adam (Man).

The essential element in the teaching is that the visible universe conforms to a pattern or design, which represents the image of the Invisible God who, himself, has neither form nor substance. Man, the crown of creation, being made in the image of God, answers therefore completely to the original pattern, which thus may be conceived as a manlike figure. This primordial or archetypal man, the 'heavenly man' of Philo and the *Adam Kadmon* of the Jewish occultists, is the true image of God, the beginning of the creation and the lord of it. Hence the first man on earth was given dominion over every living thing in it.[10]

The earthly Below is witness to the heavenly Above. Adam points us to the *Adam Kadmon*, the earthly Paradise to the heavenly Paradise, the earthly Temple to the heavenly Temple, the Jerusalem below to the Jerusalem above. There are two realms, the imperfect visible-material and the perfect invisible-spiritual, but there is a counterpart relationship between them. We see man, therefore, as wearing physically the likeness of his spiritual archetype, and that archetype is the expression of the nature of God. But neither man is God, nor the archetype is God, since the spiritual though normally invisible to man is not bodiless, and God is without form or substance. Both man and archetype are creations by means of the Spirit of God or Holy Spirit, which is to be distinguished from spiritual beings; and both man and archetype in their turn and by the same Spirit have been endowed with creative ability in their respective spheres. By way of analogy we may think of the relationship of the archetype to God as resembling the relationship between the ideas of an author and himself, and of man to the archetype as the committing of those ideas to writing.

But for what purpose was man created? His creation must have had to do with the Messianic Plan, and the soul of Adam must have been knit with the soul of the ultimate Messiah (Christ). It was therefore to be deduced that the archetypal or heavenly man was also the pre-existing spiritual counterpart of the Messiah, the heavenly Spirit-Christ. Thinking on these lines was going on in Jewish esoteric circles. In an old midrash we find this teaching: ' "Thou has formed me behind and before" (Ps. cxxxix. 5) is to be explained "before the first and after the last day of Creation". For it is said, "And the spirit of God moved upon the face of the waters", by which is meant the spirit of Messiah, of whom it is said (Isa. xi. 2), "And the spirit of the Lord shall rest upon him." '[11]

The doctrine is also expressed in the *Similitudes of Enoch*, where is is said: 'And before the sun and the (zodiacal) signs were created, before the stars of the heaven were made, his name (i.e. the name of the Son of Man) was named before the Lord of Spirits. He will be a staff to the righteous on which they will lean and not fall, and he will be the light of the Gentiles and the hope of those who are troubled in heart. All who dwell on earth will fall down and bow the knee before him and will bless and laud the Lord of Spirits. And for this reason has he been chosen and hidden before him before the creation of the world and for evermore. And the wisdom of the Lord of Spirits has revealed him to the holy and righteous. . . .'[12]

The identification of the archetypal heavenly man with the Messianic Son of Man and Elect One thus allowed for the mystical union between the Christ above and the Christ below as defined by Paul's Ebionite opponents. According to the Ebionites, 'Jesus was begotten of the seed of man, and was chosen; and so by that choice he was called Son of God from the Christ that entered into him from above in the likeness of a dove. But they deny that he (the Christ above) was begotten of God the Father, and say that he was created like one of the archangels, yet greater, and that he is lord of angels and of all things made by the Almighty . . . a manlike figure, invisible to men in general.' So reports Epiphanius, Bishop of Constantia.[13] The union between the Messiah above and the Messiah below was effected at the baptism of Jesus by the agency of the Holy Spirit, which thus became in the adoptive sense the mother of Jesus. The union was not between God and man, but between the heavenly Adam (Son of Man) and the earthly second Adam (Son of Man). So it was written in the *Gospel of the Hebrews*: 'And it came to pass, when Jesus had come up out of the water, the entire fountain of the Holy Spirit descended and rested upon him and said to him, "My son, in all the prophets did I await thee, that thou mightest come and I might rest in thee. Thou art my rest: thou art my firstborn son that reignest for ever." '[14] In the same Gospel Jesus subsequently refers to the Holy Spirit as his mother.[15]

When we turn to Paul's writings it becomes evident that his teaching is on the same lines. There is, however, the difference with Paul that he regards the heavenly Messiah as the sole Messiah, who by an act of temporary redemptive renunciation became the man Jesus. In Paul's words the Christ is 'the image of the Unseen God, the firstborn of all creation, that everything in heaven and earth might be founded on him, seen and unseen alike, whether angelic Thrones or Lordships or Rulers or Authorities. Everything was created through him and for him. He is the antecedent of everything, and on him (i.e. as the archetype) everything was framed. So also is he the Head of the Body, the Community, that is to say, the fount and origin of it, the firstborn from the dead, that in every connection he might take precedence. For it pleased God that by him the whole should be governed, and through him—his making peace by the blood of the cross—to bring everything into harmony with himself (i.e. with God), whether on earth or in heaven. You yourselves were formerly alienated . . . but now Christ has reconciled you to God in his physical body by death. . . .'[16]

Paul's Christ is not God, he is God's first creation, and there is no room for the trinitarian formula of the Athanasian Creed, nor for its doctrine that the Son was 'not made, nor created, but begotten'. But inasmuch as the visible universe is the expression of the Invisible God, the Christ, as first-product, comprises the whole of that expression in himself.

The archetypal man was necessarily conceived by the Jewish occultists as a vast universe-filling figure, and even the microcosm, the first man Adam upon earth, in his first state was held to be of gigantic stature. 'R. Eleazar said, The first man extended from the earth to the firmament, for it is said (Deut. iv. 32), "from the day that God created man *upon* the earth"; but inasmuch as he sinned, the Holy One, blessed be he, placed his hand upon him and made him small, as it is said, "and laid thine hand upon me".'[17] Adam in his sinless state was a being of transparent light, and only after his fall did he become opaque and skin-covered.

Accepting with Paul the equation of the Messiah with the *Adam Kadmon*, it required that he should cast aside his glory and 'make himself small' so as to atone for Adam's sin by the man Jesus and initiate the restoration of harmony between man and God, and between the visible universe and the Invisible God. By the resurrection there was restored in Jesus the light-body which the first man had possessed and forfeited, and the re-expansion of his stature in a manner comparable to that of the first man before the Fall. Thus ennobled and reintegrated with the *Adam Kadmon* Jesus was henceforth the Lord Jesus Christ.

So Paul writes: 'Let your disposition, indeed, be that of Christ Jesus, who though he had godlike form (i.e. as the archetypal man) did not regard it as a prize to be equal to God, but divested himself (i.e. put off the garment of light), taking the form of a servant. Appearing in human likeness, and disclosed in physical appearance as a man, he abased himself, and became subject to death, death by the cross. That is why God has so exalted him, that at the name of Jesus, every knee, heavenly, earthly and infernal, should bend, and every tongue acclaim Jesus Christ as Master, to the glory of God the Father.'[18]

Here we have the *Adam Kadmon*, the heavenly Christ, by manifestation in Jesus, reducing himself to the condition of Adam after the Fall, making himself therefore subject to death to redeem man from death. The sin of man was in yielding to the temptation of the Satan-serpent to eat the forbidden fruit and by the knowledge so acquired to be equal to God (Gen. iii. 5). The prophet Isaiah makes the lordly king of Babylon guilty of the same sin: 'Thou hast said in thine heart, I will ascend into heaven, I will exalt my throne above the stars of God: I will sit also upon the mount of the congregation, in the sides of the north: I will ascend above the heights of the clouds; I will be like the Most High' (Isa. xiv. 13–14). The heavenly Christ did not yield to this temptation to be as God, and it is again evident that Paul did not think of Christ as God, only as being created in the image of God as the archetypal man and therefore having a godlike form: otherwise to be equal to God would have been nothing to grasp at or aspire to. Instead the Christ temporarily in Jesus surrendered every attribute of his spiritual state and became wholly human and devoid of superhumanity. We meet with the same doctrine in Heb. ii.: 'Since, therefore, the children have human nature, so did he share it equally with them. . . . For where was the point of lending a helping hand to angels? It was the offspring of Abraham that needed a helping hand. Consequently it was essential for him to become *in every respect* like his brothers.' Thus it is ruled out that Jesus had any superhuman qualities. His only special endowment was at his baptism, when he received the gifts of the Spirit promised to the Messiah in wisdom and understanding

(Isa. xi. 1–4). The heavenly Christ only took over when Jesus was raised from the dead and ascended to heaven (Rom. i. 4). Then it could be disclosed that there had been this brief abdication.

Paul is very clear, as it will be needful to further illustrate later, that spiritual bodies and physical bodies do not combine. Therefore Jesus as flesh and blood human being could not identify with the heavenly Christ until he had discarded a physical body and assumed a spiritual. It would have been quite impossible for him to accept the physical resurrection of Jesus, as in the Gospels, and repugnant that the risen Jesus should be able to eat and drink. He told the Philippians: 'Our form of government originates in heaven, from which source we expect a Deliverer, the Lord Jesus Christ, who will transform the body of our humble state so that it corresponds to his glorious body by the power which also enables him to bring everything under his control' (iii. 20–1). Christ in the physical sense was to be known no more.

Because of the supremacy of the heavenly Christ, with whom Jesus is now compounded, it is not for the saints, as Paul argues, to be subject to any lesser controls as if they were still ruled by them, for the saints in Jesus Christ share the totality and the rulership by anticipation. He chides those who follow human tradition instead of Christ. 'It is in him (the archetype) that the immensity of the divine wisdom corporately dwells, and it is in him—Head of all Rulers and Authorities—that you are made complete. . . . If you have died with Christ to the elemental forces of the world, why as though still living in the world are you controlled by stipulations. . . . If, therefore, you have been raised up with Christ, seek the things that are on high where Christ is, seated at God's right hand. Set your minds on the things that are above, not on what is on earth. . . . Having divested yourselves of the former man and his deeds, and having put on the new man, renovated in knowledge, in conformity with the likeness of God who created him, there can be no question of Greek or Jew, circumcision and uncircumcision, Barbarian, Scythian, slave or freeman, but of Christ wholly and completely.'[19]

Paul adapts Jewish mystical teaching for his own purpose, and we may compare his words to what is stated in the *Similitudes of Enoch*: 'And the Lord of Spirits will abide over them (i.e. the elect), and with that Son of Man will they eat and lie down and rise up for ever and ever. And the righteous and the elect will have risen from the earth, and ceased to be of downcast countenance, and will have been clothed with garments of glory. And these shall be your garments, garments of life before the Lord of Spirits; and your garments shall not grow old, and your glory will not pass away before the Lord of Spirits.'[20]

According to Paul the community of believers represents the Messianic Body as Jesus Christ is its Head, and it is the work of redemption to transform that Body into the Messianic Body of Light, and so to bring about the same union between Church and Jesus Christ as had been accomplished between Jesus and Christ.

This teaching also has a relationship to the concept of the *Adam Kadmon*. In the archetypal man the attributes of God are made to correspond to the parts of the human body. These are the ten *Sefirot*. Surmounting the head is *Kether* (the Crown), the Head and Brain is *Chokma* (Wisdom), the Neck is *Binah* (Intelligence), the Breast is *Tiferet* (Beauty), the Right Arm is *Chesed* (Lovingkindness), the Left Arm is *Pahad* (Justice), the Belly is *Yesod* (Foundation), the Right Leg is *Netsach* (Firmness), the Left Leg is *Hod* (Splendour), and the Feet represent *Malchut* (Kingdom).[21] Of Christ's descent into Hades it is therefore said in the *Odes of Solomon*, a Christian quasi-Gnostic work, that 'the Head went down to the Feet', the feet being the pre-Christian saints, and of the resurrection which followed it is said that Hades 'let go the Head with the Feet'.[22]

By the resurrection of Jesus the universe-filling stature of Adam before the Fall has been restored, and the man Jesus has been made one with the archetypal man, the heavenly Christ.

Yet while this is so, there is a sense in which he is to be seen specifically as the Head, Wisdom wearing the Crown, and the totality of believers finally supplies the Body. By a spiritual process completed by their own resurrection they are to grow up until the Body effects a junction with the Head. Jesus and his people together personify the archetypal and ruling Spirit-Christ. Paul therefore prays for the Ephesians that 'you may be able to grasp with all the saints what is the Breadth, the Length, the Depth and the Height, that you may know, what indeed surpasses knowledge, the love of Christ, that you may be filled with *the immensity of God*. . . . That Jesus ascended implies that he also descended into the lower regions of the earth. He who descended is the same as he who ascended to the uppermost part of the heavens, that he might *fill the universe*.' The gifts then bestowed were for 'the development of the Body of Christ, until we all reach unity of faith and knowledge of the Son of God, *the Perfect Man*, *the measure of the stature of the full-grown Christ*. No longer should we be infants . . . but speaking the truth in love we should grow up collectively to him, Christ, who is the Head, from whom the whole Body closely joined together and knit by every connecting joint, corresponding to the respective action of each separate part, the growth of the Body is promoted for its harmonious development.'[23]

Paul utilises the Jewish esoteric teaching to convey his exhortations, and some of this same teaching passed on into Gnosticism from Jewish Christian sources. According to that curious document the *Acts of John* the two aspects of the macrocosm and the microcosm were already displayed on the Mount of Transfiguration:

'And at another time he (Jesus) taketh with him me (John) and James and Peter into the mountain where he was wont to pray, and we saw in him a light such as it is not possible for a man that useth corruptible speech to describe. . . . I, therefore, because he loved me, drew nigh unto him softly, as though he could not see me, and stood looking at his hinder parts: and I saw that he was not in any wise clad with garments, but was seen of us naked, and not in any wise as an (earthly) man, and that his feet were whiter than any snow, so that the earth was lighted up by his feet, and that his head touched the heaven; so that I was afraid and cried out, and he, turning about, appeared as a man of small stature, and caught hold of my beard and pulled it and said to me: John, be not faithless but believing. . . .'[24]

The account of the transfiguration, as we find it in the Gospels, is here expanded to emphasise the composite personality of Jesus Christ, not as God and man, but as archetypal man and earthly man. It was for the high purpose of redeeming the elect—and ultimately the earth itself—and incorporating the faithful in the Messianic personality that the pure image of God, which had incarnated in the first man, incarnated again in the debased image of God. The theme is beautifully expressed in the *Hymn of the Robe of Glory*, attributed to Bardaisan and preserved in the *Acts of Thomas*,[25] where we read how the son of the king and queen of the East was sent by his parents on a mission to Egypt to bring back the pearl of great price guarded by the serpent. Before he leaves his home he is divested of his robe of glory, and upon his arrival among the Egyptians he puts on their raiment 'lest I should seem strange, as one that had come from without to recover the pearl; and lest the Egyptians should arouse the serpent against me'. Eventually he succeeds in his mission.

'And I caught away the pearl and turned back to bear it unto my fathers.
And I stripped off the filthy garment and left it in their land,
And directed my way forthwith to the light of my fatherland in the East.'

There the robe of glory was waiting for him, and he put it on amidst general rejoicing. With all its mythological and cosmological trappings it is as if the hymn was dramatising the mystery of the Pauline letter to Timothy (I. Tim. iii. 16) which speaks of the Christ as:

Made visible physically,
Vindicated spiritually,
Seen by angels,
Proclaimed to the Gentiles,
Believed in in the world,
Taken up again in glory.

It is the archetypal man, the *Adam Kadmon*, as the image of God, which is the link between God and man, and as Christ the agent of man's redemption. 'There is One God, and one intermediary between God and man, the Man Christ Jesus' (I. Tim. ii. 5). And again, 'There is only one God, the Father, from whom all things derive, and to whom we belong, and one Lord Jesus Christ, through whom all things come, and by whom we are' (I. Cor. viii. 6). By one man sin entered into the world, and by one man grace has abounded. As in Adam all die, so in Christ will all be made alive. The first man was made a living soul; the second man a vitalising spirit. The first man is of the earth; the second man is from heaven. As we have worn the likeness of the earthly nature, so shall we wear the likeness of the heavenly nature (Rom. v; I. Cor. xv). For Paul the physical Jesus must no longer be the concern of believers. No longer do we know Christ after the flesh, for flesh and blood cannot enter the Kingdom of God. We must know only the Spirit-Christ so that we can be transformed into his glorious likeness through our own resurrection. We shall undergo a change, our perishable body will be exchanged for an imperishable like that of Christ. As Paul put it, 'This is what I sigh for, longing to be under cover of my dwelling from heaven; for so sheltered I shall not be left out in the cold. Yes, that is what I, living in this hutment, sigh for, not wanting to be deprived of cover but to be under cover, so that what is mortal may be swallowed up by Life' (II. Cor. v. 2–4).

By such reasoning, based on Jewish occultism, Paul is able to construct a coherent christological scheme, which through mystical Messianism explains on the one hand the relationship between God and the Cosmos in creation, and on the other hand the relationship of God and man in redemption. Out of and into the macrocosmic the microcosmic proceeds and returns. The unification of things in heaven and on earth is attained through the Messianic Head which comes down and the Messianic Body which rises up. Finally, after Christ has reigned until all enemies, the last being Death, have been subjugated, all things Above and Below will have been brought into harmony with God. Christ, the heavenly man created for the Creation, will have completed his function and hand over to the One who created him, that God may reign supreme (I. Cor. xv. 21–8; Rom. viii. 18–23).

The Jewish idea of the archetypal man, interpreted with reference to the Spirit-Christ, enabled Paul safely to avoid any diminution of the Unity of the Godhead and any suggestion that Christ was God. God has neither form nor substance; but the Spirit-Christ has both form and a spiritual body. Never anywhere does Paul identify Christ with God. His Father-Son relationship has no such implication, and the Father is 'the God of our Lord Jesus Christ'. There is One God, and one Lord Jesus Christ. The trinitarian formula, 'God the Father, God the Son, and God the Holy Ghost' is an unwarrantable adaptation of the Pauline doxology. Once we understand what Paul the Jewish mystic was driving at we can appreciate how far Gentilised Christian theology went astray.

NOTES AND REFERENCES

1. Talmud, *Chagiga*, fol. 14b.
2. Gal. i. 14.
3. I. Cor. xiii. 2.
4. II. Cor. xii. 2–4.
5. Talmud, *Chagiga*, fol. 12b and 14b.

6. Mishnah, *Chagiga*, ii.
7. See I. Cor. ii. 6–iii. 3.
8. Rom. viii. 38–9.
9. Eph. iii. 16–19.
10. Gen. i. 26; Ps. viii. 4–6 (cp. Heb. ii. 5–9).
11. *Genesis Rabba*, viii. 1.
12. *Sim. Enoch*, xlviii. 3–7 (tr. Charles).
13. Epiphanius, *Panarion*, xxx.
14. Quoted by Jerome, *Commentary on Isaiah*, xi. 2.
15. Quoted by Origen, *Commentary on John's Gospel*, iii. section 63.
16. Col. i. 15–22.
17. Talmud, *Chagigah*, fol. 12a.
18. Phil. ii. 5–11.
19. Col. ii. 8–iii. 11.
20. *Sim. Enoch*, lxii. 14–16 (tr. Charles).
21. See Jewish Encyclopaedia, article *Adam Kadmon* (Funk and Wagnalls).
22. *Odes of Solomon*, xxiii. 14; xlii. 18 (tr. Harris).
23. Eph. iii. 17–iv. 16.
24. *Acts of John* (tr. M. R. James, *The Apocryphal New Testament*).
25. *Acts of Thomas* (tr. M. R. James, *The Apocryphal New Testament*).

2. THE CHRISTOLOGY OF JOHN

THE area in which the Johannine writings were produced was the Roman province of Asia, and in particular the region fanning out to the north and south, eastward from Ephesus. A circuit of this region linked the cities of the Seven Churches to whom letters are addressed in the Revelation. The lower arm of the fan extended from Ephesus on the coast to Hierapolis, Laodicea and Colossae.

The geographical facts are of consequence because of the strong Pauline associations with the region. Paul had taught at Ephesus, having as one of his companions and co-workers Aristarchus the Macedonian, who is mentioned in Paul's letters to the Colossians and Philemon. We may also take note of Epaphras of Colossae, who visited Paul at Rome, and of whom he wrote to the Colossians, 'Invariably he contends for you at prayer times that you may stand, sound and fully assured, by the whole will of God. I can testify that he has put up a great fight for you, and for those of Laodicea and Hierapolis.'[1] Reference follows this passage to a letter of Paul to the Laodiceans, which some scholars identify with the one familiar to us as Ephesians.

Pauline teaching came under heavy attack in Asia, as we know from II. Timothy, 'You are well aware that all the Asiatic believers have turned from me.' But later on Paul's ideas, partly through pressure from the West, were restored to favour, and in considering the background to John's christology we have to remark that it is in the Pauline letters to the Ephesians and Colossians that the esoteric doctrine of the archetypal heavenly Christ finds its most pronounced expression. There is also the possibility that the letter to the Hebrews, having a kinship with Paulinism, was addressed to Jewish believers at Ephesus.

During Paul's stay in Ephesus we learn from the Acts of certain Jewish exorcists, who attempted to employ the name of Jesus to cast out demons and came to grief. The author continues, 'This became known to all the inhabitants of Ephesus, Jews and Greeks alike, and they were seized with fear, and the name of the Lord Jesus was magnified. Many of those who believed came and confessed, and made a clean breast of their practices. Several who were practitioners of magic made a bonfire of their books in the sight of all. The value was computed, and was found to come to fifty thousand pieces of silver.'[2] The story, whatever its historical merits, is at least in keeping with the conditions; for Ephesus was pre-eminent for addiction to curious arts. Here at the gate of Asia was piled up the magical merchandise of the East, charms and amulets, inscribed bowls from Babylonia, scrolls of conjurations, rigmaroles of queer Hebrew and Chaldean names to impress the superstitious, fragments of Scripture and apocalyptic writings. Teachers of every kind of strange religion could be sure of a following, and to Ephesus would naturally gravitate from Egypt men with Gnostic views like Cerinthus.

By the time John was writing, the christology of Paulinism had made substantial headway in Asia, and was being built upon and elaborated by association with Gnostic philosophy in Egypt deriving from a fusion of Jewish esotericism with Platonism in which the Jewish philosopher Philo of Alexandria had played no small part. Just as on the Jewish Christian side the archetypal man (*protos anthropos*) was identified by others, Jewish and Greek, with the Logos or Divine Reason.

The voluminous works of Philo of Alexandria (died c. A.D. 50) provide a happy hunting ground for material relating to the Logos. Speaking of the Creation, Philo tells us that light was an image of the Divine Word. It was an 'invisible light perceptible only by Mind'. From that 'all-brightness' the sun, moon, stars, and planets drew portions according to their capacity; but the very process of change from invisible light to visible light inevitably involved a diminution of light's pristine purity because it was dimmed by entering the sphere of the senses.[3] Similarly he tells us that when man was made in the image of God this did not imply bodily form in God. It was man's mind which reflected the Mind of the Universe as its archetype.[4] Those who live in the knowledge of the One are rightly called Sons of God (Deut. xiv. 1). 'But if there be any as yet unfit to be called a Son of God, let him press to take his place under God's Firstborn, the Word, who holds the eldership among the angels, their ruler as it were. And many names are his, for he is called, "the Beginning" (*arche*), and the Name of God, and his Word (*logos*), and the Man after his image.... For if we have not yet become fit to be thought sons of God yet we may be sons of his invisible image, the most holy Word. For the Word is the eldest-born image of God.'[5] In this respect 'We are all sons of one Man' (Gen. xlii. 11). Other Philonic descriptions of the Logos reach us again through Christian literature. The Logos is High Priest of God, without sin, shadowed forth by Melchizedek. He is 'an Advocate to obtain both forgiveness of sins and a supply of all good'. The Logos is the image (*eikon*) of God, by whom the whole universe was fashioned.

Another stream of thought about Mind and the Man flows from the Hermetic writings and passes on into Christian Gnosticism through various channels. But there is no need for us to pursue these developments.[6]

By the end of the first century A.D. Asian Christianity had come very strongly under the influence of the mystical persuasions which pointed to the Christ as archetypal man, the Word who was the image of the mind of God. It was a part of the world, as we have seen, which was predisposed towards such ideas. Here the Son of God Hermes had come down among men in disguise, and the Acts reports how at Lystra the apostles Paul and Barnabas were identified with Hermes and Zeus, so that the incarnation of the Word in Jesus for human salvation would not be an unacceptable proposition.

In John's time, when the younger Pliny was governor of Bithynia to the north-east, the report which the governor made to Trajan about the Christians included the information that 'they met on a certain fixed day before it was light and sang an antiphonal chant to Christ, as to a god'. The reference is most interesting for it advises us of a regular Christian practice relating in all probability to commemoration of Christ's resurrection on the first day of the week, which was held to have taken place before dawn. At this ceremony it would be appropriate to sing a dawn hymn in which Christ was hailed as the light. Significantly it is in Paul's letter to the Ephesians that we find what is probably a reference to the practice, where the writer declares, 'All visibility is due to light. This is why it is said,

> Rouse yourself, sleeper,
> And arise from the dead,
> And Christ shall shine on you.'[7]

This would be in accordance with the prophecy of Malachi foretelling the Day of Judgment and destruction of the wicked, taken to refer to the Second Advent, when 'unto you that fear my name shall the Sun of Righteousness arise with healing in his beams' (Mal. iv. 1–2).

But it is in the prologue to John's Gospel that we meet with a hymn answering so closely to Pliny's report that it may well be the very one of which the Christians had told him. When studied it can be detected that this hymn is an antiphonal chant consisting of twelve affirmations with their responses. John has chosen this hymn, of which he was probably not the author, to preface the Gospel, because it was so appropriate, and at four points has furnished comments which lead in to the Gospel proper. Omitting these comments we can readily reconstruct the hymn itself, printing the response lines in italics.

In the Beginning was the Word.
  And the Word was with God.
So the Word was Divine.
  He was in the beginning with God.
By him everything had being.
  And without him nothing had being.
What had being by him was Life.
  And Life was the Light of men.
And the Light shines in the Darkness.
  And the Darkness could not suppress it.
This was the true Light.
  It illumines all who enter the world.
He was in the world.
  But the world did not recognise him.
He came to his own domains.
  But his own did not receive him.
The Word took flesh and sojourned with us.
  And we beheld his glory.
Glory as of the Father's Only-begotten.
  Full of grace and truth.
For of his bounty we have all received.
  Yes, grace added to grace.
For the Law was given by Moses.
  Grace and truth came by Jesus Christ.

Except that the hymn introduces the incarnation of the Word in Jesus Christ its sentiments typically reflect Hellenistic-Jewish cosmogonical philosophy as expounded by Philo of Alexandria. Thus it provides supporting evidence that this thinking was well established in Asia Minor at the beginning of the second century A.D. Christian theology has been misled by failure to apprehend that John's prologue in fact reproduces an antiphonal hymn sung by Christians of his time, and once its character is disclosed it becomes easy to distinguish the commentary from the hymn itself and to see that one or two scribal changes have been made in the text of the hymn. The most notable change, which may have been due to misunderstanding an abbreviation, occurs in the second affirmation, where *Theos* (God) is read instead of *Theios* (Divine) as the response requires. The affirmation is not the end of a sentence which states, 'In the beginning was the Word, and the Word was with God, *and the Word was God*', but a distinct fresh affirmation following on logically from the first with its response. Because the Word was in the beginning with God it necessarily had a divine nature as the image of God. Through the Word in the significance of the archetype all things came into being. This is also in accordance with Pauline teaching, where Christ is always distinguished from God, and with the book of Proverbs (ch. viii) where it is said of Wisdom, 'The Lord possessed me in the beginning of his way, before his works of old. I was set up from everlasting, from the beginning, or ever the earth was . . .' Similarly in the *Wisdom of Solomon*, Wisdom is described as God's Only-begotten, 'an effulgence from everlasting Light, an unspotted mirror of the working of God, and an image of his goodness'.[8]

The last comment of John on the language of the hymn deals with the passage which affirms that through the incarnation of the Divine Wisdom (the Word) its glory was made visible, glory as of the Father's Only-begotten. John explains: 'No one has ever seen God. God's Only-begotten, who is in the Father's bosom, he has portrayed him.' John employs the Greek verb of exposition. In the Word we have the 'exegesis' of God. This is in line with the first epistle of John: 'Not only —in Christ—was Life made visible, but we have seen it, and solemnly affirm this, and proclaim to you that Eternal Life which was with the Father and was made visible to us.'[9] In this sense we must understand that strange discourse after the Last Supper, where Jesus is made to tell his disciples, 'If you knew me, you would also perceive my Father. From now on you do know him and have seen him. Philip said to him, Show us the Father, Master, and we shall be content. Jesus replied, Have I been with you all so long, yet you have not recognised me, Philip? He who has seen me has seen the Father. Why then do you say, Show us the Father? Do you not believe that I am in the Father, and that the Father is in me?'[10]

John the Greek is much closer to later Christian teaching than Paul the Jew. He can entertain godness for Jesus; but still Jesus is not God, in so far as no man at any time has seen or can see the invisible God. What Jesus is for John is the incarnation not of God but of God's divine self-expression in the Word. It is the Word of God which has taken flesh. There is a difference, even if it is a nice point of theological distinction. Since no one can see the Father, he can only be discerned through an expression of himself which has been made visible. To a Greek mind this was not difficult since statuary and even human beings could be said to display the gods. It was thus in John's time that the ruler could be regarded as God, son of the supreme God. The emperor Domitian required himself to be addressed as 'Our Lord and our God'. It was therefore quite in order for Thomas to adore the risen Jesus as 'My Lord and my God'. The title *Epiphanes* long conferred on eastern kings signified their divine nature as manifestations of the glory of God. The author of the Acts is in opposition to this kind of adulation, however, when he relates that the death of Herod Agrippa was a punishment for having accepted adoration as a god by his Gentile audience when he appeared before them resplendent in full regalia and made them a speech.[11]

There is a considerable difference between the christology of John and that of Paul, which it is essential to clarify. For Paul the archetypal man, the heavenly Christ, in taking on physical manhood for human redemption had totally divested himself of all heavenly characteristics and attributes: he had become wholly and completely man, and it was not until the resurrection that his spiritual nature as Son of God was reassumed (Rom. i. 3–4). The like idea is found in Hebrews where the author says: 'Since, therefore, the children have human nature, so did he share it equally with them; so that by death he might put out of commission him who wields the power of death, namely the Devil, and release all those inhibited throughout their lives by fear of death. For where was the point of lending a helping hand to angels? It was the offspring of Abraham that needed a helping hand. Consequently it was essential for him to become in every respect like his brothers, that he might be a compassionate and trustworthy high priest in matters relating to God, to propitiate for the people's sins; for having experienced temptation himself he is able to aid those who are tempted.'[12] Further on he says: 'Christ, in the days of his physical existence, having offered petitions, and indeed supplications, with loud sobbing and tears to him who could save him from death, was heard because of his piety. Though he was a son, he learnt obedience by what he suffered. And being perfected, he became for all who obey him the means of their eternal salvation.'[13] This thinking rules out altogether that the man Jesus was in any sense whatever more than man in his lifetime. He represented not so much an incarnation as a substitution. He could do only what any man could do, and use only the wit of man, even though he was gifted like Solomon. Every attribute that was more than or other than human was eliminated. It would be impossible, therefore, for him to speak or act in the manner of John's Gospel, or, indeed, to a less extent of the earlier Gospels. The literature illustrates a progressive change.

Unlike the Twelve to whom Jesus as man and Messiah meant so much humanly, Paul had no more use for a Christ according to the flesh, who had served his purpose by his atoning death on the cross. It was only in respect of what the heavenly Christ had done as Jesus in temporarily accepting complete and unqualified humanity that the experience of Jesus had relevance. Had Jesus not been raised from the dead, ascended to heaven in a spiritual body, become integrated with the heavenly Christ as the Lord Jesus Christ, whatever he had done on earth, even his death on the cross, would not have had any attraction for Paul. It was the proof that the heavenly Christ had indeed intervened in human affairs that made Jesus of consequence and the atonement valid. But for the future, and except in respect of the climax of the life of Jesus, there was no cause to look back to the physical Jesus, the Jesus of the time when the powers of the heavenly Christ were in abeyance. The only merit in so doing was to see him as an example of behaviour.

This is not the position of John. The situation which he had to face was that since the time of Paul, thanks to Philonism and incipient Gnosticism, Christian thinking was increasingly coming under the influence of teachers who so regarded the physical and material as evil that it was repugnant and not to be contemplated that the heavenly Christ, or the Logos, could have taken on humanity. He could only have had the semblance of humanity, not its reality. John goes a very long way with those who regarded the flesh as evil; but Jesus is the exception that proves the rule. Where would have been the hope of redemption if there had been no true incarnation, if the Word had not taken flesh? John, therefore, instead of turning his back on the man Jesus with Paul, violently attacks the docetists and sets out to demonstrate that Jesus as man, and undergoing the experiences of human pain, suffering and weariness, was always conscious of his heavenly origin and again and again demonstrated its powers. The Christ Above had not divested himself so as to become wholly human in the person of Jesus, neither in appearing as Jesus had he repudiated the flesh so as to be wholly superhuman. Instead, in the physical nature the spiritual nature had been manifested. The christology of John presents in an extreme form the fusion in Jesus of the heavenly and earthly, and the result inevitably, despite some beautiful passages and noble utterances, is a freak, a distortion of humanity and a debasement of divinity. John is too strong and too opinionated an individual himself to be able to create the portrait of a Jew who is at the same time capable of speaking convincingly as the Word of God. The Greek bias and the dogmatic argumentativeness of the author has to come out.

John, then, is waging a campaign against those who taught that the Word of God could not have occupied a physical body. 'Do not credit every spirit, dear friends. Examine the spirits to find out whether they are from God. You will recognise the spirit from God in this way: every spirit which confesses that Jesus Christ is come in the flesh is from God, while every spirit which does not admit the reality of Jesus is not from God. And this is the spirit of Antichrist, which you have heard will come.'[14]

Jesus, being Son of God in the sense that the Logos is God's only-begotten, knows all about his heavenly nature. While being a real man outwardly, inwardly he is the Logos, who speaks through his lips. The birth stories are put aside, not because John did not believe Jesus had had a human birth, but only because he is concerned with Jesus as a full-grown man, capable, therefore, in speech and action of being the vehicle for the manifestation of the Logos. Jesus must be able to say and do everything that establishes his true identity. It is this identity which assures those who believe in Jesus Christ that they too, in him, can be reborn inwardly as Sons of God by the agency of the Spirit of God, owing their new being 'not to race, nor to physical intention, nor to human design, but to God'.[15] Thus they qualify for Eternal Life. This is the point of the conversation between Jesus and Nicodemus, and the theme in various situations is repeated throughout the Gospel. If Jesus had not been really human and at the same time Son of God it would have been impossible for his human followers ever to become really Sons of God.

The onus is clearly upon Jesus, whom everyone can see is patently a human being, to convince all who can entertain it that he is genuinely superhuman. To this task he is made to address himself by his speeches and by his miracles, with the author adding his quota of statement in support.

'He who comes from heaven is superior to all,' says John.

'As he has seen and heard so he testifies, but no one accepts his testimony. Whoever does accept his testimony has confirmed that God is true; for he whom God has sent speaks the words of God, because God does not give him the Spirit stintingly. The Father loves the Son, and has placed everything in his hands. He who believes in the Son will have Eternal Life, while he who disobeys the Son will never see Life: God's wrath will abide on him.'[16]

Naturally, it is with the Jews that John's composite Jesus-Logos has his greatest difficulty, and no doubt we have a reflection here of John's personal experience with Jews he had encountered. How could a Jew, to whom the unity and formlessness of God had been revealed, acknowledge that a human being embodied in himself the self-expression of God as Son of God? Even Paul, as we have seen, recoiled from the idea that there had been such an incarnation in a literal sense. For the heavenly Christ to appear as man every vestige of superhumanity had had to be discarded. The divestment of the heavenly nature was total and complete for the lifetime of Jesus according to the flesh.

The annoyance and bitterness of John the Greek is communicated to his Jesus, and it is in the passages at arms with the Jews that his Christ loses all trace of godlikeness, being first outrageous and then angrily abusive. A few illustrations will suffice.

Jesus tells the Jews: 'If you do not eat the flesh of the Son of Man and drink his blood you will not have life in yourselves. Whoever masticates my flesh and drinks my blood will have Eternal Life, and I must raise him up on the Last Day; for my flesh is true food and my blood is true drink. Whoever masticates my flesh and drinks my blood continues in me, and I in him. Just as the Living Father has sent me, and I live through the Father, so he who masticates me will likewise live through me. This is the bread that has come down from heaven, not the kind the fathers ate, and died. He who masticates this bread will live for ever.'[17]

This teaching savours of the initiations of the Mystery Cults of Asia Minor, and John admits that many disciples of Jesus find it intolerable.

Unlike the Jesus of the synoptic Gospels the Jesus of John sets much store by miracles as witnessing to his divinity. 'The Father loves the Son, and shows him whatever he does. And he will show him how to do greater miracles than this, that you may marvel. . . . The miracles which the Father has granted me to perform, the miracles I do, these testify of me that the Father has sent me. . . . I do not require human praise, but I do know you, that you have not the love of God in you.'[18]

Jesus carries on a long argument with the Jews about his personal relationship with God the Father, whom they claim is their Father, and rounds on them: 'If God were your Father, you would love me; for I emanated and came from God. I did not come of my own accord: he sent me. How is it you do not recognise my voice? It is because you cannot heed my message. You have the Devil for a father, and would carry out your father's behests. He was a manslayer from the beginning, and could never abide the truth; for truth is alien to him. When he utters a lie he speaks his own language; for he is a liar and the father of lies. But because I speak the truth you do not believe me. Whoever belongs to God heeds the words of God. The very fact that you do not heed me proves that you do not belong to God. . . . It is my Father who glorifies me, whom you say is your God. Yet you are not acquainted with him, while I know him. Were I to say I do not know him, I should be like you, a liar.'[19]

There is much more of this pitiful sort of bickering, and Jesus is made to set himself wholly apart from his people, unrelated to them and slanging them. Thank goodness, the Jesus of history never was like that, or behaved like that! John the Greek, putting words into his mouth, simply cannot measure up to how a truly divine person would speak, or even a supremely wise man. By insisting that the Jew Jesus was really not a Jew but manifest God in a Jewish body he has effectively killed his thesis by presenting a travesty and caricature of divinity. It was John who was guilty of deicide, not the Jews.

The intention of John's christology was to silence the docetists who urged that Jesus Christ was not truly man. This he may have done, but to the discerning only at the cost of demonstrating that the man was palpably not God. When the Jesus of the Fourth Gospel says, 'I and my father are one', he is right, though not in the sense the Evangelist intended: he is one with John his creator and only-begetter.

NOTES AND REFERENCES

1. Col. iv. 12–13.
2. Acts xix. 13–19.
3. Philo, *On the Creation*, viii.
4. Philo, *On the Creation*, xxiii.
5. Philo, *The Confusion of Tongues*, xxviii.
6. See Reitzenstein, *Poimandres*, and G. R. S. Mead, *Thrice-Greatest Hermes*.
7. Eph. v. 14.
8. *Wisdom of Solomon*, vii. 22–7. See Rendel Harris, *The Origin of the Doctrine of the Trinity*.
9. I. Jn. i. 2.
10. Jn. xiv. 7–10.
11. Acts xii. 21–3.
12. Heb. ii. 14–18.
13. Heb. v. 7–9.
14. I. Jn. iv. 1–3.
15. Jn. i. 13.
16. Jn. iii. 31–6.
17. Jn. vi. 53–8.
18. Jn. v. 20, 36, 41–2.
19. Jn. viii. 42–55.

Bibliography

Acts of John, translated by M. R. James, *The Apocryphal New Testament*, Clarendon Press (Oxford, 1926).

Acts of Paul, translated by M. R. James, *The Apocryphal New Testament*, Clarendon Press (Oxford, 1926).

Apocalypse of Abraham, translated by G. H. Box, S.P.C.K. (London, 1918).

Apocalypse of Baruch, translated by R. H. Charles, A. & C. Black (London, 1896).

Apocalypse of Ezra, translated by G. H. Box, S.P.C.K. (London, 1917).

Ascension of Isaiah, translated by R. H. Charles, S.P.C.K. (London, 1917).

Assumption of Moses, translated by R. H. Charles, A. & C. Black (London, 1897).

Athenagoras, *A Plea for the Christians*, in the Ante-Nicene Christian Library, T. & T. Clark (Edinburgh, 1867).

Bacon, Benjamin W., *Studies in Matthew*, Constable (London, 1930).

Bonhoeffer, Dietrich, *Letters and Papers from Prison*, edited by E. Bethge (London, 1956).

Book of James, translated by M. R. James, *The Apocryphal New Testament*, Clarendon Press (Oxford, 1926).

Brandon, S. G. F., *The Fall of Jerusalem and the Christian Church*, S.P.C.K. (London, 1951).

Cassius, Dio, *Roman History* (Leipzig, 1890).

Cicero, *Works*, in Radin, *The Jews among the Greeks and Romans*, Jewish Publication Society of America (Philadelphia, 1915), and Dollinger, *The Gentile and the Jew*, Longman (London, 1862).

Clement of Rome, *Letters to the Corinthians*, translated by Kirsopp Lake in *The Apostolic Fathers* (Loeb Classical Library), Heinemann (London) and Macmillan (New York).

Clementine Homilies, in the Ante-Nicene Christian Library, T. & T. Clark (Edinburgh, 1870).

Clementine Recognitions, in the Ante-Nicene Christian Library, T. & T. Clark (Edinburgh, 1871).

Didache (see *Teaching of the XII Apostles*).

Dionysius bishop of Corinth, *Letter to Soter bishop of Rome*, quoted by Eusebius, *Ecclesiastical History*.

Eisler, Robert, *The Enigma of the Fourth Gospel*, Methuen (London, 1938).

Enoch, Book of, translated by R. H. Charles, Clarendon Press (Oxford, 1893).

Epiphanius bishop of Constantia, *Against Heresies* (*Panarion*) and *On Weights and Measures*, edited by Francis Oehler (Berolini, 1859).

Epistle of Peter to James, in the *Clementine Homilies*, vid. lic.

Eusebius bishop of Caesarea, *Ecclesiastical History*, translated by C. F. Cruse, Bell & Sons (London, 1874).

Farrar, Frederic W., *The Early Days of Christianity*, Cassell (London, 1898).

Frazer, J. G., *The Golden Bough*, third edition, Macmillan (London, 1914).

Genesis Rabba (see *Midrash Rabba*).

Gospel of the Egyptians, see M. R. James, *The Apocryphal New Testament*, Clarendon Press (Oxford, 1926).

Gospel of the Hebrews, see M. R. James, *The Apocryphal New Testament*, Clarendon Press (Oxford, 1926).

Gospel of Peter, translated by M. R. James, *The Apocryphal New Testament*, Clarendon Press (Oxford, 1926).

Gospel of Thomas, translated by M. R. James, *The Apocryphal New Testament*, Clarendon Press (Oxford, 1926).

Gospel of Thomas (Gnostic), in *The Secret Sayings of Jesus*, Robert M. Grant and David Noel Freedman, Fontana Books, Collins (London, 1960).

Grant, Michael, *The World of Rome*, Weidenfeld & Nicolson (London, 1960).

Grant, Robert M., *Gnosticism and Early Christianity*, Oxford University Press (London, 1959) and Columbia University Press (New York); *The Formation of the New Testament*, Hutchinson University Library (London, 1965).

Greek Papyri of the British Museum, see Radin, op. cit.

Harris, J. Rendel, *The Odes and Psalms of Solomon*, The University Press (Cambridge, 1911); *The Origin of the Doctrine of the Trinity*, The University Press (Manchester, 1919) and Longmans (New York).

Hardy, E. G., *Studies in Roman History*, Swan Sonnenschein (London, 1910) and Macmillan (New York).

Herford, R. Travers, *Christianity in Talmud and Midrash*, Williams & Norgate (London, 1903).

Hermas, *The Shepherd*, translated by Kirsopp Lake in *The Apostolic Fathers* (Loeb Classical Library), Heinemann (London) and Macmillan (New York).

Hippolytus, *Philosopheumena*, S.P.C.K. (London).

Hislop, Alexander, *The Two Babylons*, fourth edition, Partridge (London, 1965).

Horace, *Satires*, quoted by Radin, op. cit.

Hymn of the Robe of Glory, or *Hymn of the Soul*, in *The Acts of Thomas*, translated by M. R. James, *The Apocryphal New Testament*, Clarendon Press (Oxford, 1926).

Ignatius bishop of Antioch, *Epistles*, translated by Kirsopp Lake in *The Apostolic Fathers* (Loeb Classical Library), Heinemann (London) and Macmillan (New York).

Irenaeus bishop of Lyons, *Against Heresies*, in the Ante-Nicene Christian Library, T. & T. Clark (Edinburgh, 1868–69).

James, M. R., *The Apocryphal New Testament,* Clarendon Press (Oxford, 1926).

Jerome, *Commentary on Isaiah*, quoted by Schonfield, *Saints Against Caesar,* Macdonald (London, 1948).

Jewish Encyclopaedia, Funk & Wagnalls (London & New York, 1906).

Josephus, Flavius, *Works* (Loeb Classical Library), Heinemann (London) and Harvard University Press (Cambridge, Mass.).

Justin Martyr, *Dialogue with Trypho* and *First Apology*, in the Ante-Nicene Christian Library, T. & T. Clark (Edinburgh, 1867).

Juvenal, *Satires,* translated by Ramsay (Loeb Classical Library), Heinemann (London) and Putnam (New York).

Klausner, Joseph, *From Jesus to Paul*, Allen & Unwin (London).

Lebreton & Zeiller, *A History of the Early Church*, Vol. iii, *Heresy and Orthodoxy*, Vol. iv, *The Triumph of Christianity*, Collier Catholic Readers Series (New York, 1962).

Letter of Aristeas, translated by H. St. J. Thackeray, Macmillan (London and New York, 1904).

Letter of Claudius to the Alexandrians, in H. Idris Bell, *Jews and Christians in Egypt*, the British Museum (London).

Lucian of Samosata, *Works,* translated by H. W. and F. G. Fowler, The Clarendon Press (Oxford, 1905).

Manetho, quoted by Josephus, *Against Apion.*

Mead, G. R. S., *Thrice-Greatest Hermes,* Watkins (London).

Memoirs of Hegesippus, quoted by Eusebius, *Ecclesiastical History.*

Midrash Rabba, edited by J. Theodor (Berlin).

Milligan, George, *The New Testament Documents*, Macmillan (London, 1913).

Mingana, A., *Some Early Judaeo-Christian Documents in the John Rylands Library*, The University Press (Manchester, 1917).

Mishnah, The, translated by Herbert Danby, Humphrey Milford: Oxford University Press (London, 1933).

Odes of Solomon, see Harris, J. Rendel, op. cit.

Origen, *Against Celsus,* in the Ante-Nicene Christian Library,

T. & T. Clark (Edinburgh, 1872); *Commentary on John's Gospel* in the Additional Volume (Edinburgh, 1903).

Ovid, *Ars Amatoria*, quoted by Radin, op. cit.

Papias, *Exposition of the Dominical Oracles*, fragments translated by J. B. Lightfoot in *The Apostolic Fathers*, Macmillan (London and New York, 1891).

Papyrus of Ani, British Museum, London.

Parkes, James, *The Conflict of the Church and the Synagogue*, Soncino Press (London, 1934).

Passion of the Scillitan Martyrs, in the Ante-Nicene Christian Library (Additional Volume), T. & T. Clark (Edinburgh, 1903).

Paul and Thecla (see *Acts of Paul*).

Paulus, quoted by Hardy, op. cit.

Perseus, *Satires*, quoted by Radin, op. cit.

Philo Judaeus, *Works*, in the Loeb Classical Library, Heinemann (London) and Harvard University Press (Cambridge, Mass.).

Pines, S., *The Jewish Christians of the Early Centuries of Christianity According to a New Source*, Proceedings of the Israel Academy of Science and Humanities (Jerusalem, 1966).

Pliny the Younger, *Letter to the Emperor Trajan concerning the Christians* (*Letters:* the Loeb Classical Library), Heinemann (London) and Harvard University Press (Cambridge, Mass.).

Plutarch, *Moralia* (Loeb Classical Library), Heinemann (London) and Harvard University Press (Cambridge, Mass.).

Polybius, *History*, quotation adapted from W. R. Paton by Michael Grant, *The World of Rome*, Weidenfeld & Nicolson (London, 1960).

Polycrates bishop of Ephesus, *Letter to Victor bishop of Rome*, quoted by Eusebius, *Ecclesiastical History*.

Poseidonius, quoted by Diodorus, *Eclogues*.

Radin, Max, *The Jews among the Greeks and Romans*, Jewish Publication Society of America (Philadelphia, 1915).

Reitzenstein, *Poimandres* (Leipzig, 1904).

Robinson, J. Armitage, *Texts and Studies*, Vol. 1.

Robinson, John A. T., *Honest to God*, S.C.M. Press (London, 1963); *The New Reformation?* S.C.M. Press (London, 1965).

Sadler, Gilbert T., *Behind the New Testament*, Daniel (London, 1921).

Schonfield, Hugh J., *According to the Hebrews*, Duckworth (London, 1937); *An Old Hebrew Text of St. Matthew's Gospel*, T. & T. Clark (Edinburgh, 1927); *Saints Against Caesar*, Macdonald (London, 1948); *The Jew of Tarsus*, Macdonald (London, 1946); *The Passover Plot*, Hutchinson (London, 1965) and Bernard Geis (New York, 1966).

Schweitzer, Albert, *Mysticism of Paul the Apostle*, A. & C. Black (London).

Seneca, *Epistles to Lucilius*, quoted by Radin, op. cit.; *Apocolocyntosis*, quoted by J. P. V. D. Balsdon, *The Romans*, Watts (London, 1965).

Severus, *Chronicles*, quoted by Hardy, op. cit.

Shaw, George Bernard, *Androcles and the Lion*, Constable (London).

Sibylline Oracles, H. N. Bate, S.P.C.K. (London, 1918) and Macmillan (New York).

Smith, Homer W., *Man and His Gods*, with a Foreword by Albert Einstein, Grosset & Dunlap (New York, 1957).

Strabo, quoted by Josephus, *Jewish Antiquities*, Bk. XIV.

Streane, A. W., *The Tractate Chagigah from the Babylonian Talmud*, The University Press (Cambridge, 1891).

Suetonius, *The Lives of the Twelve Caesars*, translated by Alexander Thomson and revised by T. Forester, Bell & Sons (London, 1911).

Tacitus, Cornelius, *The Annals and History*, translated by Arthur Murphy, Jones & Co. (London, 1830).

Talmud (Jerusalem and Babylonian), standard editions.

Teaching of the XII Apostles, translated by Kirsopp Lake in *The Apostolic Fathers* (Loeb Classical Library), Heinemann (London) and Macmillan (New York).

Tertullian, *Apologia* (Loeb Classical Library), Heinemann (London) and Harvard University Press (Cambridge, Mass.).

Testaments of the XII Patriarchs, translated by R. H. Charles, A. & C. Black (London, 1908).

Theophrastus of Lesbos, quoted by Porphyrius, see Radin, op. cit.

Valerius Maximus, quoted by Hardy, op. cit.

Virgil, *Aenid*, translated by C. Day Lewis, quoted by Michael Grant, op. cit.; *Eclogues*, translated by H. Rushton Fairclough (Loeb Classical Library), Heinemann (London) and Putnam (New York).

Williams, A. Lukyn, *The Hebrew-Christian Messiah*, The Warburton Lectures for 1911–1915.

Wisdom of Solomon in *The Apocrypha of the Old Testament*, R.S V., Nelson (London, 1957).

Wunsch, *Sethianische Verfluchungstafeln aus Rom* (Leipzig, 1898).

Index